UNBROKEN

UNBROKEN

TINA R PAONE

TALL OAKS
PUBLISHING

Unbroken: Healing from Narcissistic Abuse & Reclaiming Me

By Tina R. Paone
Edited by Jennifer S. Gabriel
Cover Art by Miladinka Milic

Copyright © 2026 by Tina R. Paone
All rights reserved.

No part of this book may be reproduced, stored in a retrieval system, or transmitted in any form or by any means—electronic, mechanical, photocopying, recording, or otherwise—without the prior written permission of the publisher, except for brief quotations used in reviews or scholarly works.

Published by Tall Oaks Publishing
Lansdale, PA

Library of Congress Control Number: 2026908032
ISBN: 979-8-9944043-4-8 (Paperback)
ISBN: 979-8-9944043-8-6 (Large Print)
ISBN: 979-8-9944043-6-2 (Hardcover)
ISBN: 979-8-9944043-5-5 (eBook)
ISBN: 979-8-9944043-8-6 (Audiobook)
Printed in the United States of America
First Edition

Contents

Author's Note		1
Prologue		3
1	Echoes of a Troubled Past	11
2	His Vow, My Debt	21
3	The Slow Poisoning	31
4	As Abuse Got Louder, So Did My Silence	37
5	A Campaign of Cruelty	49
6	The Day I Didn't Testify	61
7	The Weight of Shame	73
8	Sugarcoated Cruelty	87
9	The Price of Freedom	97
10	My Teenage Escape	105
11	The Irony of Care	115
12	The Longest Good-bye	123
13	The Collapsing Supply	133
14	The Fairytale Amidst the Abuse	149
15	The Currency of Control	159
16	House of Horrors	171
17	The Trip to Trust	183
18	The Language of Trauma	191

19	A Map to the Past	199
20	The Paper Trail	207
21	The Ass-Backward Truth	213
22	The Inheritance of Silence	223
23	Unseen Radical Grief	237
24	The Anatomy of Abandonment	247
25	Triggers, Tremors, and Truth	257
26	The Body Remembers	269
27	The House with the Broken Alarm	281
28	Taking Back What Was Mine	291
Epilogue		303
Acknowledgments		307

TO ALL SURVIVORS:

You are strong.
You are brave.
You are amazing.

Author's Note

As a licensed therapist, counselor educator, supervisor, and trauma survivor, I wrote this memoir through a dual lens: one shaped by personal experience, and the other informed by professional training and years of experience.

Above all, this book is my story. And my truth.

This book is not meant to diagnose, treat, or analyze others. It is not a substitute for therapy. While I reference relational patterns, trauma responses, and emotional dynamics that may feel familiar, every insight offered is rooted in my journey—what I saw, what I felt, and what I've come to understand through the integration of personal truth and professional practice.

Writing this story came with tension. I wanted to tell it as it was—raw, disorienting, and deeply human. But as I wrote, my "therapist brain" often wanted to step in, explain, reframe, and add context to the discomfort. Striking the right balance wasn't always easy. I hold an ethical responsibility to honor both my role as a clinician and my right to speak as a survivor. I've taken that responsibility seriously and have worked to maintain clear boundaries throughout.

At the end of each chapter, you'll find a reflection—one written not as the narrator of my past, but as the therapist I am today. These notes are offered not to pathologize, but to illuminate . . . to validate what so often goes unnamed . . . to help others feel less alone in what they've survived or are still navigating.

As a reminder, this book contains references to childhood sexual abuse, emotional abuse, domestic violence, narcissistic abuse, and family estrangement. These themes may be difficult for some readers. Please read at your own pace and take care of yourself as needed.

If any part of this story resonates with your own, you are not alone. Please seek support from a licensed mental health professional. You deserve healing. You deserve safety. You deserve peace. And you don't have to do it by yourself.

Prologue

By the time I met Allen, I knew what it meant to live in survival mode. I knew how to shrink, how to appease, and how to read a room like my safety depended on it, because it often did. What I didn't know yet was how to recognize danger when it smiled and sounded like love.

Allen was attentive, dependable, and familiar. He mirrored everything I said I wanted. He said and did all the right things.

Until he didn't.

What followed wasn't a single act of betrayal. It was a slow, calculated dismantling—a quiet erasure of who I was, piece by piece.

We met at work in Reno. Our first real conversation happened when Allen saw a wedding photo on my desk and recognized my husband. They'd gone to high school together. That small connection sparked a casual workplace friendship.

A few months later, our cat's self-cleaning litter box jammed, and fixing it required two people. Normally I'd have helped, but I was pregnant and had been warned about toxoplasmosis. Allen lived nearby and had always seemed helpful, so I suggested we call him.

Sure enough, ten minutes later, he was at our door.

As a thank-you, we invited him to stay for dinner. The meal turned into a night of video games and nostalgic stories about high school football days. We invited him back the next night. Then the next. And the next.

It was fun—until it wasn't. But by the time I noticed the shift, he was a fixture in our home.

"Fucking Allen is here again," I'd grumble to friends as I pulled into the driveway and spotted his truck. He showed up almost daily. Sometimes he'd bring food for himself, but more often, he came empty-handed, expecting to be fed or entertained. Night after night, I found myself cooking dinner or ordering takeout because, after all, he was our "guest."

But he wasn't a guest—not really. Over time, he became an uninvited third wheel in our marriage.

My husband was in the military, which meant I was often alone. We talked regularly on the phone, but the weight of daily life—especially after we became parents—was mine to carry.

What hurt most were the moments around town, when our sons Nicholas and Christopher would spot a man in uniform and cry out, "Daddy!" Every time, their hope shattered me. I couldn't fill that void.

When the boys were three and two, my husband was deployed for longer than his usual training that took him away for a few weeks at a time. This time, he'd be gone for a year. After he left, Allen told me he'd been "asked" to check in on us—to make sure we were okay.

Now I understand exactly what he was doing. But at the time, I didn't question it. Support was support. I was working full-time as a school counselor, finishing my doctoral degree, and trying to be the kind of mother I never had. Having someone around—even just an extra set of hands—felt like a lifeline.

Then, one afternoon, Allen dropped a bomb.

"I really hate to be the one to tell you this," he began—though his tone suggested otherwise. There was a strange mix of confidence and theatrical suspense in his voice. He paused, letting the words hang dramatically in the air.

Then, finally, he let it out: "Your husband is having an affair!"

I was gutted.

Not just by the accusation—but by the way Allen delivered it.

He didn't just suggest an affair—he *insisted* that I was being lied to, cheated on, and disrespected. When I later confronted my husband, he denied everything. But Allen held his ground and claimed he'd heard it firsthand and directly from my husband. His voice was strong—calm, steady, and supportive. I had no reason to doubt him, which was my critical mistake.

My husband was a thousand miles away, and our marriage was already cracking. We'd grown apart in all the ways that mattered. His devotion to the military always felt like it came before me or the boys. And this news of an alleged affair was the last straw. I couldn't do it anymore.

In Nevada, divorce proceedings with cooperating spouses go quickly. Once we made the decision, we removed our rings, consulted a mediator, divided our assets, and determined a custody schedule. Within two months, our seven-and-a-half-year marriage was over.

As the divorce was finalized, Allen stayed close. If anything, his presence became more constant. Looking back, I now see that he was monitoring the situation to see how it played out. But at the time, I thought he was just being kind. While I worked and finished school, he stepped into the role of babysitter—always around and always available.

Now I wonder if that was the point all along. He set a stage to ensure I'd feel indebted and like I owed him something.

Things between us moved fast. Just days after I removed my ring, Allen kissed me. A week later, he told me he loved me. It was too soon for me, and I didn't say it back. But the words still meant something. I was hurting. My ex had chosen a career over our family. And Allen was there for us—attentive, affectionate, and available.

Shortly after the divorce was finalized, we took the boys to Disneyland. Their joy lit up every photo. Allen had known them since birth, and his presence felt familiar. He said he wanted what I wanted, and we seemed to share values, beliefs, and dreams. Even some of the traumas we had endured as children seemed to align.

I was thrilled when Allen started talking about marriage shortly after that trip. I was young and eager to move on. We were engaged a short time later and eloped within a year.

I ignored the red flags. I wanted to believe our relationship was good. I knew it wasn't perfect. But, I told myself, *nothing is*.

* * *

Eleven years later, I barely recognized myself.

I was hollow. My energy, my joy, my spark? Gone. Any attempt at personal growth—therapy, exercise, peace—was met with bitterness. Allen didn't see my healing as growth. He saw it as rebellion.

"You think the grass is greener everywhere else," he'd sneer. In his eyes, my efforts to evolve made me selfish and disloyal.

By then, our marriage was essentially a roommate situation. I had fallen out of love but stayed because I was afraid I couldn't financially survive another failed relationship. Meanwhile, Allen lived in a fantasy world, intentionally ignoring every opportunity that may have improved our situation.

I had been trying to convince myself to leave. And then one Sunday—five months after my father died, three months after I placed my mother in long-term care—I finally reached the breaking point. We were arguing again, this time as we drove to a furniture store. I don't remember what started the fight. I only remember that once we got home, I finally said the words "I want a divorce."

At first, Allen responded with feigned confusion, insisting I was "not thinking straight." He kept repeating, "I don't know where this is coming from," as if the years I'd spent saying that our marriage wasn't working had never happened. He acted like the cracks were brand new and my doubts were sudden and irrational.

But I'd been patching those cracks for years, and I was out of glue. This was a long time coming, and I had already visited a lawyer. When I told him that, something in him snapped.

Allen had been angry with me before, but this was different. This was unhinged. His rage was immediate. It was raw, explosive, and terrifying. His eyes turned black.

The verbal assaults came fast and hard—an overwhelming avalanche of insults and accusations. His primary point was that my dad's death had made me delusional. And each word was sharper than the last, designed to slice through whatever resolve I had left and ensure I understood that everything wrong in our family was my fault.

Upstairs, my boys hid in their rooms, until my oldest, Nicholas, couldn't take it anymore and came downstairs. At thirteen, he was still more boy than man.

As soon as I saw him, my heart split down the middle. I was terrified for him. I didn't want him stepping into Allen's rage, and I didn't know what would happen if he did.

Still, he stood there, trembling.

"Can you please stop yelling at my mom like that?" he said, softly, his voice small and shaky. Much later, he told me he was so frightened that he thought he might throw up or pass out.

Allen snapped around, his movements sharp and predatory. His face darkened as blood rushed to his cheeks. His jaw clenched. His chest rose with manufactured dominance, and his eyes—wild and unblinking, now even darker than before—locked onto Nicholas like a target.

"You think you're a man?" he spat, his voice low and venomous. "You're not."

He took a step forward—closing the space with deliberate menace. His voice escalated.

"*What?*" he sneered. "You wanna hit me now? Is that it? Do it and see what happens."

The room seemed to shrink. Allen's words were designed to provoke.

"Come on," he roared. "DO IT. Give me a fucking reason to knock the shit out of you!"

He was practically vibrating with rage, drunk on power and cruelty, begging for violence—even daring it.

Nicholas didn't flinch. Instead, he found a way to dig deep inside himself. He squared his shoulders and spoke directly.

"I'm not afraid of you anymore," he declared.

That was the final straw.

Allen's face twisted into something inhuman. In a single second, he slammed his chest into Nicholas and drove his body hard into the wall.

Nicholas hit the floor, stunned—for a second. He scrambled to stand, only to be shoved down again, harder this time.

Then Allen turned and grabbed the nearest object off the counter: a green plastic water bottle. He whipped it at the floor with every ounce of fury he had left. It detonated on impact, the plastic shattering, with tiny pieces shooting across the kitchen like shrapnel.

Just as suddenly, Allen turned and stormed out of the house. He slammed the door with such force that it rattled the kitchen cabinets. He left behind everything personal, including his wallet and his house keys. He didn't even take shoes or socks.

This wasn't just an exit. It was theater. His rage was so urgent and so righteous that mundane details like footwear didn't matter. This was the tantrum of a man-child who believed his pain outweighed everyone else's.

Once he was gone, I locked the door and collapsed onto the couch, pulling the boys close. My youngest son, Joe, was crying. Nicholas and Christopher sat frozen, stunned by what had just unfolded. All four of us wrapped ourselves around each other in a circle of grief and strength.

In that moment, I felt unity. A fierce, unspoken love pulsing between me and my sons. We were stronger than the chaos.

* * *

In the quiet after Allen's exit, something in me stirred— it was a haunting sense of déjà vu.

Allen wasn't my first storm. Long before I married him, I was manipulated by another man who weaponized his anger to force me into compliance.

Al—my mother's boyfriend—was my first example of unpredictable rage. And no, the irony isn't lost on me. Allen and Al shared more than a name; their tactics, volume, and volatility felt cut from the same cloth.

As a child, I learned that Al's fury could surface anywhere. And anytime. In fact, our family car was often his stage: and in it, we were a captive audience.

One minute, we'd be driving along. My younger brother Tony and I always sat in the backseat and were too young to name what we were feeling, but old enough to know when something felt wrong. The air was often heavy. We didn't know why. We just knew to stay quiet.

Then, without warning, Al would detonate.

With some sort of seemingly invisible slight, or some imagined betrayal, his voice would explode with venom. His foot would slam the gas, and the car would surge forward like it had been struck from behind. The whole vehicle became an extension of his rage, jerking and veering in sync with whatever tantrum had taken hold.

And then—just as suddenly—he'd yank the wheel, swerve onto the shoulder, throw the gear into park, and leap out. The slam of the door was seismic. It reverberated through the car like a warning shot.

There we'd sit. Frozen. In silence. Held hostage in a vehicle that suddenly felt like a cage.

It happened so often that the memories blur together—one rage-blind episode bleeding into the next. I couldn't tell you the details of any single incident. But the script never changed: sudden explosion, paralyzing fear, and three of us—my mother, Tony, and me—sitting silent and still, waiting for the storm to pass.

Sometimes my mother would move into the driver's seat and inch the car forward down the shoulder, slowly, like she could coax him back in with motion alone. She'd call out the window, her voice tight with desperation, pleading with him to get back in the car.

Now I understand what that was really about.

She wasn't pleading for safety. She was pleading for appearances. And for control.

God forbid someone she knew drove by and saw us like that—parked on the side of the road, her boyfriend storming off in a rage, her children terrified and silent in the backseat. That would've shattered her image. And to her, that kind of fracture was far more dangerous than the one happening inside her own family.

It wasn't better when she was the one driving. Al would rage from the passenger seat—yelling, flailing, and shaking the entire car with his fury. He'd order her to pull over, jump out, and pace like a caged animal.

These weren't tantrums. They were rituals. The emotional terrorism of a man who needed control over everything and everyone.

Always yelling. Always threatening. Always demanding to be the center of the universe.

And always, someone—usually more than one of us—nearby, scrambling to manage the explosion.

Decades later, it was happening again but in my marriage. Same script. Different actor. Allen's exit—barefoot, raging, theatrical—wasn't just about the moment. It was a performance designed to leave everyone else trembling. But this time, things were different. This time I saw what was happening and knew it was time to break the cycle.

I had no idea what that decision would unleash—or how it would set me on a path of unraveling generations of abuse, confronting ghosts I had buried, and finally understanding how I ended up married to a narcissist in the first place.

1

Echoes of a Troubled Past

Even though we'd talked at length about our future, and had picked out a ring together, Allen still managed to surprise me with the proposal.

In hindsight, it was one of many early red flags.

It happened a few months after our Disneyland trip. We were at a beach in New Jersey with the kids and extended family. One afternoon, as he and I walked along the edge of the surf, Allen pointed and said, "What's that?" He bent down, reached into the water, and came up holding the ring.

Everyone cheered, of course. I was excited . . . and a bit unsettled. I'm a private person, and having so many people around made the moment feel more like a performance than a promise.

Later, I confided in Allen about my unease. He immediately brushed off my concerns and shared his original plan to propose: by taking me on a walk across the Golden Gate Bridge and then dropping a fake ring into the water, only to pull out a real one once I started panicking about the lost diamond.

He shared this plan like it was hilarious. I didn't laugh. The whole thing felt so mean-spirited. When I said that, he told me I needed to learn how to take a joke. I remember feeling confused—*maybe I am too sensitive?*

By then, I'd grown used to suppressing my reactions and second-guessing my instincts. I was also desensitized to the discomfort of being put on display.

In many ways, I'd trained for that exact moment: my mother excelled at staging scenes, and I learned early on that how something looked mattered more than how it felt.

My mother and Al had a flair for the dramatic and a disturbing knack for making our family a centerpiece. For example, Christmas Eve became a big production for a few years. Al would dress as Santa and perch on a red wooden sleigh in our front yard, while forcing Tony and me—and whatever friends we had over—to dress as reindeer or snowmen and wave to passing cars.

It all looked festive on the surface, and some families even stopped for photos. But there was a sinister undertone: I knew who Al really was, and behind the lights and costumes stood a man with a terrifying temper and a twisted sense of power.

My mother also curated our image obsessively. One of her favorite performances was the Nights in Venice boat parade in Ocean City, New Jersey. Every July, the inlets came alive with floating lights and costumed boats. It was a family-friendly parade, an annual tradition that brought thousands of people to the waters' edge.

We participated twice. The first time, my mother chose *Rocky* as our theme—the gritty 1970s boxing film, beloved especially in nearby Philadelphia where the story is set. It follows an underdog fighter training for the match of his life. The movie is all blood, sweat, and perseverance.

Naturally, Al played Rocky—shirtless, with fake bruises and blood smeared across his face. Tony wore a bathrobe and played his opponent. My mom dressed the trainer, and Al's oldest son captained the boat as Pauly, Rocky's rough-and-tumble friend.

And me? I was instructed to put my 16-year-old body into a bikini and play the "ring girl"—the woman in a boxing match who walks the ring holding up signs for each round.

Everyone else was in full costume. I was barely dressed, standing beside Al, who was also nearly naked. At the time, I didn't question it: I was conditioned to see this kind of thing as normal. I do remember the cold, and how I hated it almost as much as I hated being exposed. But the rules were clear: don't complain, don't question, don't resist.

"Hush up," as my mom would say in a clipped, dismissive tone.

In one of the inlets, the crowd was particularly rowdy—drinking, shouting, and cheering from the shore. I remember one man yelling, "No, baby, you're not a six—you're a ten!" as I held up the "Round 6" sign.

I felt exposed, ashamed, and wildly uncomfortable. But I said nothing. That's just how it always went.

So, by the time Allen proposed at the beach, I had been thoroughly trained to swallow my real feelings and avoid conflict.

In the months to come, I got swept up in the excitement of wedding planning and barely paused to consider how we'd pay for it all. Money was tight, and Allen wasn't working. He also didn't qualify for credit, something he blamed on a past case of identity theft.

In fact, when we had picked out the engagement ring together, I lent him the money for it and told myself he'd pay me back. This is just what building a new life from the ground up looks like, I thought.

Yet while I framed the decision as a partnership, the truth was that it was a one-sided investment. It wasn't practical and necessary, like I told myself. It was the start of a pattern I hadn't yet noticed: every time a new major expense came up, I covered it. Small expenses? I paid those too.

Our first wedding was an elopement—a quiet ceremony at a couple's resort in the Caribbean, just the two of us, simple and private. But Allen insisted we'd regret not having a wedding with the boys, so we planned a second ceremony in Reno, where we lived, so family and friends could celebrate. I agreed to cover those costs too, convinced I was investing in our future.

And there were other early red flags.

As we prepared to marry, Allen suggested I let go of the woman who had been cleaning my house a few times a month. She was reliable and her services were a small luxury that brought me a sense of calm and order. Cleaning, he said, was something we could do to save money. He made the decision to fire her sound reasonable—responsible, even. And I believed that building a life together meant making choices like this together.

But once she was gone, the cleaning didn't become "ours." It became mine.

Another major source of my concerns came into our home slobbering and snorting.

I have never liked dogs. Their breath makes my stomach turn, and their unpredictability makes me tense. But Allen wanted a dog—badly. And not just any dog, but a high-maintenance, purebred English Bulldog with a price tag that exceeded four figures.

We didn't have that kind of money laying around. Or more accurately, *I* didn't have that kind of money. But Allen insisted. He said it would be good for the kids, and that "every boy needs a dog."

I gave in and footed the bill, yet again. I swallowed my unease and braced for what I already sensed: the dog would just become one more thing I'd be expected to manage.

When he arrived, I was immediately nauseous by its smell and asked what options we had to send him back, if it became necessary. Allen made me feel like a monster for even suggesting such a thing. The dog would bring my boys joy, companionship, and comfort, he claimed. And what kind of mother says no to that? I eventually agreed we could keep it.

There were other moments too—subtle things that I still didn't quite understand at the time, but began questioning later. The first time he kissed me, Allen laughed and said he had been nervous I might punch him. I giggled too, but the comment struck me as strange. *Why would I react violently to affection? Why was that the scenario playing in his mind?* I should've paid more attention to the part of me that felt unsettled by it.

Still, I was hopeful. I looked forward to our elopement—just the two of us, on a sunlit beach, far from the stress of our daily life. I imagined that getting away would give us a clean start and that I'd finally be able to exhale and feel safe.

Yet as we exchanged vows, I found myself setting quiet conditions for our marriage. During the ceremony, as the officiant spoke about commitment, I made a private promise: "I'll love this man—as long as he continues to stay good to the boys."

That should have been a warning: my vow came with a caveat. Even as we started this new chapter together, I was setting boundaries for myself and what I could tolerate in the relationship.

Ironically, when it came time to exchange rings, I slid Allen's onto the wrong hand. It was a moment of levity—something we laughed about together. Allen later joked that his grandmother had done the same thing. With her Southern drawl, she'd quip, "I put the ring on the wrong hand because I married the wrong damn man." (When I learned of this story, a cold realization ran through me. I knew the truth about his grandparents—they were married but didn't share a home, choosing instead to live in separate houses on the same piece of land.)

There was something else too. Something I couldn't quite name at the time—a way Allen spoke to me that made me feel small.

After our ceremony, a steel drum band played for us while our videographer filmed. Someone suggested we pretend to play the drums for the camera. I was all in—swaying my hips, smiling, and caught up in the joy. For a moment, I felt free.

Then Allen laughed—a loud, mocking cackle. "You can't dance," he said, shaking his head at me. "You have no rhythm. Just watch me and try to keep up."

His words cut deep. In a quiet moment previously, I had shared with him how hard I'd worked to improve my rhythm with music and how insecure I'd been about it as a kid.

That's the thing about emotional abuse—it rarely starts with shouting. It begins with subtle jabs. A joke at your expense. A smile that stings. You're told not to take it personally. You're made to feel silly for reacting. And when you've been conditioned not to trust your instincts, you don't always recognize it for what it is in the moment.

Years later, when I rewatched the wedding video, I was strangely relieved to see that I hadn't imagined it. I could pinpoint the moment Allen mocked me, and I could watch how it shifted my energy and how my joy visibly dimmed.

There was also a part of the scene I had forgotten about: as the celebration continues, Allen looks directly into the camera and says, "I'm happy with my choice."

His choice. As if I were a cut of meat. Or an appliance—useful, quiet, and meant to make his life easier.

I had already learned, long before Allen, how to diminish my presence. Growing up, my mother had a special disdain for anything she perceived as weakness—especially rest. She was quick to label people as lazy. In our house, needing rest meant you weren't trying hard enough.

Even when I was sick, I wasn't allowed to stop. If the school nurse called home, my mother would insist on speaking to me directly. The second I heard her voice through the receiver, I knew I wasn't going home.

"Get your rear end back to class," she'd snap. "You're not that sick. You're just being lazy."

And so, I went back, sick and silenced.

I learned not to trust how I felt. I learned that pain was weakness, that exhaustion was failure, and that the only way to survive and gain my mother's approval was to put my head down and keep moving.

By the time I reached adulthood, that mindset had hardened. In college, I never missed a class. In fact, I pushed myself so hard that I graduated a year early. As a professional, I worked through everything—illness, grief, and burnout. When I was at my worst, I took cold medicine, smiled through meetings, and carried on. I didn't know how to rest. I didn't even know rest was allowed.

So, when Allen mocked my dancing on the beach—when he turned a private vulnerability into a punchline—I didn't tell him it hurt. I had been trained to endure, to perform, and to stay quiet. And what I didn't realize yet was that I had married someone who knew exactly how to use that conditioning against me.

What I Know Now

For most of my life, I believed abuse was something you could point to—dark bruises, screaming matches, and broken objects or bones. It took years of clinical work, graduate training, and sitting with clients to understand that some of the most damaging forms of abuse leave no visible marks.

Emotional and psychological abuse—especially narcissistic abuse—is designed to be invisible. It builds slowly, quietly, and in ways that make you question your reactions long before you ever question the abuser. Tiny jabs passed off as jokes. Controlling behaviors disguised as concern. Mocking dressed up as humor. And manipulation framed as love.

This was the terrain Allen thrived in. And by the time he came into my life, I had already had low self-esteem, low self-worth, little self-love, and a sense of not being enough. I learned to believe that about myself as a child—from a narcissistic mother who saw emotions as weaknesses and rest as laziness.

Clinically, narcissistic abuse is systematic and repeated patterns of emotional, psychological, financial, and sometimes physical and/or sexual maltreatment that is inflicted upon another person by an individual who lacks empathy and has an overwhelming need for control. The tactics often appear subtle—gaslighting, blame-shifting, isolation, devaluation—but they serve a single purpose: to destabilize your reality and make you dependent.

Allen never raised a fist. He raised doubts—within me. Because I'd grown up in a home where my feelings were dismissed and my instincts rejected, it didn't take much for him to teach me how to ignore myself. He didn't create the pattern; he recognized it—and used it.

Gaslighting is one of the most disorienting forms of narcissistic abuse. It is the systematic denial of your reality—*you're imagining things, that never happened, you're too sensitive*—designed to make you distrust your own mind. It doesn't just distort memory; it erodes identity.

The danger of gaslighting isn't the lie—it's the way it steals your ability to believe yourself.

With Allen, gaslighting was effortless. It was him brushing off my unease about the proposal. It was him insisting a cruel prank was "funny." It was him turning my vulnerabilities into a punchline. And slowly, methodically, it worked.

The impact of this kind of abuse is quiet, cumulative, and devastating. Each moment was small enough to dismiss individually. But together, they shaped the landscape of my self-worth. I questioned my reactions before I ever questioned his behavior. I swallowed discomfort, fear, and intuition because conflict felt dangerous. I took on all the labor—financial, emotional, and domestic—because I had been conditioned to over-function.

This is the real damage of narcissistic abuse: it fractures you from the inside, until you stop trusting the one compass you desperately need—yourself.

My Healing

My healing began with vocabulary. As a lifelong learner, I needed language before I could let myself acknowledge the truth. Understanding terms like *narcissistic abuse* and *gaslighting* gave me a framework to apply to my life.

But I won't sugarcoat it: applying that language to my own story was excruciating. Every time I read a definition or heard an example, I found a loophole to protect the people who hurt me.

Maybe it wasn't that bad. He didn't say those exact words.
Maybe I'm making a mountain out of a molehill.
Maybe I don't remember correctly.
My mom always made sure I had food—that's not abuse.

One of the hardest parts of healing was allowing myself to revisit, relive, and re-feel the moments I had spent decades minimizing. I didn't just have to remember what happened—I had to understand the patterns beneath what happened.

Patterns tell the truth whether or not you're ready to hear it. And the truth was that the same dynamics—manipulation, control, minimization, humiliation—showed up again and again, beginning in childhood and repeating throughout my life. Each predator took a bite out of my sense of self until I no longer trusted my own instincts.

Some memories resurfaced with the help of people who had witnessed parts of my childhood. Others emerged only when I sat still enough to let them rise. Sometimes they came gently; other times they crashed in like waves, uninvited and overwhelming. Random recall would hit me at inconvenient times, and learning how to process those moments became part of my healing. It still is.

Healing wasn't a single moment of clarity. It was thousands of tiny acknowledgments and being able to say to myself:

This really happened.
This was real.
That was abuse.

And slowly, painfully, I began stitching together a narrative I could finally believe—the truth I had survived, and the truth I was finally ready to claim.

2

His Vow, My Debt

On our wedding day, Allen gave me a letter. In it, he wrote that he was "only doing this once"— he said I was his soulmate and the one person meant to make him happy. At the time, I read it as a romantic promise. Later, I would come to understand it for what it truly was: a threat disguised as devotion.

Even before we said our "I dos," a quiet resentment had already begun to take root. Allen was fully capable of working, but he didn't. There was always an excuse.

While finishing my PhD and buried under the weight of a dissertation, Allen insisted his job was to stay home with the boys, even though both were enrolled in full-day daycare. He made it sound like a noble sacrifice. And I convinced myself we were a team—that this chapter, me finishing my doctorate, was just one leg of the longer journey we were taking together.

I had a plan: after my graduation, we'd move back to the East Coast to be closer to my family. I was so sure of this future that I'd written it into the divorce agreement with the boys' father. Allen agreed. He even seemed enthusiastic about the fresh start in a new place.

As I secured a faculty position and everything began falling into place for our move, my doubts kept building. Why couldn't Allen pick up a short-term job, even just to help with the bills while we prepared to relocate? I was working full-time as a school counselor, scraping by on a meager salary while my credit card debt ballooned. And I wasn't just feeding my two boys anymore—I was feeding him, too.

With my patience wearing thin, Allen finally took a part-time job at a retail clothing store. It was a concession, not a commitment. He timed it perfectly, too: right before our wedding, just enough effort to keep me appeased and ensure I'd follow through with the nuptials.

That spring, we celebrated my graduation and our wedding—then packed our lives into boxes for the cross-country move. Once again, I covered everything: the travel, the rentals, and all of the logistics.

As we loaded the moving truck, it became clear that we had to make choices. Not everything would fit. Instead of parting with his boxes of *Playboy* magazines and comic books, Allen convinced me to leave behind some of the boys' toys and furniture. He claimed his things might be worth money someday.

Even then, I knew he'd never sell them. They'd just gather dust in our basement. But I conceded because it wasn't worth the fight.

Once we got to the East Coast, we stayed with my dad until our house was ready. He wasn't charging us rent—a generosity I genuinely appreciated. Between the weddings, the move, and months of covering our bills alone, I was deep in debt.

Just weeks after we arrived, I started my new faculty position in New Jersey. It was a role I had worked hard for, and something I was genuinely proud of—but the logistics were punishing. My commute was ninety minutes each way, and my classes were scheduled in the evening.

Meanwhile, Allen struggled to find work in our new hometown. The excuses changed, but the pattern didn't: I worked. He didn't.

To keep us afloat, I began seeing private therapy clients. I told myself it was just a temporary hustle, just until he found something.

Finally, Allen got hired at a local insurance agency. A few months later, he was fired. He blamed the agent: "That guy is impossible to work with," he said. He soon accepted another position at a different branch, working for a woman. And just like that, his entire demeanor shifted. He threw himself into this job with a kind of energy and enthusiasm I hadn't seen in a long time.

His new boss found him to be incredibly helpful as he volunteered for extra tasks, took initiative, and made himself indispensable. Allen knew how to present as the guy who'd give you the shirt off his back—especially with women. He always played the hero.

Take one Sunday, for example: the office was closed, but the building alarm went off because a door had been left slightly ajar—probably by the cleaning crew. Allen offered to save his boss a forty-five-minute drive by checking the door himself. But rather than shutting it and moving on, he turned it into a production, calling her multiple times with unnecessary updates and spinning this simple situation into a crisis he had expertly managed.

This was what he did: show up when it made him look good, exaggerate his effort, and reap the praise. Not because he cared. But because it fed his image.

After six months, construction on our new home was complete and we were able to move in. The house was nestled between two people I love deeply—a hundred yards from my dad's house on one side and fifty yards from my cousin's house on the other.

It should have felt like home and safety. But there was already a catch. Allen had claimed to be the victim of credit fraud, so the mortgage had to be in my name alone. In hindsight, this turned out to be a blessing. At the time, though, it felt like yet another way for me to shoulder the financial burden while Allen sidestepped responsibility.

Not long after we settled in, Allen started pressuring me to have another baby. While he had taken on a father role with Nicholas and Christopher, he had made it clear he wanted a child of his own. I believed him when he said it was about love and building a future together.

But I was also stretched thin as I tried to manage our debt, juggling a full-time university job that demanded teaching, service, and publishing; commuting long hours; working at a private practice; and parenting two boys. I even took on a third job, teaching adjunct courses through an online university. I was overwhelmed and not in a place to possibly take on more.

The pressure from Allen didn't let up though. His desire for a child of his own was constant and overwhelming. Eventually, I gave in and said I was ready. It didn't take long before I was pregnant with Joe.

This pregnancy was harder on my body than my first two. Still, I pushed myself. I was determined to contribute financially in every way I could. I increased my online teaching course load and began mentoring doctoral students for additional cash.

I could see that the balance in our marriage was off. I was carrying everything—career, parenting, and bills—while Allen didn't seem motivated to do much at all. But when I expressed frustration, he flipped the narrative and told me that my stress was my strength.

"You don't even know how to sit still," he'd say. "You'll always find something else to do."

My mother used to say the same thing. Different tone, same message: rest was failure. And still, it confused me. I was pregnant and wanted to rest. I needed to rest. But I also couldn't ignore the reality of the bills piling up and the pressure to keep our family afloat.

Toward the end of my pregnancy, Allen's mother came to visit. The timing was intentional—she wanted to be there for the birth, or shortly after. I planned to labor at home for a while before heading to the hospital, but the pressure from Allen and his mother to have the baby on their schedule was intense. Because I had been induced with my first two pregnancies, they convinced me that it was routine—no big deal. Wanting to keep the peace as usual, I agreed. But the truth is, it wasn't what I thought was best for me or the baby.

The morning of the induction, we arrived at the hospital, and my water was broken. Then we waited. Allen complained about how tired he was—and promptly fell asleep. As he snored beside me in a hospital chair, I lay there, contracting and in pain.

Eventually, he woke up, declared he was hungry, and left to get food. When he returned, he brought the meal back into the labor room. The smell was torture, and when I said that, he responded that he would "eat fast." And he did—but the smell lingered. When I gave birth to my older two boys, their father had left the room to eat out of respect. Allen's choice felt selfish and insensitive, despite his claim that it was about staying with me.

When my pain intensified, I finally got an epidural. Allen fell asleep again, and remained asleep until the nurses began preparing the room for delivery. That's when he finally stirred—just in time for the main event.

Allen looked stunned when he saw our baby for the first time.

"It's . . . a boy?" he asked, incredulously.

During the entire pregnancy and with no evidence other than a gut feeling, Allen had insisted that our baby was a girl to anyone who asked, from his family to random people on the street. He wasn't used to being wrong, and it took him a moment to adjust.

Then came the conversation about names.

"There are too many Tonys in your family," he said flatly. "We do not need another one."

We arrived on Joseph as a first name, Anthony as a middle name—after my father. We agreed to call him Joe.

I didn't take much time off work. At just six weeks old, Joe started daycare—joining Christopher at the same center. My dad stepped in to help, and so did the older boys. Joe was surrounded by love and attention. In many ways, he was spoiled. And it showed. He thrived in it.

But soon I started to see a change in Allen, especially with how he treated the older boys. If Joe cried and their sweet, well-meaning efforts to soothe him—offering a pacifier, dancing, singing, or handing him a toy—didn't work, Allen snapped at them.

"What did you do to him?" he'd bark, as if their kindness had caused the distress.

It was subtle at first, but even my oldest, Nicholas, remembers that Allen's treatment of him started to shift.

After a few months of noticing differences in our family dynamic, I knew something in our relationship needed attention and asked Allen to join me in couples' therapy. At first, he agreed, and Joe slept quietly in his carrier during our sessions. But it didn't take long for Allen to check out—emotionally and mentally. He began labeling me as the problem and eventually declared that it would be better if I just went alone.

So, I did. I stayed in therapy—mostly to survive. I was juggling a demanding career, parenting three children, running a household, and doing it all alongside a partner who contributed very little.

I also knew I needed help. There were still layers of pain, silence, and confusion from my past that I hadn't yet unpacked.

To start untangling what was happening in my present, I needed to go back—to the place where I first learned to question my reality: my early childhood.

What I Know Now

At its core, financial abuse is about control—controlling access to resources, controlling who carries the burden, and controlling the conditions under which someone is allowed to survive. In narcissistic abuse, money becomes one of the most efficient tools of domination, creating dependency and shaping the power dynamics of the relationship. When a narcissist uses finances as leverage, the victim—whether a partner or a child—learns to navigate fear, scarcity, and obligation. Research shows that financial instability, or even just the fear of it, is one of the top reasons survivors stay in or return to abusive relationships.

With my mother, financial control was subtle but powerful. When I was a child, she held the keys to anything that required her signature, and every form of support came with strings attached. I learned to do as much as possible with as little as necessary, and some of those patterns still echo through my life: like reusing paper cups in the bathroom until they're literally falling apart. It sounds like a silly thing but is driven by a deeply embedded fear of not having what I might need next time—even as a full stack of unused cups sits right beside me.

With Allen, the fear looked different. I was afraid of what he'd take if I left. I feared what I'd owe him and how he might weaponize the legal and financial system against me. That fear tethered me to a marriage where I was doing all the earning, all the planning, and all the providing—while he benefited from the illusion of partnership.

The pressure Allen put on me to have another child was also a form of manipulation I now recognize as deeply tied to narcissistic motivations. Narcissists often want children not to build a family, but to secure an anchor—a permanent tie to the person they want to control. It never looks like manipulation. It looks like longing. It looks like love. It looks like wanting to "complete the family." But underneath, it is profoundly transactional: the creation of a mini-me, a source of reflected glory, and a guarantee that a partner cannot easily leave.

After Joe was born, the signs replicated themselves: resentment toward the older boys, disproportionate anger over normal childhood behavior, subtle shaming that suggested their innocence was somehow a burden. These weren't quirks or bad moods. They were warning signs—of triangulation, conditional love, and emotional manipulation. Patterns I had lived through before that were now creeping into my children's lives.

My Healing

Healing required me to confront the reality of my situation—not the softened version I had rationalized, but the truth of what was actually happening. At first, the term financial abuse felt wrong. It didn't match the definition I carried in my mind. I was the one earning the money. I handled the bills. I managed the household finances. How could Allen have been financially abusing me?

I had to learn to look deeper.

All of my money went toward our survival—rent, food, childcare, commutes, debt, and our mortgage. All of Allen's money went toward whatever he pleased. He contributed nothing to our shared life yet benefited from everything I provided.

I had to revisit how many times I absorbed the cost of his choices: paying for his meals long before we were even dating, covering the multiple weddings and the move, buying tools and electronics he "needed," paying for a dog I didn't want, and lending him money for the engagement ring he never paid back. I skipped my own small comforts—highlights in my hair, new clothes, anything that felt like a treat—to make ends meet. Everything I did was to keep us afloat; everything he did positioned him to benefit from my labor.

I had to acknowledge how often Allen performed helpfulness in public. A great example? When we dined with friends, he would theatrically offer to pay the bill and then quietly slip my credit card into the portfolio. He was also masterful at reframing my burnout as strength, insisting I was simply someone who "didn't know how to sit still."

I believed him. Of course I did. My worth had always been measured in what I could do, not who I was. I was raised to equate exhaustion with value and productivity with love. Allen simply reinforced what my childhood had taught me.

Survival isn't the same as safety, but my nervous system had been wired for over-functioning since childhood. I confused being needed with being loved. I confused chaos with normalcy. I confused sacrifice with commitment.

And then there was the decision to have a third child—a decision shaped less by desire and more by pressure. I adored my son long before he was born, and nothing will ever change that. But I had to face the truth that having my youngest was less about building our family and more about the entrapment of me.

Healing required looking back with honesty—not cruelty, not judgment—just clarity. It required recognizing manipulation in places I once called love. It required forgiving myself for what I didn't know. It required reclaiming the parts of me that learned to survive instead of thrive.

And perhaps most of all, it required accepting that even when the patterns feel familiar—even when they feel like home—they are not where I belong.

3

The Slow Poisoning

From the outside, my childhood looked relatively normal—especially by Gen X standards. Tony and I had the kind of freedom that people now call character building: we rode bikes until the streetlights came on, walked ourselves to the corner store, and spent entire days unsupervised.

But beneath that rugged independence, things didn't quite add up. The question I dreaded most from friends was the one about the camper in our backyard—and the grown man who lived inside it.

It was obvious to nearly everyone that my mother and Al were having an affair. But for reasons I still don't fully understand, my parents not only allowed him to reside in a camper in our yard but also continued living together as if nothing had changed. The denial was suffocating.

Meanwhile, Al kept turning the camper into something far more permanent: adding flat stones to keep it from sinking, a large fire pit, boat pylons lining a makeshift walkway, and a built-up wooden staircase leading to the door.

This wasn't just a trailer—it was a homestead. A monument to how deeply he'd embedded himself into our lives, and how completely silence had become the cost of keeping the peace.

By second grade, Al was a constant presence. He would show up at school concerts and church events, always introduced as my mother's "friend." At home, he'd appear at the back door and slip in for coffee, a snack, or a shower in the basement bathroom. Al and my mom ran a business together—a book bindery—which offered a convenient excuse for the hours they spent strategizing, or doing whatever else they weren't calling it.

Back then, I didn't have the words for what I was seeing. I only knew that Al's presence and emotions made me uncomfortable.

One night, on an otherwise ordinary Monday during the summer between fourth and fifth grade, things between us changed. My dad was out playing cards at a friend's house, and my mom had taken Tony to soccer practice. Before she left, she handed me a stack of papers and told me to bring them to Al.

Since they co-owned the bindery, running small errands for Al—delivering papers, dropping off supplies, whatever he needed—was one of my regular chores. I didn't question it. Back then, I was a kid and didn't question much at all.

As I crossed the yard and knocked on the camper door, I braced myself for the inevitable: a wave of stale smoke and the bitter, choking scent of coffee. I hated that smell.

When Al opened the door to greet me, I noticed he looked sad. I asked what was wrong, and he let out a long, heavy sigh and invited me to sit on his lap. That wasn't unusual—Al was treated like family.

But this time, his touch lingered. And he mumbled something I couldn't quite catch as he began rubbing my back—slowly at first, then more insistently.

It was too much. Too intense. As a wave of discomfort settled over me, I started searching for a way out. I lied and told him I made him a present and needed to go back to the house to get it. It wasn't true, but I needed an excuse.

Leaving the camper brought only a momentary sense of relief. I knew I'd have to go back. Al's volatility was something I tried to avoid at all costs. I knew that if I didn't return, he might get even more sad . . . or mad.

I ran into the house, grabbed a piece of construction paper, cut out a heart, and scrawled "I love you" across it. It didn't feel strange to say that. Al was a friend of the family, and I wanted him to feel better. I also wanted to avoid a blowup. I hoped this little gift would make him smile.

Back at the camper, I handed Al the heart. He read the message and turned to me with big eyes: "Do you . . . do you really?" he asked pathetically. His tone was innocent, almost childlike.

"Yeah," I responded. He immediately scooped me up into a big hug and started rubbing my back again.

After a minute or two, he lifted my shirt and began caressing my underdeveloped breasts. He massaged them for a few moments before leaning forward and putting his lips over my nipples, alternating between kissing and sucking.

My body reacted to the stimulation. No one had ever talked to me about right or wrong touch. This felt good to my body, but my mind wasn't so sure. I was so confused. I kept quiet.

After a few minutes, Al lifted his head from my chest and peered out the camper window. Only my mom or dad would have stumbled upon this situation, and Al's awareness of the window suggested to me that what we were doing was wrong. But he squashed any fears I may have had by instructing me to keep watch so he didn't get caught "pleasuring me." That's how he described it.

Later that night, when my mom asked, I told her I'd returned Al's things and left it at that. I didn't say anything else.

Somewhere deep down, I believed I had encouraged what happened. Al made me feel special and told me it was our little secret—something just between us. And he made it clear that if anyone found out, I would get in trouble. Not him. His concern was never about what he had done. It was about keeping me silent.

The encounters became regular. Although his tone eventually became much more sinister, at first he told me this was love—and his touching was how a man showed love to a woman. He insisted that my body's physical reactions were examples of me being "turned on," and I believed him when he said it was normal.

What I Know Now

Childhood sexual abuse is not always violent. Most of the time, it comes wrapped in confusion, secrecy, and moments that feel simultaneously wrong and strangely intimate. This is what is known as grooming.

In clinical work, grooming is the slow, calculated conditioning of a child's mind and body, much like love-bombing functions in an adult narcissistic relationship. It is intentional, incremental, and designed to erode boundaries one thin layer at a time.

What happened to me in Al's camper wasn't a single moment of abuse—it was a slow poisoning of my sense of self, my understanding of love, and my trust in my own body.

Grooming always follows a pattern. The abuser builds closeness and then exploits that trust. They test reactions with small boundary violations, which escalate over time. They normalize what is not normal, creating secrecy and dependency and calling it love.

Al's actions were not accidents or impulses. They were deliberate. And they were devastating—not only because he violated my body, but because he violated my developing beliefs about safety, touch, affection, and truth.

One of the most painful and least understood aspects of childhood sexual abuse is the body's automatic response. A child's body can experience physical stimulation even while the mind freezes or recoils. This involuntary biological reaction is often weaponized by abusers as "proof" that the child wanted or enjoyed it. This is one of the deepest betrayals a survivor can endure—having a body that responded in ways the brain could not understand, and an abuser who used that confusion as a tool.

Grooming didn't just steal my innocence. It shaped how I interpreted love, danger, and trust for decades. It rewired my nervous system, trained me to silence myself, and left me believing that discomfort was normal and my needs were irrelevant. The slow poisoning began in that camper, but its effects echoed throughout my adulthood.

My Healing

For years, I carried a belief that is tragically common among survivors: I must have done something to cause my abuse. I "let it happen." I could have—or should have—stopped it.

Like so many who endured childhood trauma, I internalized responsibility that never belonged to me.

The truth is simple and undeniable: children do not have agency in abusive dynamics.

When it happened to me, I froze. I went quiet. I appeased. I did what I thought I needed to do to get through it. And those survival strategies—silence, compliance, and self-blame—followed me well into adulthood. I normalized discomfort. I questioned my memories, my instincts, and my worth. I mistrusted myself before I ever mistrusted anyone else.

Naming what happened to me as "abuse" brought freedom, but it also brought a kind of grief I wasn't prepared for: the grief of realizing that the people who should have stood beside me would never speak of it. Even as an adult, the continued silence of my extended family adds another layer of pain. I know they remain quiet out of fear, discomfort, or the familiar safety of denial. I also know that their refusal to acknowledge what happened doesn't erase my story. It just makes the landscape of healing lonelier.

It took more than thirty years before I could face the fear that lived in my body—the flashbacks, the hypervigilance, the shame, the constant feeling of being "dirty" or damaged. I had to learn that the feelings in my body were not defects—they were echoes of trauma that had never been soothed or acknowledged.

My healing came from naming it as a child, naming it again as an adult, and continuing to name it every time shame tries to take back the narrative. It came from understanding that the confusion was not my fault, the physiological responses were not my consent, and keeping silent was not my responsibility.

And as I move through my healing, I am learning—slowly, steadily—that reclaiming my truth is the first step toward reclaiming my entire self.

4

As Abuse Got Louder, So Did My Silence

To most of the world, Al came across as quite the charmer. He was the kind of charismatic man who chatted up neighbors, cashiers, and complete strangers with ease. He made fast friends. He could fix a broken sink or patch a leaky roof, and that made him seem useful—like someone you'd want to keep around.

But I don't know how else to say it: Al was a real asshat. The public image he curated was a far cry from reality. The truth was that he carried himself like he owned the world and expected everyone else to fall in line.

His hands were massive, cracked, and calloused from years of manual labor, thick with the grime he never quite managed to wash away. He was almost a caricature of himself—reeking of old coffee and cheap cigarettes that he'd try to mask with even cheaper cologne. He used old-fashioned words—like "beau" instead of "boy"—and, in later years, took to wearing a fedora. It was like he thought he was some sort of old-school Southern gentleman.

Beneath the surface was a sinister man who believed he was always, always right—and that everyone else existed solely to meet his needs.

His moods could turn on a dime, and when he entered a room, his presence swallowed it whole.

A great example? One year in grade school, I planned my first real sleepover for my birthday. My best friend and I picked out games, and my dad bought a bunch of snacks. It was supposed to be a night of carefree fun, just for me—a night that, for once, I didn't have to share.

The evening started off exactly how I'd hoped: full of laughter, whispers, and the kind of carefree magic that only comes from being a kid with your friends.

Then, out of seemingly nowhere, Al's voice tore through the moment. He came lumbering from the camper, across the yard, and into our living room, booming, "Where's the birthday girl?" He was loud, theatrical—and hungry for attention.

It got worse. As soon as he was inside, Al dropped to all fours and began crawling around like an animal—growling, snorting, and lunging at my friends. At first, they giggled nervously, unsure if it was supposed to be a joke. But it didn't take long before confusion turned into discomfort.

My best friend fled to my brother's room to hide. The others scattered, running through the house, dodging Al's grasp. I stood frozen, holding my breath, watching it all unfold like a nightmare I couldn't stop. This was supposed to be a joyful night to celebrate my birthday: what was happening?!

I was mortified. And when he finally left, I was overwhelmed with shame. The night I had looked forward to for weeks was ruined. All I could think was that none of the girls would want to be friends with me after it.

My mother, of course, was there, too. But she didn't seem to be bothered by what unfolded. When I finally worked up the courage to tell her how uncomfortable Al had made my friends feel, she called me ungrateful. Then, she demanded that I hug him and thank him for coming to my party. When I did what she ordered, he picked me up off the ground and pressed his mouth against my face, neck, and head in a barrage of forceful, unwanted kisses.

Looking back, I realize I could never have stopped him from walking in. The situation was out of my control. But I still wonder how it ever became normal for a grown man—who didn't live with us—to walk into a little girl's sleepover like he belonged there. He wasn't invited, and he wasn't family. He should never have been anywhere near us.

That manufactured normalcy took root in my childhood imagination. By the time Al began touching me, I was well-trained to play along and keep the peace. I also had no roadmap for what was safe or appropriate. There were no adults around to give me knowledge, language, or permission to name the abuse.

Al regularly invited Tony and me to his camper for sleepovers. At first, we went willingly, tempted by the promises of games, candy, and fun. The sleepovers were also a chance to feel special. Al always made great efforts to ensure we could be alone.

One time, our "game" involved Tony stationed at one end of the camper and me at the other, with the doors shut between us. Al moved back and forth between our spaces. I don't know what the game involved for Tony. When Al was with me, he stroked his penis and talked about "gum." I remember wondering what bubble gum had to do with anything—confusion that only grew once he ejaculated into a washcloth and proudly displayed the goo for me as a symbol of my ability to please him.

But as the camper sleepovers continued, I became skeptical that what was happening was okay. In the darkness, Al told me I was his girlfriend. But in the light of day, he was quick to remind me to stay silent, warning that our interactions would end if we were ever caught.

I also wasn't always on board with Al's demands. There were times I was forced to do things I didn't want to do: one time, he gave me specific instructions to put my mouth on his erect penis, and I was disgusted. The only thing I knew about penises was that they were used for peeing, and I didn't want my mouth to touch pee.

I wanted to say no when he would insist on certain games, too, like strip poker. But I was also trapped. I didn't dare suffer the wrath of saying no. Al was an adult, and his temper kept everyone in line.

I did try, in small and strange ways, to make the abuse stop. For a period of time, I was rude to Al, hoping he'd think we weren't friends anymore. That only made him angry. I stopped bathing and wiping after using the bathroom, hoping my filth would repel him. He never seemed to notice.

The more I began suspecting that what was happening between us was wrong, the more I started searching for answers. The internet didn't exist, and I didn't really know what I was looking for. I just hoped I'd recognize it when I found it. In the self-help sections of libraries and bookstores, I scanned titles with a quiet desperation.

Sometimes a book's title or blurb hinted at something familiar, but as soon as my heart quickened, fear rushed in to shut it down. Al had made one thing very clear: no one could ever know. If I told the truth, the consequences would be catastrophic for me—or so he said.

Still, one afternoon, I checked out a small stack of books that felt close to what I needed. As the librarian slid them across the counter and said "Have a good day," I held my breath, fearful that she'd notice the titles and say something. She didn't.

My mom would drive us home from the library and would sometimes ask about the books we checked out. This time, thankfully, she didn't. At home, I put the stack in my bedroom closet and waited until a quiet moment when no one was around.

Of course, the books only reinforced what I had already suspected: what Al was doing was completely wrong. Although relieved to have this fear confirmed, I was overwhelmed with deep shame and a vague sense of guilt that I had been a "willing" participant in all of it. I wasn't ready to tell my mom. In the end, I never had to.

A few days later, she found the books in my closet and confronted me, angrily. I finally let it out. I said Al had been touching me and I wanted it to stop.

My mother's response was not compassion. It was not care. It was not even centered around my basic safety. She cared about one thing and one thing only: her reputation.

"Who else did you tell about this?" she hissed. I responded that I had told my cousin Michele, who was nine months older than me. This news caused her to erupt with anger.

"You can't tell Michele anything, Tina," she scolded me. "She can't keep a secret and will tell Aunt Dody!" Her reaction said everything. Her priority was to consider what others might think of her, and the idea that Aunt Dody—her sister—might know was too much.

After some time, my mother said she'd speak with Al. I was thrilled, thinking that the nightmare was finally over. This was a short-lived victory, however, because when the time came to confront him, she made me go with her. It was awful, but my strength came from the knowledge that maybe, finally, it would stop.

But Al was equally as talented at flipping the script, and as soon as she got the words out, he began crying dramatically. He dropped to his knees, admitting to everything and pleading for us to forgive him. This was his way of teaching me to become a woman, he said. It would never happen again, he said. As he sobbed, he wrapped his arms around my mother's waist, heaving into her.

When the scene ended and we finally walked away, my mom made me a promise: "Tina, if this ever happens again, we will leave—I'll close the shop and we will leave." It was a statement I'd never heard before, and I wondered if finally, my nightmare would end.

But whatever hope those words gave me didn't last long. By the next day, all had been forgiven and forgotten. And within a few weeks, we were taking a family trip to Busch Gardens and Virginia Beach . . . with Al. While I didn't want him there, I held onto the hope that having both of my parents and my brother there would keep me safe.

Busch Gardens was bigger than any amusement park we had ever been to in our lives. For a little while, Tony and I got lost in the joy of the rides.

But then we lined up for the sky ride, which took two people at a time in little capsules that traveled through the air from one end of the park to the other. When we got in line, we got separated. My mom traveled alone in the first capsule, my brother and dad were in the next one, and Al and I were in the rear.

This was very unfortunate—you can't escape on a sky ride, its little cars dangling high and out of earshot of park guests. And sure enough, once in the air, Al lunged at me, grabbing my body into a bear hug and groping at my chest. His mouth found its way to my breasts and he began to suck on my nipples.

As I demanded him to stop—but he didn't—I began to fear that the ride would fall off the cable if I moved too much. All I could do was scream, hoping someone would hear me. They didn't—the capsules were too far apart—but my screaming was enough to make him stop.

The day we got home from that trip, Al penetrated me with his penis for the first time. I was twelve. I don't remember much other than leaving the camper, going back to my room, closing the door, and shutting everyone out. I had been raped. And I was numb.

In the end, telling my mom what happened to me backfired in the most horrifying way. The abuse not only didn't stop—it got worse. Al, having been exposed, only grew angrier and bolder.

Looking back, especially as a mom myself, I can't believe what my mother allowed to happen to her own daughter—consistently and right in front of her.

Sometimes I'd test her. One time while we were driving in the camper, Al suggested we play a game. This particular "game" required me to squeeze Al's penis so hard that it hurt and then run to the back of the camper's "living room" to get away from him. I was only a preteen, but my mom was not fazed at all by this scene. In fact, she giggled and laughed through it.

Another time, Tony and I were swimming in our above-ground pool as our mom and Al lounged on the deck nearby. Suddenly, out of nowhere, Al announced, "Hey, let's go skinny dipping!"

Tony and I said no. Unfazed, Al jumped in and removed his bikini swimsuit—attire I already found gross because every other man in my family wore swim trunks. And then in one quick movement, he pulled off my swimsuit and tossed it across the pool.

I was horrified—and scared! Tony noticed and swam quickly to retrieve my swimsuit. Meanwhile, I slipped from Al's grip and hoisted myself up onto the side of the pool.

But Al was faster. He grabbed at me and pulled me back into the water. I was incredibly aware of his nudity, and my own, and the fact that his penis was dangling near my butt. I wanted out of this situation and started screaming.

My mom, watching, became concerned—but not about the scene unfolding in front of her. She was worried about the noise I was making.

"Tina—shut up! You'll wake up the neighbors!" she snapped.

Her message rang loud and clear: using my voice was taboo. I was being assaulted right before her eyes, but the bigger issue was what the neighbors would think. My experience—and my reaction to that experience—was an inconvenience, a nuisance, and an embarrassment.

I realized I could never trust my mother to help me. She simply didn't care.

Her continued complacency—bordering on encouragement—told me that Al's behavior was perfectly acceptable and normal. Her words and actions convinced me that telling anyone would only make trouble for myself and others. I believed my voice didn't matter, and so I struggled to find the courage to use it.

There was nowhere to turn, no one to trust, and no one to help, so I kept to myself and said nothing. My self-esteem, already low, began to spiral downward. I was trapped. There was nothing I could do to make the abuse stop.

By this time, Al also had stopped trying to convince me that what I was experiencing was pleasure. He was annoyed he'd been found out and relied on force to get his way. I have always been petite, and I didn't have the physical strength to fight him off so I'd try other ways to make him stop.

"You better not get me pregnant," I joked one time. As a preteen, I didn't really understand how pregnancy happened, but it was something I heard in a movie that got a guy to stop having sex with someone, so it seemed worth a shot. And it did work . . . sort of. He didn't rape me that day; instead, he just rubbed his penis on my vagina for what felt like hours.

Afterward, he allowed me to get dressed and asked to speak to me in his "living room," the area of the camper with a small sofa and chair.

"I was just thinking . . ." he said, his voice drifting like it was some kind of beautiful dream. "When you're sixteen, I want you to have my baby."

I didn't react. I couldn't. I knew better. If I flinched, if I showed how repulsed I was, I'd pay for it later. So, I kept my face still and silent, praying he'd forget he ever said it.

What I Know Now

Childhood sexual abuse is not just a violation of the body—it is the slow, systematic dismantling of trust, safety, and identity. And when the abuser is not a stranger, but someone woven into the fabric of the family, the damage has layers: there's the trauma of the abuse itself, and the betrayal of the adults who were supposed to protect you.

Abusers rarely groom only the child—they groom the entire environment. They start small: testing boundaries, normalizing the abnormal, cultivating secrecy, and slowly reshaping the family system until the unthinkable feels routine. By the time any overt abuse occurs, the child has already learned to doubt their instincts and silence their fears. That's the devastating power of grooming: it prepares everyone around the abuser to accept what should never be accepted.

This kind of manipulation is especially common in individuals with narcissistic personality traits. Clinically, narcissism is often understood through three broad patterns. Some people present as *grandiose*: loud, arrogant, superiority-seeking, and dominating. Others fall into a more *vulnerable* or covert style, marked by fragility, hypersensitivity, and a constant posture of victimhood used to manipulate through passivity. The most dangerous form, often called *malignant narcissism*, blends these traits with antisocial behaviors—aggression, cruelty, and a profound lack of empathy.

Al embodied narcissism long before I had the language for it. He was grandiose in public, a victim in private, and cruel behind closed doors. His emotional manipulation—dramatic tears, pleading apologies, performative remorse—was never about accountability. It was about control.

The more devastating betrayal came from my mother.

When she prioritized her reputation over my protection, she taught me a lesson I carried for years: that my safety was less important than her image, that my voice was a liability, and that keeping silent was my responsibility. In her eyes, the abuse of her daughter by her own boyfriend was less shameful than the possibility of others discovering the truth.

Years later, I confronted this same belief from another angle. In my marriage to Allen, I minimized the problems because I had been so thoroughly conditioned to keep the peace. Even as my sons and I endured his wrath, I couldn't fully see it—let alone name it. My mother's voice was still loud in my mind, and I had absorbed her lesson completely: whatever happens in a family stays behind closed doors. Challenges are to be contained within four walls, never revealed, never acknowledged, and certainly never allowed to hint to the outside world that something is wrong.

This is not just emotional neglect. It is complicity. It is the environment in which children learn to doubt themselves instead of the adults hurting them. In that silence, confusion grows. I remember wondering things like:

"If he's sorry, does that mean it wasn't abuse?"
"If my body responded, does that mean I wanted it?"
"If my mother doesn't stop it, does that mean it's okay?"

Now, as a therapist, I know what my child self could not: A child cannot consent. A child cannot seduce. And a child cannot be responsible for the emotions, impulses, or rehabilitation of an adult. My body's involuntary response was not consent, nor complicity—it was biology. And my silence was not agreement—it was survival.

My Healing

In healing, I had to learn to separate what happened to me from who I am. When I finally named the abuse with honesty—not with euphemisms or softening—I saw that I never received what every child deserves: protection, validation, safety, and care.

A crucial part of my healing was learning to see myself not through the distorted lens of the abusers, but through the truth of who I had been: a child. A ten-year-old girl who had been convinced she was older, complicit, and powerful enough to "handle" an adult man's behavior. I had internalized the belief that because my body reacted, I must have wanted it. That lie took decades to unwind.

To bridge the divide between my adult self and my child self, I sat with photographs from those years—snapshots of a girl I had long believed was grown. But when I looked at her face, her size, and her innocence, I finally allowed myself to say:

I was a ten-year-old child.
He was forty years older than me.
It was never my fault.

Understanding the patterns of sexual abuse—and the ways grooming, secrecy, fear, and bodily responses were used against me—has been both clinically meaningful and personally liberating. Although my healing will be a lifelong challenge and an ongoing practice, I am learning to call out the lies I was taught, speak truth even when it makes others uncomfortable, and refuse to internalize the shame that was never mine to carry.

5

A Campaign of Cruelty

The betrayal I felt ran so deep, it hollowed me out. I stopped believing anyone would care, let alone help. If my own mother could witness those moments and do nothing—or worse, laugh—then who in the world could I possibly trust?

Silence became my shield. I kept my head down, did what was expected, and tried not to draw attention to myself. But that kind of pain doesn't stay hidden forever. It finds a way out, even if just in glimpses.

A woman named Mrs. Kelly was my seventh-grade teacher. I'd had her in previous years, and she was the only adult at school I had ever seriously considered confiding in about what was happening at home. In fact, the year before, I'd written her a letter and carried it in my backpack for weeks, trying to summon the courage to hand it to her. Eventually I tore it up. What stopped me wasn't just fear—it was uncertainty. What if Mrs. Kelly was like my mother and told me to let it go?

My mother's voice echoed constantly in my mind: "No one wants to hear about your problems, Tina. Don't make a big deal." She warned me that if I ever spoke up, I'd destroy our family. Not the abuse. Not the lies. Me.

Now, of course, I understand her words differently. What she really meant was that telling the truth would shatter the image she worked so hard to curate—the illusion of a perfect family she needed more than my safety or my voice.

One of our daily assignments at school was to respond to journal prompts that Mrs. Kelly wrote on the chalkboard. We turned in our notebooks each day. At first, it felt light—creative, reflective, even fun. But midway through the year, I must have let something slip. I don't remember the prompt, but whatever I wrote revealed just enough of the weight I was carrying.

The next day, as the bell rang and class ended, Mrs. Kelly slipped me a tri-folded note. My heart pounded. I waited until I was safely in the next classroom before unfolding it.

I skimmed it quickly, then folded it back up just as fast. I was terrified my classmates might somehow sense what it said—like my secrets could seep through the paper.

After a minute or so, I unfolded it again. This time, I read it slowly.

"Dear Tina, I have a pretty good idea of what you're trying to say about your mother's boyfriend. Remember it is your body and NO ONE has the right to make you feel uncomfortable with talk or touch! If you need me, I'll be here for you. Let me know. – Mrs. Kelly"

"Wow, she knows," I thought, a wave of relief washing over me. "Someone finally sees me."

Then a girl sitting next to me noticed the note and asked what it was. I panicked, folded it up, stuffed it away, and said it was nothing. The momentary safety I'd felt vanished. Relief gave way to fear.

Just as quickly as I'd been seen, I was hiding again. While it felt good knowing than an adult had picked up on the clues, I wasn't ready to say more.

Tony and I—and everyone else—knew about our mom's affair with Al for quite a few years, so it was no surprise when our parents finally told us they were getting divorced. It was also no shock to learn we would be moving into a new house with our mother. Those days, it was common for mothers to retain primary custody after a divorce, while fathers typically had visitation rights.

Although we were the only family I knew with divorced parents, and we had no roadmap for what to expect, I had hope that leaving behind the old house, the camper, and the pool would provide a fresh start. Maybe my mother was making changes that would create a better environment for us all.

In hindsight, I'm not sure why I didn't see it coming—but it still stunned me. One day, my mom divorced my dad; the next, Al moved with us into our new house.

Within a week, he was standing in the doorframe of my new bedroom.

Conveniently enough, upon moving in, Al had chosen my room and explained that its location close to the bathroom would be ideal for me. In reality, it was the bedroom located furthest from all the other sleeping spaces. Since my mom wasn't home that night and my brother was already asleep, if I upset him, it was only me that would deal with his wrath.

"Can I come in?" he asked.

He's already in, I thought to myself. *Why did he even bother asking?*

I also knew refusing him entry would cause an explosive outburst, and I didn't want to deal with that even more than I didn't want him there.

"I don't care," I responded, coldly. Al took a few steps forward and sat down on the edge of my bed. He began rubbing my back.

I told him to stop, and he refused. "Doesn't this feel good?" he said softly.

"No," I replied, more forcefully this time. "Stop it and get off of me!"

His reaction was immediate. In one quick swoop, he flipped me over and began fondling my breasts.

Something about this day was different. This time, I fought back. I flailed my arms and twisted my body over and over. I refused to back down. I was disgusted—and done—with this ongoing abuse. And I felt stronger than I had in the past, both emotionally and physically.

The persistent rejection eventually worked. Al huffed a grunt and left. I was so relieved. I was able to get him to stop!

And in that moment, I swore to myself that it was never going to happen again.

The next morning, I found Mrs. Kelly and pulled her aside to confirm everything she'd feared.

"My mother's boyfriend is hurting me," I said. "And last night, he tried to do it again. I told him to stop, but he wouldn't get off of me."

Mrs. Kelly immediately wrapped her arms around me. A hug is such a simple gesture, but one that I didn't regularly receive at home. She promised to be there for me, and I believed her. Finally, an adult was listening to me. Finally, I felt safe.

At the time, I knew nothing about mandatory reporting or what happened when a child disclosed abuse. And no one let me know what to expect, which made the future full of terrifying unknowns.

The very next day, I was called to the front office at school. I went to Catholic school, where Franciscan nuns were often in charge. Our principal and school counselor were there to greet me and didn't waste time. Gently, but directly, they asked me questions.

Eventually, the counselor picked up the phone and dialed a number. As she spoke, everything became very real:

"Hi, yes. I'd like to report a case of child sexual abuse."

As I half-listened to the end of the conversation I could hear, I was both frozen and in a panic. I wasn't worried about what came next with the authorities; I was worried about my mother. She was going to be furious. I knew I absolutely needed to get to her first, before they did, and soften the blow somehow. I didn't know how or what I'd say—but I needed to try.

At the end of the day, Mrs. Kelly pulled me aside and asked if she could call me later to check in. I agreed, suggesting she call after 9:00 p.m. to give me a chance to talk to my mom first.

"Sounds good. Good luck," she said. "And keep a stiff upper lip."

I'd never heard that phrase but I assumed it had something to do with being strong. I didn't feel strong at all.

That evening, I took a deep breath and told my mom that Al had attempted to touch me again the previous night. I told her I fought him off.

She looked at me blankly. She didn't have time for this conversation, clearly, and wasn't interested in it. She sighed heavily. "Stop complaining, Tina; he's just trying to be friendly."

I wasn't surprised by her response. But I also knew she needed to know that this time was different.

"I had to do something about it, and I told Mrs. Kelly," I said.

Her response, as I feared, was rage—immediate, sharp, and directed squarely at me.

"If you have a problem, you come to me," she hissed. "This should have stayed inside the family, but you had to go and tell one of your stupid teachers! What's over is done with, just forget about it!"

She was so angry and venomous that I never told her that there was more and a call had been made to the authorities. That night, silence felt much safer than the truth.

As promised, Mrs. Kelly called to check in. Her follow-through meant the world to me, and I quickly told her that my mom was very upset.

Years later, when we reconnected as adults, Mrs. Kelly shared that she assumed my mother's anger was because she had just learned what had happened to me. It had never occurred to her—because it felt unthinkable—that my mother's rage wasn't about the abuse at all. It was about the fact that I had broken the silence and exposed the truth to a teacher.

The next day at school, I heard my name over the intercom, summoning me to the front office. My mother was there—unannounced—and told the staff she was taking me to lunch.

When I climbed into the car, she was seething. She'd gotten the calls and now knew that the county's Department of Children & Youth was involved.

She didn't ask if I was okay. She didn't ask what had happened. She demanded to know who I'd told.

I said it again: I had told Mrs. Kelly.

"Why can't she keep her nose out of our business?" she snapped.

"Maybe because I asked her for help," I replied.

She drove in silence, her face tight with rage. Eventually, we pulled into a parking lot and Al climbed in the front passenger seat.

"We aren't leaving here until you two work this out," my mother hissed at us. *What does that even mean?* I thought.

Al lit a cigarette, the smoke curling thick through the car like it always did. Then he turned toward me, slowly, deliberately. His eyes were hard—filled with both anger and fear. His voice—booming, sharp—cut through the silence:

"Why did you call them, Tina? WHY?"

It was abundantly clear: the two adults closest to me in life didn't see a child in pain. They saw a threat.

My mom drove us to a local pizza shop, and we ordered slices at the counter. The air was thick with tension as we slid into a booth.

"There's nothing we can do; she already called Children & Youth," my mother finally said, flatly.

Al's voice rose. "Terri, I didn't rape her. I'm not a pervert . . . she messed up everyone's life!"

"Al, you know as well as I do, what you did was wrong," she replied. It's the only time I can remember my mother defending me, and for a brief moment, I felt a flicker of hope. Maybe she'd finally had a change of heart?

But Al had different plans. His face went red, and he wagged his finger an inch in front of my face. "You go back to that school and tell that fucking teacher of yours to stay out of our lives!" he demanded. "Do you understand me? Do you?"

I was so scared that I thought I might pee my pants. But I also felt empowered by what Mrs. Kelly had said. So, I summoned what little preteen sass I could muster.

"For your information, I told her what was going on, and I will keep telling her until the time comes when I decide not to say anymore!"

Al's face contorted, twisted by a fury so sharp it looked like pain. He was a volcano on the edge of eruption.

"I will not let some punk kid ruin my life," he spat.

My mother recognized that she was losing control of the moment and snapped. "Stop it, both of you," she hissed.

We finished our lunch in silence and quietly piled back into the car. My mother dropped Al off first, then drove me back to school. Just before I stepped out of the car, she turned to me and said something she'd promised once before.

"Tina, if this ever happens again, I'll leave Al. I'll close the shop. We'll move away."

This time, her words rang hollow. I wanted to believe her, but I knew better—her actions had already told me everything I needed to know.

And sure enough, by the time I got home that night, the promise was broken.

"I hope you're proud of yourself," she sneered as she saw me. "Al is a nervous wreck because of you—he's too afraid to even come home!"

When I tried to explain, she doubled down. Once again, she accused me of tearing the family apart. She was incredulous that I didn't feel gratitude for everything Al did for our family.

"You are killing me," she said. "You are killing Al. Your grandparents will die if you say things like this."

I ran to my room, shattered. My cry for help had only unleashed more rage.

But deeper inside me, there was a bit of an awakening. Even then, as I weathered my mother's wrath, I learned a truth: survival would require breaking the silence, and I had taken the first step.

The next day at school, when I was called to the main office to meet with someone from Children & Youth, it felt like crossing a threshold. I stepped into a new chapter—one filled with fear and uncertainty, yes. But there was also something else: resolve.

No matter what happened, I would never let Al touch me again.

The caseworker's questions were careful and compassionate—but still probing. I wanted to tell the whole truth; I really did. But the echo of my mother's rage reverberated in my mind and made it hard to speak. I answered sparingly and withheld the most vivid details. Deep down, I was terrified the investigator would see me the way my mother so often had: not as a child in pain, but as a whore, a slut, or—worst of all—a liar.

Still, saying anything at all felt like everything. It was the first time I had shared my truth with someone who I thought might actually help.

That evening, my mom demanded a recap of the conversation. I gave vague answers, hoping they would be enough. They weren't. Her voice sharpened; her fury ignited.

This marked the beginning of my mother's full-blown campaign to break me. I wasn't a daughter to be protected—I was a liability to be silenced.

The attacks became a ritual. Every evening, without fail, she appeared in my doorway—primed to unleash her fury, which escalated as the minutes ticked by. It always began the same: guilt trips, passive-aggressive jabs, and calculated silence. But it never stopped there. Soon came the yelling, the name-calling, the deep, cutting shame. She twisted my words, questioned my motives, and emptied her own self-loathing onto me, as if it were mine to bear.

"You're just making everyone think you're a slut," she'd say. "You don't want people to believe that about you, do you?"

Imagine being a child, lying in bed, and bracing for the sound of your mother's footsteps—not out of comfort, but because you knew what was coming would hollow you out.

What she accused me of most often was being "an evil little girl." At that age, all I knew of evil came from Catholic teaching: evil was the devil, and the devil was destined for hell. If she was right—if I was evil—then speaking out, testifying, telling the truth wouldn't just destroy the family. It would mean I would burn for eternity.

Even at thirteen, I knew: this wasn't about me. It was about preserving her life with Al. Still, her voice became my own. "You're stupid. You're selfish. You're the reason everything's falling apart." My mother said the words. And I came to believe them.

Dissociation is a powerful tool. As the nightly tirades continued, I taught myself to keep my body present and my mind far away. I coached myself silently: "Don't let it in. Don't react." Crying only prolonged the pain, so silence became my armor.

"If you tell your grandparents, they'll die," she'd say, again and again reminding me that it was my silence that kept the world safe. "I'll take Tony and leave. You'll be alone—with even more mental problems than you already have."

Her words weren't just cruel—they were convincing. The force behind them made me believe they were true.

It was psychological warfare—deliberate, relentless, and mean. She cornered me in my room every night for anywhere from thirty minutes to three hours. And when it ended, I'd sit in the dark—too numb to cry, but relieved it was over.

At the time, I didn't recognize her behavior for what it was: emotional abuse. It didn't leave bruises. I just thought she was mean. It wasn't until much later—through therapy and healing—that I understood how manipulative and devastating her words really were.

I started working part-time at a pizza shop, which is where I met Teresa, the thirty-one-year-old daughter of the owner. She had a full-time job during the week, but worked at the shop on weekends. She was strong, sharp-witted, and had a no-nonsense attitude I admired.

Not long after I made the initial report to Children & Youth, Teresa and I got to talking about *Cagney & Lacey*, a show we both loved. I told her I wasn't allowed to watch it anymore, because, according to my mom, it made me "do things." Naturally, she asked what I meant, and that's when I told her about Al. I explained that my mom said the show was "giving me ideas"—as if the courage to report abuse could be traced back to fictional female detectives.

Teresa didn't hesitate. She listened, she believed me, and she supported me. Her validation felt like a lifeline. I felt real love from her—a protective, big-sister kind of love. And she convinced me to talk to another friend of hers named Linda, someone she believed would be a strong support for me.

Over the next several months, as my mother's nightly assaults continued, I spent a lot of time talking on the phone to Linda. She became a steady voice in my life—encouraging me to keep fighting for myself, for justice. I suspect she had her own history with abuse, and maybe, in helping me, she was also healing something within herself. I'll never know for sure.

What I do know is this: whenever I called, she answered. She listened. She validated me. She offered a counter-narrative to everything my mother was trying to drill into me. Linda reminded me—over and over—that I wasn't wrong; that I deserved to be protected. She urged me time and again to tell my dad the truth.

I never met Linda in person. I never even knew her last name. But during one of the darkest times in my life, she was a light.

What I Know Now

Children rely on their caregivers for food and shelter, and for reality-checking—learning who they are through reflection. In healthy families, this mirror affirms the child's worth, offering stability and guidance. But when the mirror is warped, the child doesn't question the mirror. She questions herself. And that is exactly what I did.

As my mother launched her campaign to silence me with nightly tirades, manipulation, and threats, she didn't just call me names. She tried to rewrite my identity by calling me "evil," "selfish," "slut," and "crazy." These weren't offhand insults; they were words turned into psychological weapons and used again and again until they sank into my bones. It was conditioning—a deliberate attempt to make sure I saw myself as the problem, rather than the abuse and the abusers.

And it worked. When my mother told me that if my grandparents found out about the abuse they would die, she made my truth lethal. She put their lives in my hands and then blamed me for holding the weight. If I spoke, I might "kill" the people I loved. So, I did what so many children in abusive systems do: I chose silence, and I called it protection.

This, too, was gaslighting. Not the kind that makes you doubt whether something happened, but the kind that twists your empathy and uses it against you. It turned my compassion into a cage.

I did have a few champions—Mrs. Kelly, Teresa, and Linda—women who noticed, listened, believed me, and offered glimmers of safety. But this is part of the trauma, too: being seen, but not fully saved. Their support mattered deeply, but they couldn't override the power my mother had at home. Their voices were gentle; hers was relentless.

Over time, I internalized the message that my truth was dangerous, my needs were disruptive, and my reality was too much. It was far easier to stay small and silent. So, I learned the art of dissociation. I found ways to leave my body while my mother's words rained down on me. And I mistook that numbness for strength.

My Healing

Only now, with distance and training and healing, can I see the absurdity and cruelty of what was put on my shoulders. No child is born evil. I was not a slut. I was never responsible for managing the emotions—or the mortality—of the adults around me.

Healing from this kind of systemic betrayal required radical truth-telling and rewriting the story my mother worked so hard to implant in me.

In therapy, I learned the language for what happened: emotional abuse, psychological warfare, gaslighting, and dissociation. I had to then bring that language into my everyday life—hold it up to my memories, my body, and my beliefs—and begin to sort what was mine from what was never mine to carry.

I spent time, intentionally, imagining myself sitting with thirteen-year-old me in my childhood bedroom, lying awake, waiting for my mother's rage. I told her what no one told me then:

You are not evil.

You are not ruining anyone's life.

You are telling the truth—and that is something to be proud of.

Slowly, this work unlocked something profound within me: the realization that the woman I am today is exactly the mother my inner child needed.

My healing has meant stepping into that role—protective, steadfast, validating—and refusing to abandon her the way others did. It has meant allowing myself to feel anger on her behalf, sadness for what she lost, and pride in what she endured.

I couldn't stop my mother's campaign of cruelty then. But I can stop it now—by refusing to carry her words as truth, by speaking my own, and by choosing, every day, to stand with the little girl who never stopped fighting, even when all she could do was survive.

6

The Day I Didn't Testify

As a kid, you just wait—for decisions to be made, for consequences to fall, for adults to do whatever they're going to do. You don't act. You endure.

Waiting for whatever came next with the investigation was its own kind of torture. I never knew when or how the next step would come. Or even if it would.

Meanwhile, I was furious at the inaction that made me feel, once again, invisible. I was still living under the same roof as my abuser, and enduring nightly verbal assaults by my mother for having dared report it. It didn't seem like anyone was doing anything to change that.

What I didn't understand at the time was that Children & Youth were quietly working to gather enough evidence to take meaningful action. That process was complicated by my mother, who lied or downplayed the truth at every opportunity—clinging desperately to the life she had built with Al, no matter the cost.

During that time, I continued connecting with a victim's advocate. This woman was someone assigned to my case who sporadically checked in. Frustrated by the lack of progress, Linda continued to encourage me to share more of my story, and as I grew to feel safer with the advocate, I revealed additional details.

Finally, one afternoon, the advocate called the house to update me on the investigation— progress was being made. Unfortunately, Tony answered the phone, and she mistook his voice for my own. He listened intently and then turned to me, demanding to know, "Who is sexually abusing you?"

I panicked. "It's Al, all right?" I said as I grabbed the phone from him. I don't recall Tony's reaction to my answer. Later it occurred to me that, at such a young age, he likely failed to even understand the gravity of the situation.

That same day, a new phase of investigation began. Children & Youth came to our home to interview me. Although Al and my mother were at work, I feared that they would return unexpectedly. I was physically shaking as I shared details. The investigators informed me that I would need to make a full report at the police station.

I thought to myself, *Holy shit, this is actually moving forward. He's going to be held accountable.* And in the very same breath, another thought hit me just as hard: *holy shit, my mom is going to kill me.* Not literally—but I knew she would tear me apart with her words, breaking me down the only way she knew how.

When she found out she was required by Children & Youth to take me to the police station to file an official report, her rage took on an even more sinister tone. She insisted I was ruining my life. This information would kill my grandparents, she said, and their stress-related deaths would be mine alone to carry. Then in the next breath, she accused me of wanting the abuse: I liked it, and that's why I kept going back to Al's camper, she claimed.

Her anger only ever showed up when we were alone. In public, she performed—doing just enough to convince the world she was a good mom.

Since the law required it, she couldn't get out of taking me to the police station to file a statement. What she hadn't expected to see was Mrs. Kelly already waiting when we arrived.

Her presence moved me. This was during summer break, and she showed up in a way that went far beyond her role as my teacher. Seeing her meant more than I could put into words.

My mother's twisted face indicated that she saw it otherwise. "Why is she here?" she hissed.

"She's here to help," I said.

"As long as she's here to help," my mother replied coldly. For whatever reason, she seemed to believe Mrs. Kelly was there to help me recant and protect Al. I wasn't going to tell her otherwise.

As I made the report, Mrs. Kelly sat next to me, and I was flooded with so much shame. I was so afraid my beloved teacher would see me the way my mother did: dirty, broken, and to blame. But she didn't. She stayed and offered quiet reassurances, gentle squeezes on my arm to let me know I wasn't alone.

Afterward, as my mother drove me home, I felt a flicker of pride. I had been brave. I had told the truth.

A week or two after the police interview, my mother informed me that Al was in the hospital. Internal bleeding, she said. He'd had a nervous breakdown. This was also my fault. She used his illness as another weapon, another way to convince me that my truth had caused destruction. Another way to convince me that if my grandparents found out, they'd surely die.

Al was the victim. I was the villain. Again.

Finally, one Tuesday afternoon, something happened. I was working a shift at the pizza shop when the phone rang. When I picked it up, my mother's voice crackled on the other end, sharp with rage: "Al's been arrested."

My hands began to shake. She told me the police had come to their workplace, put him in handcuffs, and taken him away.

I was stunned. Equal parts relieved and terrified. After everything, he was finally being held accountable.

But my mother wasn't done.

"Write down this number," she barked. "Call the judge. Tell them to release him. Fix this mess you made."

I was thirteen. No judge was going to take my call, even if I wanted to make it.

Later that week, the story broke in the *North Penn Reporter*, the local paper that landed on doorsteps across our community. The story didn't mince words. On September 6, Albert Windfelder, age fifty-one, had been arrested "on charges of indecent assault and endangering the welfare of children after being linked to several incidents involving a thirteen-year-old girl."

In the days that followed, the charges escalated publicly to include statutory rape, involuntary deviant sexual intercourse, and corruption of minors. The newspaper reports confirmed that Al had been formally charged and remanded to the county prison on $50,000 bail.

My mother paid Al's bail. Of course she did. Even this wasn't enough for her to prioritize my health and safety. Again, and again, she chose to protect her partner, her image, and her lifestyle over me—her daughter.

Meanwhile, my phone conversations with Linda continued. She continued to encourage me to think about talking to my dad. She felt that if he knew, he might step in to help. I wasn't so sure, but agreed to try.

When I finally told him the truth, his reaction caught me off guard. He didn't get angry at me, which is what I'd expected. He was livid about what had happened to me. His voice was calm but forceful, his words full of reassurance. He promised he would help.

For the first time in a long time, I believed an adult might protect me!

We drove to my mom and Al's house together. When we arrived, he asked me to wait outside while he went in alone to talk to her and Al.

I sat there, heart pounding, lungs tight—holding my breath with hope.

When he finally emerged, I barely recognized him. His face was heavy with something I didn't yet understand. He avoided looking me in the eyes.

"Maybe we should just let this whole thing go," he suggested flatly. "It'll be better for everyone if you just forget about it."

It felt like the floor dropped out from under me. What had they said in that house? What kind of power did they still hold over him? How did my father go from protector to enabler in one conversation? I was crushed. And alone. Again.

I still had one last sliver of hope: that maybe, somehow, the justice system would do what the people around me refused to. I had already made a report to the police. Now we would just wait.

The days leading up to the preliminary hearing were rough. My mom's tirades weren't isolated to evenings anymore—every time she spoke to me, she issued new threats. One of the worst was her promise to remove me from the few things that brought me even the smallest amount of joy or escape—band, choir, cheerleading, my job, and my friends. These were lifelines to me. Without them, I would be completely trapped.

I couldn't turn to anyone for help. My mother insisted our extended family was disappointed in me. She repeatedly told me the news would kill my grandparents. She even implied that if I wanted to run away, no one would have me. "Go ahead and testify, then go live with Mrs. Kelly," she'd say, making sure to twist the knife just so. "But she won't take you either—and you know that."

I was drowning in shame, guilt, and confusion. I wanted to fight. I wanted Al to go to jail. But I was losing steam. According to my mom, I had no one. And I believed her.

A few days before the hearing, after Al had been released from jail, my parents told me they had hired a lawyer "for" me. But the message was unmistakable, and the decision had already been made: the case was going to be dropped. I would forgive and forget.

When we finally sat down with the lawyer, I sat between my parents as he asked me directly, "What do you want to do?"

There was nothing simple about that question.

No matter what I said, I would lose. I knew that. By then, my mother had already issued a string of threats so venomous, so exacting, they had flattened my spirit and shattered my will to fight. I had spent weeks—months—being worn down by her campaign of control. Her voice lived so loudly inside my head that I wasn't even sure where her thoughts ended and mine began.

I didn't feel like I had any choice at all. This was a trap.

"I guess I don't want to testify," I said, my stomach clenching.

I regret those words to this day. I also know I was a child, and my mother had broken my spirit. My dad wasn't going to be the hero. My grandparents, aunts, and uncles were not people I could turn to—my mom made sure of that. No one was coming to help.

With that, the lawyer told us how the court hearing would go. I was to respond to each and every question, he said, with the statement, "I do not wish to testify."

That afternoon, as we left the lawyer's office, my mom beamed with happiness. She knew she had succeeded. She had won. Al would go free.

I've kept this lawyer's business card for decades. Recently, I googled him and realized he was still in practice. I reached out multiple times, but he never returned my emails, calls, or requests for an appointment. That told me everything I needed to know about him. My childhood suspicions were correct. He was only interested in getting paid—not justice.

Up to that point, my only reference for court was what I saw on TV dramas—grand rooms with dark wood, high benches, and a clear separation between the victim and the accused. When we finally stepped into the courtroom for the hearing, it looked nothing like that. The furniture was made of light oak, and the witness stand was a single chair with a mic. The set-up was directly across from the defendant's table. Directly. Al and his attorney were right in front of me.

Wait, what? I remember thinking. *This is how it works? This sucks.* Over and over in my mind was one single thought: This. Sucks.

I had to get away. So, I ran. I ran out of the courtroom and down the hallway. I didn't have a destination in mind. I just needed to get away. This whole situation just . . . sucked, and I wanted to get out of it.

I was ready to use my voice that day. I wanted to testify. I wanted Al to go to jail.

But I was also a thirteen-year-old girl making $3 an hour at a pizza shop and completely dependent on the adults around me. My mother used that fact to control me. And one by one, the adults in the courtroom—my mom, then dad, then the lawyer and the victim's advocate—came and talked to me. They all convinced me to go back into the courtroom.

With question after question from the district attorney, I answered as I had been instructed: "I do not wish to testify."

And when I say that I answered every question with that phrase, I mean it. The DA asked me my name, my age, and things like "Do you know why you're here today?" And I'd repeat the same line. Word for word. Flat and unwavering. "I do not wish to testify."

It should have been painfully obvious that something was amiss. Now, from my adult perspective—especially as someone who's spent years working with children—it's impossible not to see it for what it was: a child parroting a rehearsed phrase and terrified to step out of line.

And with each repeated phrase, I felt like I was disappearing more and more. The little girl who had suffered and survived was being erased, syllable by syllable. I had rehearsed these words out of fear—but every time I spoke them, I hated myself more.

And if you were sitting in that courtroom as an adult, watching a scared little girl repeat the same robotic sentence over and over, wouldn't you think something was wrong? Wouldn't everything in you scream that something about this wasn't right?

Even at thirteen, I knew what my mom, dad, and Al were asking me to do was wrong. They wanted silence. They wanted to erase what happened and for Al to walk free. And I had no choice. Obedience to my mother was nonnegotiable, and no one else intervened. Not the judge, not the lawyer my parents hired, not even Children & Youth.

Sure enough, a few days later, that story appeared in the local newspaper as well. "Indecent assault charges dropped," the headline read. The story said it was because the thirteen-year-old girl refused to testify. As a result, the charges were dismissed.

My mother's betrayal that day shattered something foundational in me. From the moment I said the words "I do not wish to testify," I was on my own. The only person I could trust was myself. That belief, that instinct to rely solely on me, and me alone, shaped my relationships for years to come.

After the investigation, the hearing, and the dismissal of my case, my mother went back to living in the fantasy world she'd created. Her goal was to ensure I also kept the peace by refusing to acknowledge that piece of my past. "Just forget about it," she'd tell me, anytime it would come up over the years to follow.

I was still five long years away from being an adult, from having the freedom to move out and make my own choices. I had no idea how I'd survive that long.

As if the pressure from my mother to just let it go wasn't enough, another tactic emerged to ensure my silence: the wrath of God.

I'd been baptized and was attending Catholic school at the time. Not long after the hearing, Al and I were brought to meet with priests at our church. I don't know who arranged it or why—only that I didn't have a choice. The plan, it seemed, was for Al to confess his "sins" and for us to somehow "repair" our so-called relationship.

We were separated for the conversations. I sat with Father Ricci, a priest I'd always liked—warm and approachable, especially with kids from Italian families like mine. But I said almost nothing. I was scared. I knew that speaking openly would make things worse. Meanwhile, Al was with another priest. I imagined him spinning some story, playing the victim, as he always did.

Even as a kid, the hypocrisy was obvious. Was that all it took for God to forgive a child abuser? A confession and a few Hail Marys? And then you can go right back to the harm you were causing.

Looking back, it's eerie how closely the Catholic Church's long history of abuse mirrored my own upbringing. People knew. People always knew. And yet the silence served the abuser—not the abused.

That day, we left the church in silence. And at a stoplight on the drive home, Al turned to me and said, "You know this is partly your fault too."

With one sentence, he rewrote the narrative once again. This was gaslighting in its purest form—the abuser assigning guilt to the abused in order to absolve himself.

For a moment, I thought maybe he was joking. But he wasn't. He was still twisting reality, and I was still trying to survive it. I wanted to scream that he was wrong—but deep down, I also believed him. That belief—the lie that I was to blame—would haunt me for years. It would become the root of a shame so deep, it kept me silent well into adulthood.

From that point on, every day began with new challenges. I was trapped with two abusers: my mother and Al. Al attempted to touch me several more times, but I was able to fight him off. So, his abuse took on new forms: unwanted hugs and kisses.

The hugs were especially problematic. More often than not, they involved him lifting me off the ground—suspending me in the air like a doll. I hated it. I felt trapped and powerless. Sometimes, he'd press his mouth against my neck and face in a barrage of wet, unwanted kisses. It was gross. I knew better than to squirm or pull away, but my body's instincts often betrayed me anyway. When I'd inadvertently flinch or recoil, there were consequences.

Those consequences most often came in the form of guilt—him pleading with me, saying how much he loved me, and how he needed to hug me. Other times, it was anger—accusing me of being disrespectful or ungrateful, reminding me of all he had supposedly done for me.

And sometimes, it wasn't even him who reacted—it was my mother.

Despite how many times I told her I didn't want him to hug me, she insisted I not be rude. "Just let him hug you," she'd say, brushing off my discomfort. Neither of them ever respected my bodily autonomy. Hugging was no different. Those bear hugs left a lasting imprint. They shaped the way I would experience hugs for the rest of my life.

What I Know Now

The legal system is not built for survivors. It is built for procedure, decorum, and the comfort of those with power—often at the expense of the people who have been hurt the most.

When I was forced to sit in a courtroom directly across from the man who abused me, I wasn't being protected. I was a terrified thirteen-year-old girl who had already disclosed and survived abuse and was now being required to perform a script. As I repeated the phrase "I do not wish to testify" over and over, it should have been obvious that it was a phrase that had been drilled into me by the very adults who were supposed to shield me.

No one in that room—no judge, no lawyer, no advocate—stopped to ask why a child might be parroting the same line to every question. No one pressed pause to say, "Something about this isn't right." That is what systemic betrayal looks like: coercion happening in plain sight, and a system that looks away.

One of the most devastating patterns in narcissistic abuse is emotional inversion—when the abuser and their enablers make the victim believe that speaking up is the real harm. That telling the truth will "destroy the family." That choosing your own safety makes you selfish, dramatic, or cruel.

When a child hears that message enough times—from a mother who minimizes, from a father who gives up, from professionals who stay silent—it carves itself into her sense of self:

No one cares.

Just drop it.

You're making things worse.

Those aren't just words. They are tools of control. They don't just silence a child—they teach her to erase herself.

My Healing

Healing from this kind of betrayal has meant grieving on multiple levels: grieving what happened, and grieving what should have happened and never did. It has meant mourning not just the abuse itself, but the complicity, minimization, and emotional abandonment that surrounded it.

Part of my healing has been naming coercion for what it was—no matter how nicely it was dressed up in family language or legal terms. What happened in that lawyer's office and in that courtroom was not choice. It was pressure. It was fear. It was a child doing what she had been conditioned to do to survive.

Reclaiming my voice has been central to my healing. The words "I do not wish to testify" were taken from me, rehearsed into me, and used to erase my story. Writing this now, telling the truth in my own language, is a way of taking that voice back—not because it will change the outcome of that case, but because it restores something inside of me that was stolen.

Silence was my survival then. Truth is my healing now.

As I learned more about narcissistic abuse and manipulation, I also began to see my father differently.

There is a particular kind of heartbreak in having a parent who could have helped and chose not to. I still don't know exactly what was said inside that house that changed my father's stance so completely. I will never know. What I do know now is this: his failure to protect me did not mean I was unworthy of protection. It meant he was not capable of offering it at the time.

Recognizing this didn't erase the hurt or disappointment, but it shifted the narrative away from "He didn't care about me" toward a more complex truth: he was likely caught in my mother's web, too. Understanding how thoroughly she silenced me allowed me to see how easily she could have silenced him.

There is something deeper, too—something about the way I have moved through the world for most of my life that I now understand is rooted in my childhood.

I have been an advocate for as long as I can remember. My education led me to a counseling degree that helps others dig into themselves and heal their own trauma. Professionally, I became a respected voice in anti-racism work, guiding students and colleagues toward greater awareness and justice.

Much of my success grew from the very roots of my abuse—creating a complicated, layered dynamic that takes time and courage to unravel. It is strange and painful and powerful all at once: the understanding that even in the darkest soil, something resilient took hold and refused to die.

7

The Weight of Shame

"I do not wish to testify" were words spoken by a terrified child under pressure. A child trained to protect the very people who were hurting her.

They were also my words. Because I didn't know what justice looked like. I only knew obedience. And fear.

That moment lives at the center of so much of what came after—because it taught me something dangerous: that silence keeps you safe. That compliance is survival. That if you just do what they say, maybe it won't get worse.

That belief followed me into adulthood, into motherhood, and into marriage to Allen. Because once you've been conditioned to abandon yourself, it's almost inevitable that you'll end up with someone who benefits from that abandonment and takes advantage of your vulnerability to benefit themselves.

Although I'm not his counselor and can't formally diagnose him, I am a therapist—and I know enough to confidently say Allen meets the clinical characteristics of narcissistic personality disorder (NPD). And I've done enough work to recognize that he wasn't the first. My mother and Al met the criteria, too.

The irony, of course, is that most people who qualify for the diagnosis never receive one. They avoid therapy, reject accountability, and deflect blame. After all, the problem is always someone else.

Narcissistic predators are experts at identifying vulnerability. They look for gaps—and when they find one, they pounce. One of their easiest entry points is the absence of a safety net. They sense when you're isolated, overextended, or emotionally exhausted. They recognize your ache for connection and consistency. And so, they become exactly what you've been missing: a steady presence, a shoulder to cry on, and the answer to your unspoken prayers.

But with a narcissist, that version of them is only ever temporary.

Once they've gained your trust, the support starts to fade—slowly and subtly, at first. That's how they condition you to settle for breadcrumbs. You start chasing the person they were at the beginning; begging for the love and care they once gave so freely.

It's a cycle of abuse that's hard to explain to anyone who hasn't lived it.

From the outside, Allen and I looked like a typical family. We were a family establishing a new home. I had a stable job, the boys were thriving, and we even volunteered with Nicholas's soccer team one season. On weekends, we showed up for neighborhood events, smiling like everything was just fine.

But the reality underneath the polished exterior was a different story.

As Joe grew from a baby into a toddler, Allen's behavior toward the older boys continued to shift in unsettling ways. Joe was curious and energetic—the kind of toddler who threw himself fully into whatever fascinated him. His behavior was totally normal for a little one still learning to navigate the world.

But Allen twisted those moments into something else. Every outburst became an opportunity to assign blame to Nicholas or Christopher. If Joe cried, Allen said one of the older boys upset him. If Joe got frustrated, Allen claimed it was because they hadn't helped him quickly enough or had done something to him.

It wasn't just discipline—it was a pattern. A quiet but persistent campaign that painted the older boys as troublemakers while casting Joe as innocent, fragile, and in need of protection. Over time, the difference in how Allen treated them became impossible to ignore. Joe received affection, patience, and praise. Nicholas and Christopher received correction and suspicion and were called names.

And I—exhausted, overworked, and trying so hard to keep our family afloat—wasn't yet ready to call it out. I continued in therapy, knowing that I needed to do the work to unravel my past. But the truth was . . . I was barely keeping my head above water. Each week, I showed up to my sessions not as someone ready to grow—but as someone just trying to survive. There was no space for deep healing from my childhood.

I'd also been heavily conditioned by that very upbringing to know how to adapt to dysfunction—and to understand that a family's external image often hides what goes on behind closed doors.

Allen never seemed to question the imbalance in our marriage, and truthfully, I didn't have the awareness to understand it at the time either. I just knew things were "off."

About a year after Joe was born, Allen left his job for a new one. Three months after that, he was fired. After that, he insisted he couldn't take just any job—it had to be the right one. With that declaration, he seemed to stop trying to look altogether.

Meanwhile, I juggled multiple employers just to keep us afloat. I was running on fumes and still unable to climb out from under the weight of our growing debt.

It didn't register as another form of abuse, because it felt so familiar.

The truth was, I was pushing myself way too hard. I was trying to be everything to everyone and didn't know how to rest. It was only when my body forced it that I finally stopped.

One day, during a routine work meeting, I suddenly felt horrible. My vision blurred and the room tilted. I excused myself quietly, trying not to cause a scene, and stepped into the hallway.

That's where I collapsed.

My dad and uncle drove almost two hours to get me and take me home. I was humiliated. But more than that, I was scared—and not for the reasons you might assume. My first thought wasn't about my health. It was "I'm causing trouble." I felt nothing but guilt for being an inconvenience and needing help.

That reaction wasn't new. I had been trained to feel that way.

Growing up, my mother made it clear: being sick meant you were a burden. Needing rest, care, or attention wasn't allowed unless it was on her terms. Tony and I received perfect attendance awards at school year after year—not because we were never sick, but because staying home simply wasn't an option. Pushing through was praised.

Self-care, in our house, was also selfish. Especially beauty—that belonged to our mother alone. She curled her hair, painted her nails, applied makeup, and selected matching jewelry—but she never showed me how, and was critical when I tried on my own. If she caught me spending too long in front of a mirror, she'd snap, "You're full of yourself. Stop looking at yourself."

With Allen, the rules were the same—just dressed in different language. If I came down with a virus, or one of the kids did, Allen inevitably ended up with the same thing. But somehow, he was always sicker. I could take an afternoon to rest—maybe a few hours in bed if I really pushed for it—but when Allen got sick, it became a full-scale shutdown. The same mild bug that I powered through would leave him incapacitated for days.

He wore what I came to call his "sick uniform"—a pair of sagging sweatpants and a stretched-out thermal shirt with a frayed hole near the collar. He'd pull a hoodie over his head and tuck the fabric behind his ears, leaving them jutting out awkwardly. Then he'd sink into the couch, limbs heavy and useless, eyes glazed over, the television flickering across his blank face. He didn't move. He didn't speak. He simply collapsed inward, wrapped in self-pity, performing his suffering for anyone who might be watching.

His "injuries" were just as dramatic. If he bumped his knee or jammed his toe, he'd shout theatrically and complain about it for days. But when he was actually hurt—like the time he broke a bone after falling in the garage—he went silent. That was the tell. His real pain never needed an audience. But the rest of it? It was performance and a tool to control the emotional attention in the room.

That same dynamic played out with money, too. While he claimed to support our efforts to cut back on expenses, I noticed that it was only when it came to my needs. I was expected to stop spending money on myself: no more highlights in my hair, no new clothes, no small indulgences. He made me feel selfish for even considering them, as if basic care was a luxury I didn't deserve.

Meanwhile, Allen never hesitated to buy the best electronics, upgrade tools, or stock up on overpriced lawn supplies. He'd offer long-winded, performative justifications—about durability, investment, long-term savings—that left me feeling foolish for even questioning the expense.

And if I disagreed, or made a choice that didn't work out, the failure was mine to carry.

Take something as mundane as hammers. You walk into a store and see three options: a $10 hammer, a $20 hammer, and a $30 hammer. Allen would insist—every single time—on the $30 hammer.

It didn't matter if the $10 version was perfectly adequate for what we needed to do, nor that we were actively trying to get out of debt. If I pushed back and suggested the more affordable option, he'd shrug and say, "That's fine . . . if that's what you want, but don't blame me if it breaks," his voice dripping with condescension.

This wasn't a small, passive-aggressive jab—it was a calculated move to protect himself from ever being accountable. If the hammer broke, it was on me. If it didn't, he still got to wear the mask of generosity and wisdom—he had let me choose the hammer, after all.

It wasn't ever about the hammer—or whatever item we were discussing. It was about control. And eroding trust in my judgment, one small decision at a time.

In an effort to stabilize our finances, I began seriously considering opening a private practice. I was confident I could build a solid client base, and I figured Allen could at least help with administrative tasks.

Over the next several months, I laid the groundwork—securing a business license, recruiting therapists, asking family for financial support, and renting a space. Building a business from scratch was both exciting and overwhelming—a leap toward independence that felt equal parts empowering and exhausting.

My first counseling practice opened with two employees and myself. Over time, we grew. I expanded the space; at our peak, we had eleven therapists and an outstanding reputation for our specialization in play therapy.

At first, Allen acted enthusiastic. I hoped his involvement would give him a sense of purpose. But his interest quickly waned. Soon, he was spending more time playing video games and less time helping with the practice. Most days, he simply loafed around.

After about six months, I asked him to step away from the day-to-day operations—his lack of motivation had become a real problem. He didn't argue. He simply slipped comfortably back into the one role he seemed to thrive in: that of an unemployed dad.

And in some ways, it probably looked good. To neighbors and teachers, he appeared to be a devoted, stay-at-home father—the kind people praise for being "hands-on."

The trouble was, his interest in fatherhood really only extended to one child: Joe.

He nurtured his relationship with Joe obsessively—while finding new ways to tear down Nicholas and Christopher. If Joe cried, it was their fault. Blame came swiftly, and it was nearly always followed by yelling.

A good example: when Joe was a toddler, he didn't like being alone in the bathroom. Most kids go through that phase. But Allen turned it into a power play. He demanded that either Nicholas or Christopher sit with Joe every time he showered, peed, or pooped. It didn't matter if they were eating dinner, doing homework, or trying to unwind—if Joe wanted company in the bathroom, they were expected to provide it.

One day, Nicholas had enough. Joe was in the shower, and Nicholas quietly stepped out. Almost immediately, Joe started screaming.

Without gathering any additional information other than the sound of Joe's cry, Allen exploded. "WHAT DID YOU DO TO HIM? GO TURN THE WATER BACK DOWN!" he screamed, accusing Nicholas of scalding his brother by turning up the temperature.

Nicholas tried to explain—he hadn't touched the water. He was just tired of being forced to sit and watch his little brother bathe while Allen played video games.

But logic didn't matter. In Allen's eyes, Joe was always the victim. And Nicholas and Christopher were always to blame.

With Allen, the rules were always shifting. What applied to one child never seemed to apply to another, especially when it came to Joe. He could have a lollipop as an afternoon snack, but if Nicholas asked for the same thing at the same time, he was denied—because it would "ruin his appetite." Joe had nearly unlimited access to his iPad at night, while Nicholas and Christopher were expected to follow our family's rule: devices were to be plugged in downstairs by 8:00 p.m. sharp.

That's how narcissists parent—not by guiding or supporting, but by choosing favorites, manufacturing loyalty, and keeping everyone else off balance. Love becomes transactional and is earned through obedience, while punishment is always waiting just beneath the surface.

And it's not just emotions they distort. Narcissists twist reality itself—until even the physical world starts to feel unstable.

When Christopher was little, he carried stuffed animals for comfort. First it was Lamby—a small, worn sheep. Then, after Lamby mysteriously vanished, it was Hamsty, a little plush hamster. These weren't just toys. They were companions. He didn't take them out into the world, but they were always close by—in the car, in our home, at my father's house. He was petrified of losing them so they remained in our trusted spaces.

So, when Lamby disappeared without a trace, I tried to tell myself it was just a fluke. A misplaced toy. Allen blamed Christopher for being careless. But something felt off. Christopher wasn't careless—not with Lamby. Still, kids lose things. I tried to let it go.

Until it happened again.

Hamsty vanished the same way. One day there, the next day gone. No explanation. No recovery. And again, the blame fell on Christopher.

That's when doubt turned into something sharper. It didn't make sense—not the disappearances, not Allen's reaction, and definitely not the sinking feeling in my gut that whispered: *this isn't normal*. It reminded me of the stories I grew up hearing about Al's ex-wife. Stories that never quite added up, but were always told with such conviction that you questioned your own instincts.

Because that's the thing about narcissists—they don't just manipulate people. They manipulate reality. They make you question what you saw, what you heard, what you know to be true.

The goal isn't just control. It's confusion. Disorientation. Chaos that keeps them at the center of your world—and you, spinning.

In narcissistic family systems, everyone gets a role—though no one chooses it. There's the narcissist, of course, whose needs dominate the entire emotional ecosystem. Then there's the *enabler*, often a partner, who upholds the narcissist's version of reality, smoothing things over or minimizing harm to keep the peace.

Next is the *golden child*—the one who gets praised, protected, and idealized. This child becomes an extension of the narcissist's ego, rewarded for their loyalty and compliance. Then there's the *scapegoat*—the one who absorbs the blame, catches the criticism, and is often punished for daring to push back. The scapegoat becomes the emotional dumping ground, while the golden child is shielded, often at the scapegoat's expense.

There can be other roles in a family too. There's the *truth-teller*—the one who dares to call out the bad behavior and refuses to stay silent, even at great personal cost. The *mascot* uses humor or charm to diffuse tension and distract from pain. And then there's the *lost child*—quiet, invisible, and overlooked, they learn to survive by not needing anything at all.

Regardless of the labels assigned, there is one suffocating rule that everyone abides by, even if they can't name it: absolutely everything revolves around the narcissist's moods. Every family member learns to anticipate their reactions, suppress their own needs, and accept blame that was never theirs to carry.

And one of the favorite weapons of a narcissist? Shame.

Allen could have taught a master class in tearing down adolescent boys. His treatment of Christopher and Nicholas made one thing painfully clear: Allen was the one with all the control and all the power.

Like most boys, Christopher had gross habits. For a brief period of time, he picked his nose and, for reasons only kids understand, wiped it on his bedroom wall.

When Allen found out, he didn't respond like a parent should. Instead of correcting the behavior with patience or guidance, he turned it into a punishment rooted in humiliation. He made Christopher go to his room and scrape the dried boogers off the wall. If the consequence had ended there, it might seem reasonable. However, Allen took it to another level and threatened to make him eat them, too.

It wasn't any better for Nicholas. As a therapist, I know why kids bite their nails. It's not rebellion—it's anxiety. And living in a toxic home made Nicholas anxious.

So, Allen turned that, too, into a lesson. When he caught Nicholas biting his nails, he would either clip off any remnants remaining or cut his own nails and toenails and then put the tiny pieces in a plastic bag. The next time he caught Nicholas, Allen would pull out the bag and threaten to make him eat from it. It was humiliation disguised as discipline—sadistic, calculated, and meant to break him down.

"If you want to snack on these so badly, then here you go," he'd say. The entire charade was meant to shame Nicholas into compliance.

In all its forms, shame chips away at self-worth, leaving a person feeling broken, disgusting, or less than. Shaming children is especially damaging because it rewires how kids see themselves. It does not teach them not that they made a mistake, but that they *are* the mistake.

Most of us retain only a few early memories, and the ones we do hold onto carry weight and often reveal something essential about how we were shaped. Research encourages us to examine those memories and ask: what do they tell us about how we learned to be in the world?

For me, the answer was clear: shame was there for me from the very beginning.

My earliest memory is from when I was two or three years old—small enough that the world felt big and unpredictable, but old enough to recognize when my mother was annoyed. We were in the parking lot of the local pharmacy. As she pulled me from the car, she snapped, "Do you have to pee?"

I did, but I said no. I knew what yes meant.

Yes meant being yanked into her arms, cradled awkwardly at arm's length, and made to squat mid-air over the parking lot pavement while she hissed, "Just go." It had happened before, and I didn't like it. So, this time, I lied.

Inside the store, I couldn't hold it. I felt the warmth spread, the wetness running down my legs. I was wearing a dress, and a puddle formed beneath me.

A pharmacy worker came over quietly and placed a newspaper on the ground to cover the spot. My mother's eyes cut through me. She grabbed my arm, yanked me close, and whispered, venom in her voice: "I asked you if you had to go. You should be ashamed of yourself."

Now, as a mother of three, I've potty-trained children. I know what's normal. I've said the words I needed to hear as a child—because they're true: "It's okay. It was just an accident."

But my mother believed shame would teach me control. And her ridicule wasn't limited to bodily functions. My mother's disapproval became part of me. I didn't just feel shame for what I did—I felt it for who I was.

That humiliation in the pharmacy taught me this: never be a burden and never let your needs disrupt someone else's day. Even needing to pee, I learned, was asking too much.

Ironically, I was potty-trained early. But I quickly learned never to admit when I needed to go. And I certainly didn't want anyone to see me. At school, I'd wait until classes were in session so I could sneak into the bathroom when the halls were quiet—just so no one would hear me. I treated even the most basic needs as something to be hidden.

I grew up believing my body's basic needs were shameful. Anything my mother deemed unladylike—farting, burping, pooping—was not only off-limits to conversation but treated as a personal flaw.

Even stomach aches were dismissed. If I lingered in the bathroom too long, she'd yell through the door and accuse me of wasting her time. My body's needs were never met with care, only contempt. An upset tummy, nausea, or diarrhea were all inconveniences I was expected to ignore.

Of course, getting my period was no different. It arrived when I was eleven—a year after Al's abuse had begun. I was mortified and couldn't hide it from my mother. She handed me a panty liner and a thick, diaper-like pad. No conversation. No comfort. Just silence and supplies.

But I learned something new with that milestone: some bodily functions were discussed—just not in ways that made me feel safe.

That afternoon, while Tony and I played in the backyard, Al stepped outside and shouted loud enough for the entire neighborhood to hear:

"Tina became a woman today!"

He said it like a joke. Like a punchline. The kind that wasn't meant for me, but was about me.

Obviously, my mother had told him.

What I remember most about that day wasn't the blood or the pain. It also wasn't a milestone on the journey to adulthood. All I remember is shame. The deep, relentless shame.

What I Know Now

Shame is one of the most powerful weapons in the narcissist's arsenal. It's not corrective—it's corrosive. It doesn't help a child learn; it teaches a child to disappear. Where guilt says, "I *made* a mistake," shame insists, "I *am* the mistake."

In narcissistic families, shame isn't just a feeling—it's an organizing principle. It's how roles are assigned, enforced, and policed. These roles don't develop naturally; they're engineered to protect the narcissist's ego at all costs.

There is the *golden child*, who is idealized, overvalued, and used to reflect the narcissist's superiority. There is the *scapegoat*, who absorbs the blame, anger, and projected flaws the narcissist refuses to hold. There is the *lost child*, who withdraws and becomes invisible to avoid conflict. And there is the *enabler*, who smooths things over, keeps the peace, and protects the narcissist's image.

Of course, family systems are complex. While these are the roles my family members held, there are others as well—for example, the *mascot*, who uses humor or distraction to diffuse tension, or the *hero*, who overachieves to compensate for the family's instability. And in smaller families, it's common for one person to occupy multiple roles at once, shifting between them as needed to preserve the dysfunctional balance.

But there is one constant across every permutation: shame is the glue that holds the system together. The golden child is shamed for any crack in perfection. The scapegoat is shamed for simply existing. The lost child is shamed for needing anything at all. The enabler is shamed into loyalty.

These roles become self-fulfilling. The golden child performs. The scapegoat absorbs. The lost child vanishes. The enabler apologizes for everything. Everyone orbits the narcissist's emotional gravity—and shame is the force that keeps them from breaking away.

For me, shame started with my mother. The belief that bodily needs were disgusting. That being seen, helped, or cared for was an inconvenience. That dependence was weakness. Even the normal vulnerability of being a small child felt like something I needed to hide.

Like most children raised in narcissistic systems, I didn't ask for help when I felt shame—I disappeared inside myself. I learned early not to trust my own instincts, not to express needs, and not to expect comfort. Eventually, I came to believe that my existence itself was a burden.

This is why narcissistic partners don't initially feel dangerous—they feel familiar. They replicate the emotional blueprint you were raised with: love that must be earned, comfort that comes with a cost, peace that depends on your silence. It doesn't feel toxic; it feels like home.

My Healing

The early patterns of living in a narcissistic home didn't fade as I grew up—they simply transferred. They resurfaced in my marriage to Allen, where financial control, favoritism, humiliation, and affection that had to be earned kept me doubting my own reality.

Eventually, a question rose up from somewhere deep inside me—quiet but insistent: *Whose peace had I been working so hard to protect?*

What I had lived through wasn't a misunderstanding—it was a carefully designed distortion meant to keep me small, compliant, and silent.

Healing began the moment I allowed myself to name that truth. It meant grieving everything that distortion stole from me. It meant rewriting my internal narrative one honest sentence at a time. It meant offering my younger self the compassion, protection, and validation she never received.

For me, healing began with learning to talk to myself the way no one ever spoke to the little girl hiding in the pharmacy aisle. It meant saying:

My needs were never too much.
My exhaustion was not weakness.
My body was never something to be ashamed of.
My truth was never dangerous.

Slowly, with practice, that compassion began to soften something inside me. It didn't erase the past, but it loosened its grip. And over time, I came to see that I had been raised with three rules: don't need, don't feel, and don't speak. Those rules followed me into my marriage, shaping how I loved, coped, and survived. It's only through healing that I am learning—finally—to do all three again.

8

Sugarcoated Cruelty

Shame taught me to hide my pain, silence my needs, and carry burdens that were never mine to hold. I spent a lifetime trying not to be a problem—swallowing my hurt, minimizing conflict, and blaming myself for things that were never my fault.

But the trouble with shame is that it doesn't just live in the past. It shows up again and again, until you finally recognize it. And by the time I had a family of my own, shame was showing up in all the same ways—only this time, it was threatening to swallow my children too.

As things with Allen kept devolving, our home often felt volatile and unpredictable. I was constantly stuck in the middle, trying to shield the boys from Allen's temper and protect them from consequences they didn't deserve.

If something went wrong—something got broken, someone tracked in mud, left lights on, forgot to feed the cat—I'd instinctively say it was me. Not because I thought it would fix things, but because I thought maybe it would diffuse Allen. If I took the blame, maybe he wouldn't come down on the older boys. But it didn't work. He still got angry. And then, instead of going after them, he turned it into another reason to accuse me of favoritism.

"You always protect Nicholas," Allen would sneer, his voice tightening into a sing-song mockery he reserved when he wanted to be sure

I felt as small as possible. "He's your favorite," he'd coo, drawing out the vowels in each word with theatrical disdain. "You make excuses for him because he's just your precious little boy."

The English bulldog—the one I never wanted but was convinced to buy—only made things worse. Allen never trained the dog, so by the time it became Nicholas's "job" to clean up after it, it lived most of the time in the garage and hadn't been trained to poop on the grass. Instead, it regularly defecated in the garage and on the driveway. Then Allen would drive over the piles on his way into the garage and smoosh them into the blacktop.

Somehow, this was always Nicholas's fault. "You should've cleaned it up before I got home," Allen barked, as if the offense was not the dog's accident but Nicholas's failure to anticipate it. As punishment, Nicholas would be forced to scrape the remaining bits of poop off the driveway while Allen complained about his "half-ass job."

Allen judged everyone—and made sure we all knew it. He had a cruel nickname for nearly everyone in our orbit– and if they didn't laugh along, the problem was theirs: "They're too sensitive," he'd scoff. "God, nobody can take a joke anymore."

Even the boys weren't spared. He referred to Nicholas as his "red-headed stepchild" and Christopher as the "Jolly Green Giant" or "Mongo," a slang term meaning huge, extreme, or stupid. It wasn't funny—it was unnecessary and mean. These were my boys, and those words stuck to them like burrs.

But I didn't say anything. It was a familiar pattern for me. My mother judged people just as ruthlessly—only her version was even quieter and colder. No one escaped her scrutiny. The checkout clerk was too slow. The woman in front of us at church was wearing too much perfume. The neighbors couldn't control their dog, which is why it barked. Teachers who asked too many questions about our home life were "busybodies." She'd pass judgment on people she'd never met and make cutting remarks about people she claimed to care about. She was never trying to be funny—she was just right. Always.

Growing up surrounded by that kind of constant criticism taught me that being good wasn't about kindness or integrity—it was about avoiding judgment. To this day, I assume when I walk into a room, I am being picked apart, measured, and dismissed. Because when judgment is the air you breathe, self-worth becomes conditional. And silence becomes survival.

There were also moments so strange and uncomfortable that they almost defy explanation—like the way Allen forced the older boys to massage his feet. It wasn't a request; it was a demand, wrapped in entitlement and delivered with the expectation of obedience. If they resisted or complained, his mood would shift instantly—as if their reluctance was a personal offense.

Eventually, they stopped pushing back. They learned that it was easier to just do it than face the consequences of his rage. What should have been a clear boundary—a child does not serve the adult—became one more example of how Allen blurred lines, manipulated power, and taught them to abandon their own discomfort for the sake of his.

Things at the counseling practice also weren't well. From the outside, it still looked like a success: the schedule was full. But inside, Allen had grown hostile. He was demanding to the staff, and even worse, he would berate and humiliate the very clients who came to us for help.

And the most maddening part? The business was in my name. My mother had loaned me the money to open it. Allen didn't own any part of the practice. He wasn't a therapist either—he should have had no say in the day-to-day operations of a business he knew absolutely nothing about. But being married to me, he seemed to believe it was all his by default.

To Allen, any disagreement wasn't a business issue; it was a personal attack and a challenge to his authority. When something as minor as a billing issue arose—a refusal by a client to pay a no-show fee, for example—Allen's voice would rise and he would quickly threaten to call the police.

Our online reviews stopped being about therapy and started being about him. His unprofessionalism wasn't just embarrassing; it was destructive.

By the time Nicholas was thirteen—the same age I was when I was forced into dropping the sexual abuse charges—he reached his breaking point and tried to run away from home. He packed his backpack with what his teenage brain deemed essential: a few bottles of water and two loaves of bread. He didn't have a destination—maybe the homeless shelter on Broad Street, he later told me—but it didn't matter. Anywhere felt safer than staying near Allen.

He made it about halfway down the main road near our house before my dad spotted him and brought him home.

When Allen found out, he didn't express concern or ask what happened.

"If you do that again," he told Nicholas, "I'll call the cops. You'll go to jail."

Just to make sure it stuck, Allen actually arranged a tour of the local jail. He called around looking for the old "Scared Straight" program—a controversial intervention strategy developed in the late 1970s with the goal of deterring juvenile delinquency by exposing at-risk youth to the harsh realities of prison life. It had long been dismantled as a program that was well-intentioned but lacked the therapeutic support that teens needed to be able to process it.

Still, Allen convinced an officer to let him run his own version—and dragged Nicholas through the cell blocks, pointing out where he'd end up if he ever tried to run again.

For a while, Nicholas believed it was about protection. He told me Allen just wanted to show him what could happen out in the real world—that it was a lesson, not a punishment. And at the time, I didn't question it either. The way Allen framed it to me made it sound like love. He said it was about helping Nicholas understand the consequences of dangerous behavior. That he was trying to keep him safe.

Now I know better.

This wasn't guidance. It was punishment. This flavor of parenting was Allen's specialty. His words sounded protective, concerned, even loving—but underneath, the intent was cruel and strategic.

He knew how to say the right thing, always. On paper, it looked like fatherly concern. Strangers would have called him devoted, engaged, even admirable!

That's what made it so hard to name, and why it was so easy for me to doubt my instincts. Because the words were always loving. The tone was even gentle. But the message—the truth—was control, shame, and threat.

My mother's cruelty had come in sharp tones and cutting words, easy to identify even when it was hard to bear. But Allen's? Allen's cruelty came dressed as love. And that kind of abuse doesn't just hurt—it confuses you to your core.

I understood Nicholas's urge to run. My own desperate attempts to flee the chaos of Al and my mother defined my teenage years. It was rooted in the logic of a child who decides that the unknown is safer than home.

Long before I was a mother, I was a teenage girl doing everything I could to escape the suffocating world I'd been born into. There were so many late nights I'd lie awake calculating exit strategies, and long hours I filled with extracurriculars just to avoid going home. Watching my son try to flee reminded me just how young I had been when I started looking for ways out.

What I Know Now

Cruelty doesn't always shout. Sometimes it whispers. Sometimes it smiles. Sometimes it arrives disguised as guidance, wrapped in phrases like *"This is for your own good."*

And when you grow up in a home where cruelty is either normalized or sugarcoated, the line between safety and danger becomes so blurred that your body reacts long before your mind can understand why.

This is the nature of covert narcissistic abuse—the kind delivered quietly, strategically, and with just enough sweetness to confuse you. It hides in sarcasm, ridicule, entitlement, favoritism, and "lessons" that are really punishments. It hides in the subtle ways someone tells you who you're allowed to be, how small you're expected to stay, and which parts of you must be sacrificed to make their life easier.

My mother's cruelty was sharp and cold. Allen's was warm and sticky. One stung, the other suffocated. But both conditioned me to the same belief: if you're upset, you are the problem.

Narcissistic abusers rely on confusion, because confusion keeps you compliant. Sarcasm becomes "joking." Punishment becomes "teaching." Control becomes "care." And by the time you realize what's happening, you've already learned to question your worth.

Once again, shame was the thread stitching these patterns together. It shaped how I saw myself and how my boys began seeing themselves. Shame punishes identity, not behavior.

Nicholas and Christopher weren't disciplined; they were shamed into scapegoat roles they never chose.

Even the counseling practice—something built from my professional skill, my labor, and my sacrifice—became a playground for Allen's need for dominance. What should have been a symbol of independence and stability for our family instead became another arena where he could assert control. His interference wasn't partnership; it was intrusion disguised as concern. It was another way to twist facts, rewrite outcomes, and keep me doubting my own judgment.

He called it "helping." But the truth is, he couldn't stand the idea of me succeeding without him. He needed to plant himself in the middle of something I had created so he could claim ownership over it too.

And when the divorce finally came, I was so desperate to untangle myself from him that I handed the practice over just to move on. It felt like cutting off a limb to save my life. In doing so, the loan my mother had given me to start the practice was effectively erased. The understanding was always that I would make her whole once the practice was thriving. But because of Allen's control, the chaos he created, and the impossible position I was in, that never happened.

So once again, Allen walked away ahead—this time with a debt-free practice that I built and my mother funded, while both of us were left to absorb the loss. This matters now because my mother is incapacitated, and every dollar of her money needs to be dedicated to her care. And it's also another example of how the systems around narcissistic abuse—financial, emotional, relational—always seem to tilt in the abuser's favor. Another place where my silence, my shame, and my attempts to keep the peace ended up costing me more than I could articulate at the time.

What made it even more devastating wasn't just the financial loss—it was the attempted theft of my life's work far beyond the practice itself.

For years, Allen insisted he stood beside me in my work on empowerment, anti-oppression, and anti-racism. All through our marriage, he positioned himself as the "anti-racist ally," repeating my words as though they were his own revelations. He echoed the values I had studied, practiced, and taught—the values that shaped my identity as a counselor, educator, and advocate.

The moment I realized it was all performance is burned into my memory. After we divorced, Joe asked to buy a sweatshirt emblazoned with blatantly racist imagery. I objected immediately. Allen shrugged and told me it was no big deal, that there was "nothing to do" to stop it. There was no conversation about harm and no alignment with the very principles he loved to repeat when they made him look enlightened.

That was the truth I kept running up against: Allen didn't want purpose—he wanted proximity to purpose. He didn't want to build anything with me; he wanted to absorb what I had built and use it to elevate himself. And when the marriage ended, he walked away with the practice—the name, the clients, the mission—as if he had earned it.

He hadn't. He had simply taken it.

My Healing

I understand that language is hard, and sometimes saying the real words hurts. We instinctively soften the edges: a loved one "passes away," a pet "crosses the rainbow bridge," someone we miss is now "in a better place." We do it to cushion the impact, to protect ourselves and others from the sharpness of reality.

But when you're a survivor, softening the language doesn't soften the harm. It erases it.

The trouble with sugarcoating cruelty is that it becomes another form of silence—another way to make myself smaller so someone else can stay comfortable. My healing required reclaiming the right to name what actually happened, without minimizing it, excusing it, or translating it into something more palatable. I learned that abuse isn't defined by how loud it is, but by how deeply it wounds.

Healing meant going back—through old pictures, journals, memories—and examining every moment that felt "off," every place my intuition whispered but I didn't yet have the language to understand. I had to ask myself again and again:

When did the erosion start?
When did I stop trusting myself?
When did I learn to call cruelty love?

Undoing years of conditioning was slow and disorienting. But the clarity that emerged was powerful.

Most of all, healing meant giving myself permission—perhaps for the first time in my life—to tell the truth without fear. To stop protecting the people who hurt me and to stop carrying the burdens they handed me.

As I examined my own story, I began to see how my experiences echoed through my boys' lives—how the patterns I had inherited were unconsciously being reenacted in our home. Their reactions, their fears, their way of shrinking or bracing around conflict mirrored the child I once was. And in that reflection, I saw clearly what I had never allowed myself to see: that my lack of healing was harming them.

This awareness became the doorway into understanding generational trauma. Healing wasn't only about reclaiming my voice—it was about stopping the transmission of pain from one generation to the next. Owning that truth was painful, humbling, and ultimately transformative. It allowed me to shift from survival to responsibility, from repeating what I had learned to intentionally choosing something different.

My healing was for me, yes.

But it was also—and perhaps most urgently—for them.

9

The Price of Freedom

As a teen, I was always searching for someplace safe. Someplace where I could finally exhale. That place arrived in the form of a boy named David. He was my first love.

David was the older brother of a classmate. We met when I was eleven, and I immediately thought he was cute. He had dark hair—short in the front, long in the back. Okay, yes, it was a mullet . . . but I loved it! He had soft, puppy-dog eyes and a quiet coolness that made my heart flutter.

David was fifteen, an age at which he was far more interested in the things teenage boys cared about than in his kid sister's friend. But still, he was always kind to me.

As David's sister and I became close, their home became a kind of refuge for me. I liked sleeping over—I was able to soak up the warmth of a family home that felt different than mine. And when I was lucky—when David wasn't out with friends or playing in his band—I'd catch a glimpse of him. Like so many young girls with big imaginations, I dreamed that maybe, someday, I'd marry him.

Once I got to high school, survival meant staying busy—really busy. I joined every club and activity I could find, filling my days with anything that kept me away from home. I started volunteering at the elementary school and signed up for chorus, concert band, marching band, and color guard. I worked most weekends and began spending Saturday nights at my friend's house, turning weekend sleepovers into a routine escape.

Being home meant being on high alert. My heart pounded whenever I changed clothes, convinced Al might barge in. In the bathroom, I latched the door and checked it again. And again. But the bedroom door had to stay unlocked—Al and my mother made sure of that, inspecting it without warning. So, I learned to adapt. I changed with the speed of someone being hunted: a shirt over my head before the old one came off, jeans swapped one leg at a time. Anything to stay covered and safe.

Al had a habit of sitting in the sunroom, chain-smoking cigarettes. Often, when my mom was gone, he'd call me in to sit with him. He'd tell me we should "rap" about life—that was his word for it. Rap. It sounded ridiculous, like he was trying to be cool or wise. But I knew what it meant: it was time for Al to park himself on a soapbox and deliver a monologue about how the world worked, while I nodded in silence.

There was no saying no to Al. Any refusal triggered backlash—anger, guilt, manipulation—and the consequences always felt too overwhelming to face. So, I complied. I sat there for his smoke breaks, pretending to listen and trying not to breathe too deeply.

One "rap session" stands out more than the rest. Al launched into a speech about the best time for a girl to get pregnant. He said—confidently—that the most likely time to conceive was just before or just after a girl's period. I was still a kid, with no real sex education. My mother never spoke to me about things like that. So, I believed him. Of course I did. Who else was I supposed to believe?

Later, I learned how wrong he was. But the damage was already done. That misinformation followed and shaped me, impacting decisions and outcomes in ways I couldn't have predicted.

The language he used also left its mark. Al always referred to women as "girls" or "broads." Always. No matter their age. As if to remind us that, in his world, we were meant to stay small. Powerless. Beneath him.

When I was sixteen, David and I finally got together. We fell hard and fast. With him, I felt normal. I could breathe. Despite everything that happened with Al, I consider him to be the person I lost my virginity to. That's how safe he made me feel.

It wasn't long before I found out I was pregnant. Of course, Al was wrong in his teachings about a woman's cycle, and I'd been having sex at the worst possible time when the goal was to prevent pregnancy.

When I first saw the two lines on the at-home pregnancy test, I was terrified. A baby? At sixteen? My heart pounded as I tried to steady myself. But then I began stitching together a version of the future that felt almost magical. David loves me. I love him. We'll figure this out. Love is enough.

Beneath the panic and the fantasy, something else stirred—something more primal, more desperate. *This is it*, I thought. *This is how I get out!* This baby was my miracle, my escape route. I was meant to get pregnant so I could finally leave the violence! I wasn't thinking about buying strollers or affording diapers or how I'd finish school. I was thinking about freedom.

Optimistic, I called David and shared the news.

"I don't want it," he said immediately. He insisted we were too young, it was too much, and we weren't ready.

I was shattered and begged him to reconsider. I saw us running away, starting fresh, building something better. But as the days passed, our conversations went in circles. David couldn't see himself as a father, and I couldn't imagine not keeping the baby. I wanted to create a life—something real—out of the ruins I was already living in.

I clung to the hope that we could do it together. That love could be enough. Though we loved each other and he continued to reassure me that we would figure it out together, my brain continued to interpret it as a promise that we would keep the baby and flee together.

Eventually, I confided in a woman who was dating my dad, someone I felt I could trust. Unfortunately, things didn't pan out the way I'd imagined, and I came home one evening to find my dad, my mother, and Al waiting for me. I knew it wasn't good.

As I walked into the room, my dad scoffed and told me I looked "provocative." I was wearing a pair of leggings and a loose sweater—a normal, casual outfit for the time. But I understood what he was implying.

My mother didn't hold back and used the words he only hinted at. She sneered that I'd been busy "spreading my legs" and accused me of "dressing like a whore."

Al sat in the corner, silent, watching it all unfold.

After what felt like hours of beratement and humiliation, I finally escaped to my room and crawled into bed. The darkness offered no peace. My mind wouldn't stop racing. David and I could figure this out. We just needed a plan.

But by the next morning, my mom had already contacted David's parents and invited them to the house. The specific details from that day are fuzzy now, but I remember the feelings with painful clarity. The path I thought I was on—one that might have led to freedom, escape, and love—suddenly veered off into a direction I didn't choose and couldn't stop.

Once everyone was seated in our living room, my mother took control of the conversation.

"What are we going to do?" she asked, directing her question to no one in particular. It was performative. She already knew how this conversation would end.

She launched into her monologue. We were too young to have a baby. We'd be poor, miserable, trapped in a trailer park, and "walking sideways because the trailer will be too narrow." It was a joke, maybe, if the moment hadn't been so cruel.

"You'll be white trash," she said flatly. In her world, "white trash" meant lazy. And laziness was the ultimate sin.

As she spoke, David's parents nodded along. And just like that, it was decided: I would have an abortion. No one asked me what I was feeling or what I wanted. As usual, my voice didn't matter. I was a passenger in my own life—strapped in, silenced, and taken where they decided I should go.

Then came the second blow: both sets of parents told us we were no longer allowed to see each other. David was twenty; I was sixteen. "He's an adult," my mother said. "And if I find out you're seeing him, I'll call the police."

David and I were devastated. It felt unthinkable that they could rip everything away from us so easily. We begged for one last moment together, just to say good-bye. Under my mother's watchful eye, we stood around the corner from the front room, holding each other and sobbing.

David and the baby had become my lifeline. My way out. In one moment, both were taken from me.

From the other room, my mother's voice cut through the air, sharp and cold. "That's enough, Tina. It's time."

Through tears, I followed David and his family to the front door. Just before they left, his mother turned to me, her face stricken with pain.

"Why didn't you just come to me, Tina?" she said softly. "I would've gotten you on birth control."

I was stunned. The idea had never even occurred to me. I had never imagined an adult—any adult—who might listen, support, and protect me in that way. It was a foreign concept. It also didn't matter. It was too little, too late.

Once again, Al had remained silent in the corner, bearing witness to the scene unfolding in front of him. Just before they left, he reached out and took David's hand in his.

"Son, it's okay; I know this is a hard thing, but it's okay," he said. David immediately pulled away. Al tried again, repeating, "Now son, now son, I know how you feel . . ."

David's hands curled into fists. He knew what Al had done to me, the physical and emotional pain he had caused me. He hated him for it. Sensing the escalation, his father quickly stepped between them and gently nudged his son toward the door.

As they walked out the door, it felt like everything went with them, including all of my hope.

Once the door had closed and the house was quiet—Al turned to me.

"I think you should keep the baby," he said.

I stared at him blankly. I could hardly believe what I was hearing. After everything—after the decisions made for me, the voices speaking over me—now he had something to say?

Then a wave of nausea hit me. I heard Al's voice—just as clear as if he were standing beside me—the words I'd heard four years earlier: "When you turn sixteen, I want you to have my baby."

It was vile the first time it came out of his mouth. Now, it was haunting.

And the final twist? The due date I'd been given for this baby: October 20. Al's birthday. As if the universe needed one more way to drive the knife in.

What I Know Now

When a child grows up in an environment charged with fear, surveillance, and emotional unpredictability, the body isn't looking for logic—it's looking for escape. Safety. Autonomy. Breath. A way out of the cage.

That's what pregnancy represented to me at sixteen. It wasn't naivete or recklessness. It was survival. At that time, anything—*anything*—that promised freedom felt worth clinging to.

The adults around me didn't ask, listen, or try to understand. They made decisions for me, spoke over me, and reinforced a lesson I'd been taught my entire childhood: *Your voice doesn't matter. Your body doesn't belong to you. Your future is not your own.*

And then there was Al. He wasn't just a bystander in these moments—he was a predator cloaked in stillness. He was always watching. Weighing. And waiting. When abusers remain silent during moments that demand protection, their silence is its own form of violence. And that moment—when he finally spoke up to say, "I think you should keep the baby"—wasn't compassion. It was control.

Trauma doesn't make you weak. It makes you resourceful. My teenage self was not foolish. She was not reckless. She was surviving the best way she knew how, without guidance, safety, or a single adult willing to put her well-being first.

My Healing

As I reflected on my teenage years, I couldn't help but remember the disappointment I carried—the belief that David should have done more to fight for us, that he should have supported the pregnancy I saw as my way out. For years, I quietly blamed him for not rescuing me from the life I was so desperate to escape.

What I eventually understood is that he was just a kid, too. He didn't have the full story—not even close.

It wasn't until we were married, years removed from the chaos, that I could finally unravel the belief that he had abandoned me. The truth was simpler and far more compassionate: what I thought I had made clear about the abuse was not clear at all. I gave him fragments—shadows—of a reality that was impossible to grasp unless you were living inside of it.

My situation back then was so extreme, so far outside the realm of what most people consider normal, that expecting a teenage boy—or his parents—to understand it was unrealistic. In fact, no one truly saw my life for what it was until I began my healing journey . . . and until I began writing this book.

With that clarity, I was able to see my sixteen-year-old self differently—not as foolish or reckless, but as a girl who was unprotected and trying to survive. My hope wasn't naïve; it was resourceful. I reached for love because I had never been given safety. I imagined escape because I had lived too long in fear.

Healing meant letting David be human—and letting that younger version of myself and him off the hook. It meant releasing shame that wasn't mine, trusting my own instincts again, and finally naming what happened to me without minimizing it.

Most of all, healing has meant honoring the girl who kept going despite everything. She is the reason I'm here, the reason I survived, and the reason I can now tell the truth—with compassion, clarity, and no more apology.

10

My Teenage Escape

After the breakup and abortion, I was wrecked. I missed David constantly—and missed what might have been—but I also knew there was no way forward. Not with David. And not then.

Later that year, I started growing closer to a boy named Billy. What began as a casual friendship quickly deepened. We spent nearly all our free time together, and when we weren't in the same room, we were on the phone late into the night, filling the silence with stories, laughter, and teenage confessions.

Things were easy with Billy. There was no drama, no manipulation, no walking on eggshells. His family was stable and intact. Their home—just a short walk from my dad's barbershop and close to school—offered something my home did not: warmth, consistency, and a sense of being safe without needing to earn it.

Billy's parents were kind and approachable. They didn't hover or interrogate—they simply made space for me. I started spending every possible moment at their house. Between school, work, and extracurriculars, I kept myself busy enough to avoid being home at all. I'd slip in just before bed, quietly tiptoe to my room, and leave again at sunrise.

A few months into our relationship, I told Billy everything. Al was no longer raping me, but his abuse continued, I said. And there was no sign that my mother was ever going to do anything about it.

Billy didn't flinch—and he asked how he could help me run. The only escape I could see was the one I'd stumbled on before: pregnancy.

We were two teenagers who believed that creating life could be the key to saving mine. We started trying, though our early attempts were futile.

In talking to Billy, I also realized I had a lot of unanswered questions about what had happened during Al's arrest and the court case. Billy's dad worked at the local newspaper, so I asked if he could possibly access information about the investigation that I couldn't. Within days, he gave me the police logs from the time of Al's arrest and connected me with a man named Steve, a former police officer who had become a pastor.

Steve hadn't worked my case but remembered being at the station the day Al was arrested. Just knowing someone had witnessed that moment felt deeply validating. But what Steve offered next mattered even more: he and his wife ran YouthQuest, an agency supporting teens in crisis. They could help me leave my home.

I didn't know then that YouthQuest was evangelical-affiliated. But at that point, I wouldn't have cared. I just needed a way out. This seemed like a good option to me. Billy and I stopped trying to get pregnant and pivoted to this new plan, reshaping our future around the hope of my escape.

With Steve handling the arrangements, I prepared. The whole plan felt crazy at times, and my emotions flipped back and forth—one moment excited, the next absolutely petrified.

One day after school, Billy and I—along with another friend—bagged up my personal items. We worked quickly, knowing that if Al came home, it would all be over. Billy kept the bags at his house for safekeeping.

I went to work as normal that afternoon. YouthQuest had instructed me to call them once I had escaped. I left a message, and Steve called back within the hour. "Did you run away?" he asked. I wanted to scream. I knew he needed to hear the words from me, but of course I had run away! That was the entire point.

Steve told me that he and his wife would pick me up at the end of my shift. Then, about thirty minutes later, the phone at the pizza shop rang—it was my friend who had helped me pack.

"You can't go home," she said urgently. "Your mom called. She went into your room and saw everything was gone."

Panic surged through me. Plans needed to change. I immediately called Steve. Fifteen minutes later, I was in his car and en route to what they called a "safehouse." I'd heard that word and imagined some fortified cabin in the woods, hidden and locked down. Instead, my safehouse was just a warm, quiet home belonging to a kind couple from their church.

I spent my first night there. I don't remember much—just kindness and calm, and the powerful sense that, for the first time since the abuse began, I was truly safe. That night, I slept well.

The next morning, Steve brought me to YouthQuest's offices. We spent the day preparing to meet the foster family who would take me in.

The family lived just one street from my school—and from Billy's house. That alone gave me a sense of ease. Still, for the first few days, I wasn't allowed to tell anyone where I was. Despite being in a safe home, I was scared. I couldn't see Billy or my other friends, and their absence made those early days heavy.

One of YouthQuest's policies required someone to inform my mother that I was safe, but not returning home. Steve handled the call. My mother wasn't given a choice—she had to sign over temporary custody to the agency.

My foster parents, Denise and Bruce, were young and kind and had a five-month-old baby. I stayed in their attic, which they had converted into a bedroom. They made breakfast each morning, checked in on me daily, and folded me gently into their routines. I stayed active at school and on weekends—Denise even took me to my activities and showed up to some. Sometimes, my mom did too. She'd approach me afterward, making small talk, never once naming what had happened. That was her way—everything was surface-level. We would never dare talk about something real; it was just business as usual for her.

In time, Denise and Bruce began noticing signs of the life I'd come from. I didn't wash my clothes regularly. I didn't shower often. Not because I didn't care, but because I'd never been taught to. Denise started leaving notes:

Do your laundry—it's been a week.
Take a shower—it's been a week.

This was different than anything I had experienced before. This wasn't shame. They were noticing. That meant something to me.

Still, as much as I appreciated their care, I knew I couldn't stay forever. The religious undertone of everything—from the family to YouthQuest itself—began to weigh on me. I was already pushing back against Catholicism at the time. I couldn't take on another faith, especially when faith had never been a place where I found comfort or safety.

Living in a safe, abuse-free foster home was life-changing. Another unexpected gift was that it reconnected me with my dad.

Since his divorce from my mother, my dad had not been a consistent presence in my or Tony's lives. My leaving home seemed to wake him up. He realized I wasn't okay, and he wanted me out of foster care and with him. We began talking more and more. He worked to show me he could be a safe place. I was skeptical, but also grateful. For once, it felt like an adult in my family was truly seeing what I was going through.

With support from YouthQuest, I eventually left the foster home to live with my dad, a move that also meant moving back into my childhood home. It was the first time I'd slept there since leaving with my mom years before. At first, it felt awkward. But I soon settled in.

Things seemed to be going well—until they weren't. My mother convinced my dad that she and I needed to reconnect, and he encouraged regular visits between us, thinking it would help.

Over the next two months, my mom showed up often—for dinners and outings and other attempts to "rebuild" our bond. Eventually, she convinced both of us that things would be different if I moved back in with her. I wanted so badly to believe her. Maybe it was the child in me, still longing for a mother's love. So, with their encouragement, I packed my things and returned.

Within days, I realized I had made a huge mistake. Al was still there. So were the "bear hugs." My mom still excused it all. Nothing had changed, and I was trapped again.

This time, I didn't even try to call my dad. I felt betrayed—he had worked so hard just to hand me back over.

Days bled into weeks. Weeks into months. Al remained volatile, controlling, and terrifying. I loathed every moment I spent in that house. Billy and I reignited our efforts to get pregnant—it felt like my only way out. I studied ovulation, tracked my cycle, and even bought an ovulation kit from the local drugstore to increase our chances.

One night, I came home from Billy's to find the kit laid out on my bed. My mother found it, and the confrontation that followed was brutal. But by then, I had mastered the art of dissociation. As soon as I sensed the storm coming, I'd retreat inward. I'd stop listening. I'd hold my breath and wait for her to leave.

Years later, I realized how deeply that survival mechanism stayed with me. Even now, when my husband speaks at length—about something as simple as an observation about one of the kids—I dissociate. It takes me right back to those bedroom night sessions with my mother. The pattern is the same. I only hear criticism, so I hold my breath and wait for it to end.

Finally, months later, just before the start of our senior year, I finally got the news I was hoping for—I was pregnant! Billy and I were thrilled. We couldn't wait to tell his parents and grandmother.

The announcement didn't go as we'd hoped. Although loving, his parents were furious. They'd had Billy as teenagers and knew how hard this road would be. Their anger stung, but we still made plans—we mapped out when I'd tell my mom, and when I'd finally leave for good.

The universe had other plans though. A few weeks later, I felt a sudden sensation—like I'd lost control of my bladder. I rushed to the bathroom. I was bleeding. Billy and his father rushed me to the emergency room, where the doctors confirmed what I already knew in my heart. It was a miscarriage. I would need to come back the next day for surgery to clear my uterus.

The thought of undergoing surgery without my parents knowing was terrifying, but telling the truth carried consequences I wasn't willing to face. So, I made myself invisible. I changed the billing address at the hospital to Billy's house, burying the paper trail along with the rest of my grief.

My sorrow was bottomless—deeper than anything I'd ever known. The baby was gone. I had clung to the pregnancy like a lifeline, convinced it was the only way out. But now, that door had slammed shut. I was going back to the same house. The same abuse. The same waking nightmare.

I wanted to know my rights, if I even had any. So, I began looking for resources—anything I could use, anything within reach.

Working at the pizza shop gave me access to the community—and one of the regulars was a detective at the local police department named Bob.

One day, heart pounding, I called the station and asked for him by name. I was terrified—afraid I'd get in trouble, afraid of what my mother would do if she found out I was talking to the police again. But I also knew I had to take the risk. No one was coming to save me.

They put me through. "Hi Bob, this is Tina—you know, the girl from Vincent's Pizza."

He recognized me, and after I explained why I was calling, he asked me to come to the station immediately. I couldn't believe it—I was thrilled. I jumped in my truck and drove straight there.

At the station, I told him everything: the abuse, the current situation, and my plan to leave. I even brought the newspaper articles about Al. I asked the question that had been eating at me: was it legal for me to leave home, being just shy of eighteen?

Bob gave me the clarity I needed. Even if my mother called the police the day I left, she'd have to locate me, convince the police to act, and force my return. If I could keep my location secret for just a month and a half, I'd be legally free. At eighteen, she'd have no rights over me.

That was all I needed. I made my decision: I was going to leave—for good this time.

By the time I was planning my second escape, things at home had gotten worse. My mother's daily rants were relentless, and Al's temper was more explosive than ever. Billy eventually convinced his grandmother to take me in.

This time, I planned carefully. I moved my things out gradually, hiding them at Billy's grandmother's house. And in early August 1993—two months before my eighteenth birthday—I left my mother's home for the last time. I stayed with Billy's grandmother until February of the following year.

At some point, my dad received the hospital bill for the surgery and ER visit. He confronted me on the sidewalk outside his barbershop. I told him the truth, took the bill, and walked away.

In that moment, he looked devastated—his only daughter had now been pregnant twice before eighteen. But I think he also finally saw the impact of his absence. He began to step up. He supported my counseling and even attended sessions with me. Over time, he worked to rebuild our relationship. This time, his promises felt different. Still, I remained with Billy's grandmother.

I also had a new problem: debt. The surgery cost thousands, and my part-time pizza job barely paid anything. After some digging, I found my way to the welfare office to apply for medical assistance. I had no idea what I was doing, but I drove myself, waited in long lines, filled out the forms, and met with a case manager. Eventually, I was approved, and my medical bills were covered. It was the only time I used public assistance, and I was grateful it existed.

That February, I moved back in with my dad. He had a new mantra: "You don't have to do anything you don't want to do." He encouraged me to maintain a relationship with my mom, but never forced it.

What I Know Now

As a therapist, I often see clients struggle with this painful contradiction: they were forced to grow up quickly, yet never truly allowed to grow up. They carried adult responsibilities without ever receiving the safety, structure, or emotional grounding that should have come first. This is called *parentification*—a role reversal where the child becomes the caretaker, the protector, or the problem-solver long before they're emotionally ready.

That was me.

By seventeen, I could manage a crisis better than I could manage joy. I could spot danger in a heartbeat but didn't recognize safety when it finally appeared. I wasn't looking for happiness. I was looking for relief.

Trauma rewires the nervous system like that. It doesn't take away intelligence—it hijacks decision-making. When your home feels like a war zone, anything that looks like escape becomes a lifeline. That's why pregnancy felt like freedom. It wasn't about wanting to become a mother—it was about wanting control over my life for the first time.

Survivors often look back at their teenage choices with shame, asking themselves, *Why did I do that?*

A more accurate question is: *Why did I feel so unsafe that these were my only options? Who failed to protect me?*

Risk-taking, secrecy, and desperate planning weren't recklessness. They were resilience. My attempts to flee weren't dramatic—they were logical. They were the responses of a child who believed the only person who might save her was herself.

My Healing

Intellectually, I knew I deserved protection and care. Emotionally, I didn't feel it. Even now, when my husband gives me a gift or does something kind, my first instinct is to think, *I didn't earn this.* But love isn't a transaction. It's a presence.

Healing began with noticing that instinct and asking, gently, "*Who taught me I couldn't rely on anyone?*"

It also meant grieving the parts of my youth I didn't even know I'd lost—years shaped by fear, silence, and responsibility that no child should ever carry. And it means honoring the girl who never stopped imagining that something better was possible.

I have had to learn to flip the script inside my mind. When I feel unworthy of kindness, I picture myself giving a gift to one of my children simply because I love them—not because they earned it. I remind myself that I, too, deserve love without conditions.

Some days, I can see it with clarity: I survived. I built a successful, meaningful life. I broke the cycle.

And the truth is it's not easy. There are other days I slip back into the posture of that small, terrified girl—holding my breath, waiting for criticism, and bracing for impact. But at least I know when it's happening, and in those moments, I can choose to be kind and compassionate to that version of me.

11

The Irony of Care

My relationship with my mother can be called complicated at best. The truth is, it was deeply wounding. She should have protected me. Instead, she looked away. Sometimes, she even bore silent witness to the abuse. In many ways, her treatment of me caused far more lasting harm than anything Al ever did.

And now, in one of life's cruelest ironies, I've become more of a mother to her than she ever was to me.

When she was sixty-eight, our mom had a major hemorrhagic stroke that rendered her incapacitated. It happened suddenly and without warning, as these things do. And that's how I ended up in a room again with Al.

It was the first time I'd seen him in years—in fact, the last time had been when Nicholas was just a baby. I was living in Nevada, and before our visit, I had made one thing crystal clear to my mother: I would not bring my ten-month-old son into her home unless she could guarantee that Al wouldn't be there.

She balked. "He lives here too," she said, as though that somehow excused it.

I stood firm, and eventually, her desire to meet her grandson outweighed her loyalty to him. One morning, she called and told me Al had gone out and I should come over for a quick visit.

Of course, he came home early. I'm sure that had been the plan all along. He walked through the front door with a big grin on his face, acting like everything was fine—like years of abuse could be undone with a smile.

My stomach turned as I watched his eyes land on my baby.

I didn't say a word. I calmly packed up Nicholas, looked at my mother, and told her I would never bring my children back into that house. And I meant it. No matter what she said in the years that followed, I never changed my mind. It was the first boundary I ever truly held with her.

Now, this reunion was much worse. It brought us all back to the table under the guise of caregiving. Except Al clearly wasn't there to care—he was there to control.

I'll never forget being beside my mother's ICU bed, the machines beeping steadily around us, when Al stepped out for a cigarette. While he was gone, a doctor came to update us on her condition. When Al returned and learned that the conversation had happened without him, he lost it. He wasn't upset about missing the information—he was furious that the world had dared to continue without him. That's the heart of narcissism: the belief that everything, even a medical crisis, should pause until you return.

Alone in the room with us, and with dramatic flair, he ripped off his fedora and flung it into the wall, shouting at us, "That's not your mother—that's my wife!"

Tony and I exchanged a glance but said nothing. We knew better. Though it was surreal to watch one unfold in a hospital, we were used to Al's outbursts. This wasn't grief. It was grandiosity. It was about him. Always him.

And despite all his theatrics, a truth lingered in the room: our mother had never married him. Al had asked her countless times, but for whatever reason, she never said yes. Maybe, deep down, she knew better. Or maybe that's just me trying to give her too much credit. But either way? He was not in control of her affairs, and that was deeply upsetting to him.

Soon after her stroke, Tony and I—working with an attorney—filed for emergency guardianship. It was a necessary and practical step. Our mother could no longer manage her medical care, finances, or insurance—and, true to form, she had never established a power of attorney. Like many narcissists, she believed she was invincible. In her mind, illness was something that happened to other people, as if sheer willpower could protect her from reality.

But there we were, standing in the very situation she'd refused to prepare for. The judge approved our petition quickly, naming Tony and me as our mother's emergency guardians.

Al did not take that news well.

Within a week, he began to spiral—just as he always had when control slipped through his fingers. He hired a lawyer, and not just any lawyer—the same man who had represented him during my childhood abuse case years before.

Soon, he filed for an adjudication claiming our mother wasn't incapacitated at all. Despite her obvious cognitive decline, Al insisted she was of sound mind. A court-ordered evaluation—and then a second—found that she, in fact, was incapable of making decisions for herself.

Tony and I agreed to let Al continue living in our mother's house, but we refused to relinquish control over her medical and financial affairs. There were more hearings, more filings, and then more hearings.

After a year of rehab, our mom returned home for a few months. But stability didn't last. Soon, a series of small strokes caused her to lose the few abilities she had regained. At that point, she moved into a permanent assisted-living facility.

Meanwhile, Al's attorney kept chipping away at us, filing motions and mounting objections. And eventually, their efforts worked. The court removed Tony and me as her guardians; in our place, they appointed a stranger: a court-appointed guardian who didn't know our mother, didn't know us, and didn't seem to care. We were blindsided. But in a twist of irony, so was Al. He wanted control of my mother's care, and he didn't want me or Tony involved. But he also didn't want some other person involved.

While we were all shut out, the system failed in every way imaginable. The court-appointed guardian was negligent. The court-appointed attorney, who was supposed to provide oversight, did nothing. Our mother's accounts fell into collections—despite the fact that she had more than enough money to cover her needs.

The deeper we got into the system, the more disturbing the truth became: this wasn't just incompetence. It was collusion.

In some jurisdictions—including ours—the court-appointed attorneys, guardians, and judges work together on so many guardianship cases that they fall into a toxic rhythm. A pattern of protecting one another, shielding negligence, and maximizing personal gain. Whether they intend to harm the most vulnerable people in their care or not, that is exactly what ends up happening.

And here's what I learned: when it comes to guardianship, it's not the person who matters. It's the estate. The money. That's where the real power lies. That's what draws the attention. That's what gets fought over. The care of the human being becomes secondary—if it's considered at all.

After months of court hearings, filings, delays, and dysfunction, Tony and I were finally reinstated as our mother's guardians—he for the estate, and me for the person. We stepped in, not because it was easy or convenient, but because we were still her children. Despite everything we'd endured growing up, we did what needed to be done: managing her care, attending her medical appointments, overseeing her finances, and making sure she had what she needed.

But caring for her after her stroke wasn't just logistical—it was also emotional. It was strange to witness: her body was still that of a grown woman, but her cognitive functioning was that of a toddler.

As a child therapist, I'm trained to listen for meaning in what's not said—to pick up on the clues in nonsensical statements. And with my mother, those clues came fast and loud.

She couldn't form complete sentences, but what she could say often alarmed me. Once, while struggling to crochet—a skill she had once mastered—she told me she was making a "dick cover." Later, her doctor flagged that her pessary had been forcibly displaced—something that doesn't happen by accident. It only moves through significant force—usually the result of someone attempting intercourse with a person wearing one.

Eventually, I received a call that confirmed what I already knew: Al is a predator. As my mother's legal guardian, I was informed that the nursing staff had walked in on Al forcing our mother to give him a hand job. He would no longer be permitted to be alone with her.

Even in her incapacitated state—helpless, disoriented, and childlike—she was being violated by Al. His needs always came before anyone else's. And when the facility set a clear boundary—and that he could only visit in common areas, never alone—he was furious. "No one is going to tell me how to be with my wife," he bellowed.

Wife. They had never married. But to him, that word was a claim. A license. A declaration of ownership.

After that, Al may have visited her once more, out of spite. And then never again. He disappeared the moment he was told no.

And that's what it was always about for him—not love. Not loyalty. It was always about access, power, and control. The moment he couldn't have those things—when the system finally told him no—he threw a tantrum and vanished from her daily life. But not entirely. He kept living in her house, enjoying all the comforts of her home for free.

Meanwhile, I was just trying to hold it all together—navigating my new reality one day at a time. I was focused solely on survival: showing up as my mother's legal guardian, parenting three boys, juggling multiple jobs, and managing the slow-burning frustration in my marriage. There was no room left for more heartache—let alone any healing from my past. I was doing everything I could just to keep one foot in front of the other.

But grief has a way of cutting through even the strongest armor.

After nearly a year and a half of navigating day-to-day life, my father died—suddenly, without warning. With that single, shattering loss, the fragile structure I built to contain my pain collapsed. I couldn't outrun it anymore. I had to face everything I'd buried.

What I Know Now

Caring for someone who never truly cared for you creates a kind of psychological whiplash—one only survivors can fully understand. From the outside, the world sees strength and loyalty. They see a dutiful daughter stepping up. What they don't see is the internal war inside me: the grief, the rage, the longing for a mother who never existed, and the aching absence of everything I needed but never received.

The grief I carry is layered. I grieve the mother I lost to a stroke, but I also grieve the mother I never had—the one who might have offered safety, comfort, or protection. I grieve the childhood that never felt secure. And I grieve the adult version of me who still hoped she would one day say, *"I'm sorry. I believe you. I should have protected you."*

Layered over that grief was the constant presence of my childhood abuser—the man who threaded himself into every chapter of her life and mine. When Al used the word "wife" at the hospital, it wasn't devotion. It was a declaration of ownership. His behavior during her decline was a perfect echo of what he had always done: manipulate, dominate, destabilize, and seize control wherever he could.

And then there was the guardianship system—a structure that looks legitimate from the outside but was as hollow and harmful as the dynamics I grew up in.

Abuse doesn't end when someone becomes incapacitated. Sometimes, that's when it becomes most visible.

I didn't step forward as my mother's guardian out of loyalty or out of some need to redeem the past. I did it out of principle—and because trauma doesn't get the final word in my life. I refuse to let Al define her story or mine. I refuse to let a broken court system cement the narrative.

Taking responsibility for her care was my way of reclaiming agency. My way of saying:

"You didn't protect me, but I will not become the version of you that looked away. I will not let abuse be the legacy that shapes my actions."

My Healing

Choosing to become my mother's guardian was simultaneously grounding and destabilizing. It affirmed my identity as a protector, a doer, and someone who shows up when life becomes unbearable.

It also reopened wounds I thought I had long buried.

Being forced to interact with Al—to witness his volatility and entitlement up close again—was retraumatizing. And at that time in my life, I wasn't ready to confront any of it. I was in survival mode: working multiple jobs, raising three boys, living in a marriage that was cracking beneath the surface, and trying to hold together a life built on a shaky foundation.

It took time—and truthfully, my father's sudden death—to break me open enough to finally face what I'd been outrunning.

I started doing the hard work. I spent time identifying my core values—peace and happiness—and recognizing the choices, relationships, and dynamics that were pulling me away from them. Once I had that clarity, everything else became a series of honest questions: *Am I at peace? Am I happy?*

Where the answer was no, I learned to change direction.

Healing also meant understanding that I am not my abusers. My kindness is not rooted in guilt or shame. My care is not born from obligation. My willingness to show up for others is not proof of weakness—it is evidence of who I am at my core.

I don't choose compassion because that's what was modeled for me. I choose it because it's mine. Because it is the truest expression of who I am when no one is trying to rewrite my story.

12

The Longest Good-bye

My dad dying unexpectedly broke me open. The pain was unbearable—but also undeniably clarifying. Without him, I could no longer buffer myself from the chaos. I could no longer pretend things were okay. His death didn't just devastate me—it forced me to face the truth about my marriage to Allen.

The night before he passed, I had taken the boys to a local carnival. On our way home, we drove past my dad's house. I noticed the lights were on and called to check in, but he didn't answer. I thought about stopping by but told myself he was fine, and I'd see him in the morning.

The next day, after a morning run and a quick shower, I walked the short distance to his house to make sure he was up. My brother Tony was scheduled to take him to a doctor's appointment.

Inside, the TV was blaring. There was no smell of coffee brewing, the usual sign that he was up and moving. But I also knew he wasn't supposed to drink anything before the appointment. I walked in and called his name. No response. No footsteps. No voice from the kitchen.

It wouldn't be the first time I'd walked in and found him slow to rise. Usually, he'd emerge from the back room, smirk, and say, "What—did you think I was dead?" Then always with a wink: "I'm still here, baby."

Then I saw his feet. He was face down on the hardwood floor, his legs frozen mid-stride, as if he'd simply fallen forward and never gotten back up. He was wearing his wind pants and the soles of his feet were dirty. He had never liked wearing shoes, even outside.

My stomach flipped. "Daddy!" I screamed. I ran to him and touched his arm. I barely remember what happened next, other than sprinting home to call 911.

Allen heard me and ran to my dad's house. When I followed, he blocked the door. "You don't want to go in there!" he said. I pushed past him. This was not going to be a time for Allen to exert control. I had already seen everything, and I needed to be there.

I don't remember a lot of details. I know the police arrived first and someone pulled me off my father's body. Then the paramedics came, and they covered him with a white sheet. Family began to gather as I floated through the house in shock.

When Tony arrived, he found me sitting on the patio steps, folded into myself. He sat beside me, calm and steady, and told me of what I couldn't tell myself: "This wasn't your fault." I had been beating myself up for not having visited the night before, and I needed to hear that. Especially from him.

By this time, the boys and I had grown incredibly close to my dad. After we moved back, he became everything I had always needed—steadfast, present, and deeply involved. He didn't just show up because he lived next door; he showed up because he wanted to.

The aftermath of his death revealed something I had refused to acknowledge. In the rawness of my grief, I finally saw my marriage for what it had become. Allen didn't comfort me. He competed with me. Every time I cried, he made it about his pain. Every story I told about my father, he hijacked it. Even at the funeral—without being invited—he stood up to speak and center himself in my dad's life story.

Perhaps the strangest part of this story is what happened to the dog—Allen's dog. The beloved English Bulldog he insisted we buy. Three days after my dad died, the dog suddenly got sick.

There had been nothing wrong with him up until this point. But that afternoon, as I was gathering neighbors and friends to work on photo boards and crafts for my dad's funeral, Allen came storming into the house, interrupting everything. He was frantic, demanding ice and attention, insisting the dog was seriously ill.

And just like that, the focus shifted.

A few of my friends ran outside to help him. Allen left shortly after for the vet. When he returned, he was solemn and deep in grief. The dog had been put down, he said. And now, we needed to dig a hole and celebrate its life.

Some of the neighbors who had been helping me honor my father's life pivoted without question. They consoled Allen and the boys as they dug the hole to bury the dog.

I understood, of course. Even with my aversion to the dog, I knew his death would affect the rest of my family. But everything about it felt . . . off.

It was no longer about my dad. It wasn't about my shock, my loss, or the trauma of finding his body. It became about Allen's grief. About how unfair it was that, on top of everything else, he lost his dog.

It took that—Allen trying to steal my grief—for me to finally see things clearly. Within a few months, I said the words, "I want a divorce," and Allen stormed out of our house without his shoes.

While clarity came quickly, untangling myself from Allen took much longer. Just because I saw the truth didn't mean I was free from the consequences of finally speaking it aloud.

A few hours after his dramatic exit from our home—shoeless and now technically homeless—Allen came back.

He had to. His departure had been so theatrical, so fueled by rage and indignation, that he hadn't paused to gather so much as his wallet, his keys, or a pair of shoes. And when the adrenaline wore off and the cold reality of having no shoes and nowhere to go set in, he showed back up.

I didn't want to let him in, but he cried and begged. He had nowhere else to go—a fact he used to guilt me into letting him stay. After hours of his groveling and apologies, I was too afraid and too worn down to deny him anymore. So, I eventually agreed to let him sleep on the couch.

That first night, I locked myself in the bedroom, shaking with panic, convinced he might find a way in before morning. I didn't sleep. I just waited.

And when the sun finally rose, I did what I hadn't been able to do before: I said it again—calm, direct, unshakable—"Our marriage is over."

"Just wait until after Christmas," he begged. "Let's not ruin the holidays for the boys."

I knew my decision wouldn't change. Allen's promises that things would get better were lies—I felt that in my bones. But for the sake of the kids, I agreed to wait.

As Allen moved into the basement, I prepared. This was a decision that had been years in the making, so I already knew I had the unconditional support of my brother and my therapist. By January, I was ready to file and ready to be free.

Allen, true to form, had done nothing to make the situation better, despite his promises. And now, facing the prospect of having to leave our house with nowhere else to go, he stalled.

In a last-ditch performance, he started seeing a counselor—telling me he was "doing better." He begged me to join him for one session. I agreed, and I was also clear: I'm done and I want a divorce. A week later, he stopped going. The counselor hadn't taken his side, and he couldn't manipulate him into manipulating me.

Once it became clear the divorce was inevitable, Allen pivoted again—insisting we "self-file" to save money. He said that if we didn't self-file, we would need to hire two attorneys.

Allen knew exactly how to exploit my fear of financial collapse. All our credit cards were maxed out, and I couldn't afford a drawn-out legal fight. I knew that the bills for his lawyer would somehow become my obligation, so I agreed that we didn't need to involve them.

While I gathered paperwork and completed court documents, Allen continued to camp out in the basement—eating my groceries, using my shower, and occupying my space. My so-called "guest room" could not have been comfortable. It was just an unfinished basement: cold floors, concrete walls, and no plumbing.

But he stayed. Squatting in my house kept him close and in control—exactly what he wanted.

In Pennsylvania, a contested divorce requires a mandatory one-year waiting period—and I knew if our arrangement became contentious, Allen would use every extra minute to manipulate and delay. He talked a good game about wanting things to be amicable, but his actions told a different story. He dragged his feet at every step, turning the process into a slow, grinding war.

Before we married, he'd signed a prenuptial agreement that protected my retirement, the proceeds from my first home, and the educational savings for my two older boys. But now he claimed the prenup didn't matter. He wanted access to my accounts, and he made it clear: if I didn't comply, he wouldn't leave.

A lawyer could have helped resolve this. But I was thinking ahead—how I'd buy him out, raise the kids, cover the mortgage, and start over. I was already in debt, and legal fees would only drain me further. Allen had told me he'd get what he wanted, one way or another, and I believed him.

Every conversation became a battlefield. Every object in our home, a negotiation. It was never about fairness—it was always about control. A lamp, a chair, a bookshelf—even the showerhead. His tone shifted depending on the tactic. Sometimes, he'd try to manipulate my logic: "You don't need that," he'd insist. Other times, it turned to accusation: "You're not going to keep all the good stuff and leave me with the junk."

This wasn't about splitting assets. It was about dominance. About watching me bend. About proving that no matter what I owned on paper, he still had the power.

Allen had his own equation for justifying everything he took. According to him, our eleven-year marriage entitled him to more—more money, more things, more say. Why? Because it was longer than my first marriage, which had ended after seven and a half years.

That fact seemed to give him a twisted sense of pride. He brought it up more than once, smirking as he reminded me that he had "lasted longer," as if our relationship had been a contest he had won.

It wasn't about love or commitment. It was about outlasting someone else. About proving that he'd done what another man couldn't. And when it came time to divide our lives, he used those eleven years like currency—proof, in his mind, that he was owed. That he'd put in enough time to collect a return.

It didn't matter that I was the one who built the counseling practice. That I brought in the income, raised the children, and paid the bills. In Allen's eyes, time was the only thing that counted—and it belonged to him.

In the end, the divorce agreement was completely lopsided. I gave in to almost everything he demanded—over half the equity in the house, half my retirement, a portion of the inheritance my father had left me, and the business I had built from nothing.

The counseling practice was perhaps the most ridiculous thing he took. Allen's lack of interest, and his proven inability to manage it, was what made his demands for 100 percent of it so absurd. Yet I let him take it. I just wanted it to be over.

On my final day, I packed a small box of personal items—old notebooks and a few early marketing brochures that featured my image. Allen made a show of demanding the box back, insisting I was "removing company property." It was petty, absurd—and exactly the point. One last power play to assert control and remind me that, in his eyes, I didn't matter.

What made it worse was how normalized it all seemed to the people around us. One younger therapist stood by, watching it unfold, seemingly oblivious to the dynamics at play. The entire exchange was humiliating—and clarifying. It affirmed what I already knew deep in my bones: teaching therapists to recognize abuse that doesn't leave bruises isn't just important—it's essential. Because if even trained professionals can't see it, how can we expect anyone else to?

To be clear, it didn't surprise me when Allen shuttered the practice without warning a few years later. There was no plan and no notice—just a paper sign on the door. Therapists were blindsided. Clients—hundreds of them, all in the middle of their healing—were suddenly cut off.

Allen had applied for COVID relief during the pandemic, taken the financial benefits, filed for loan forgiveness—and then walked away. When people asked what happened, he said he'd "retired early."

This is how narcissists operate: control the narrative, burn the evidence, and walk away from the wreckage like it never existed. And in this version of the story, Allen got to look like he'd cashed out, like he'd built something and exited on top.

But I know the truth. He didn't just destroy something I built. He destroyed something people relied on. Because to him, people aren't people. They're tools. Props. Reflections of his ego. And once they stop serving him, he discards them—without a second thought.

There was one final act of manipulation while we were still technically married. Allen used my grief as leverage and finagled his way onto a Disney Cruise meant for me, the boys, and my brother's family—a trip we planned to honor "Nonno," which is what the boys called my dad. We chose to use a bit of our inheritance to create joyful memories. Allen, as always, used it as a free vacation.

But the day we left, our finalized divorce papers arrived in the mail. As we pulled out of the driveway, I felt relief: it was over. Although Allen's presence would linger—on the cruise, in our lives, and deep in my nervous system—the papers were stamped, signed, recorded.

I thought I was finally free. But Allen wasn't finished with me yet.

What I Know Now

Grief has a way of stripping away our defenses. It doesn't just break the heart—it dissolves illusion. It forces us to look directly at what we've spent years trying not to see. For me, the death of my father shattered the fragile story I had been clinging to—that my marriage was stable, that Allen was a supportive partner, that if I just held everything together, everything would be fine.

In the rawness of that loss, I finally saw my life clearly. I saw how Allen made my grief about him, how he competed with my pain instead of comforting it, how even my father's death and funeral became yet another stage for his ego. The chaos with the dog, the drama, the way he overshadowed my loss—none of it was random. It was a pattern. It was who he had always been.

Grieving my father, my marriage, the life I believed I had, and the future I thought we would build was anything but tidy. Grief is hard—whether you are mourning a person, a relationship, or the dreams that never materialized. But grief also reveals truths we are too afraid to face until everything else falls away.

My Healing

My dad's sudden death made me feel instantly orphaned. My mother was already incapacitated, and now my father—the one person who had finally shown me some measure of safety—was gone in an instant.

Understanding that death can feel like abandonment became a turning point. It opened the door to recognizing all the ways I had been abandoned long before that day.

His death didn't just devastate me; it delivered a fierce, unflinching clarity. Something in me knew I could no longer live the way I had been living. That clarity was my dad's final gift—an unexpected gift of freedom. It set me on a path toward my authentic self. Looking back, I can see that it was the catalyst that pushed me toward intentional healing rather than accidental survival.

Another layer of healing began the moment I told Allen I wanted a divorce. His reactions were dramatic, chaotic, and cruel—and at times, I caught myself thinking, "He wasn't this way before I told him I wanted a divorce." But that was a story I had been telling myself. He had *always* been this way. I just hadn't recognized it.

As I learned more about narcissistic abuse, coercive control, and the patterns of power and domination, I started to map those frameworks onto my own life. And when I did, everything snapped into focus. Naming the abuse didn't mean I had failed—it meant I was finally seeing clearly. That clarity was the first step in reclaiming my power.

From there, healing became a series of choices. Hard choices. Brave choices. Choices that cost me things I once thought defined my stability: the financial security I had built and the business I created. Letting go of all of it wasn't indifference—it was a declaration. A decision that my sanity, safety, and self were worth more than any asset.

For the first time in my life, I chose me.

13

The Collapsing Supply

With Allen, the damage is done in shadows. He is a master of disguise—appearing to the world as the generous guy who'd give you the shirt off his back. The doting husband. The devoted stepfather. The selfless friend. The perpetual victim.

None of it is real, but his performance can be so convincing and so well-practiced that it can be nearly impossible for others to see—let alone believe—who he truly is.

Delay tactics were often a first line of defense. Allen dragged out his search for a new home in every way possible. One of his more absurd suggestions was that he move into my late father's house. To him, it made perfect sense. His own grandparents had lived separately as neighbors, so why not us?

It was laughable. And completely unacceptable.

Finally, Allen bought a house a short drive away. But even after he got the keys, he continued sleeping in my basement for several more weeks—refusing to let go of his oversight of my life until the very last possible moment.

When he finally left, he took everything that wasn't bolted down. That's not an exaggeration. He took items we had never discussed or agreed on. I saw that it was spite and let it go.

But the thing that stuck out the most—the thing that seemed like the most obvious and pathetic attempt at maintaining control—was the box of old sex toys he took. As he did it, he repeated his mantra of "you don't need these." Yeah, he was right. I didn't need sex toys. Neither did he. It was ridiculous and so clearly about revenge.

I let go of it all—money, belongings, the business I had built from scratch. In their place, I chose peace, stability for my children, and room to breathe. I made myself a quiet promise of a future no longer tethered to fear.

Time would prove that this was a false hope. As a new stage of our relationship as co-parents began, the abuse didn't end at all. It just changed forms.

In the months after our divorce was finalized, Allen continued treating my house like it was still his. He walked in without knocking. He opened the fridge to take whatever food he wanted. Even my bedroom wasn't off-limits: when he learned I repainted it, he waltzed right in to see the new color for himself.

Allen picked up on the guilt I carried about the end of our marriage—and he used it to get what he wanted, again and again. And when I found the courage to push back or say I wasn't comfortable, he would counter by insisting he had "a right to see where his son was living." For a while, I believed that could be true.

Everything was harder because I was just starting to understand Allen's behavior patterns and didn't know how to hold boundaries. And he knew it and kept finding ways to insert himself into my life. The first year, he invited himself to Thanksgiving. He showed up again on Christmas Eve. Each time, I told myself I was trying to keep the peace for the boys, even when keeping the peace meant pushing down my own needs and pretending everything was okay when it wasn't.

There was subtle stuff, too. One day, a few months after he moved out, Allen shared a social media story about a man and his ex-wife who remained close friends after their divorce. In the narrative, the man continued to visit, bring gifts, and offer support. On the surface, it sounded ideal—mature, healthy, and cooperative. But post-divorce "friendships" only work when both people genuinely want them to, and I definitely did not. I only wanted to co-parent Joe.

Early the next year, my beloved Philadelphia Eagles made it to the Super Bowl. I was so excited to watch the game with Joe, who shared my love of football and my devotion to the team. This was the first time in his young memory that "our" team had made it to the top. But as the big game approached, Allen insisted that Joe watch it with him, not me. This was absurd. Allen had never even been an Eagles fan. Still, I didn't argue. I let it go, trying—once again—to keep the peace.

Around this time, the two older boys were starting to see through Allen's subtle digs and quiet attempts to rewrite history. But Joe was still young, without the tools to question the stories he was being fed.

Parental alienation is one of the most damaging dynamics that can emerge from divorce, and it's disturbingly common when a narcissist is involved. It happens when one parent systematically undermines the child's relationship with the other. They make disparaging remarks about the other parent, distorting reality in ways that are nearly impossible to trace. And over time, it has an impact. The child begins to internalize this manipulation, question their own instincts, and then withdraw from the targeted parent.

What I didn't know then—but would later learn—is how textbook my experience was in cases involving narcissistic exes.

Allen was careful never to say anything blatantly cruel about me—at least, not in ways that would be obvious to Joe. His criticisms came coated in sugar and wrapped in "concern," which made them difficult to recognize—even for me.

Early on, if Allen wanted more time with Joe on a weekend, it didn't matter what our custody arrangement had been. And he wouldn't ask me himself, which would be the normal course of action among co-parents. Instead, Allen would put Joe in the middle, coaching him to make the request himself.

"You can ask your mom," he'd say, "but she'll probably say no. Go ahead and try—just don't be upset with me when she says no."

If I said no, I was the bad guy. If I said yes, I'd walked straight into his trap. Either way, Allen got what he wanted: power, control, and a growing wedge between me and my son.

It was maddening. And for a long time, I didn't fully understand just how damaging it was for Joe. Worst of all, I was still seeing Allen's side over my own—second-guessing myself, doubting my instincts, and questioning what was truly best for my child.

As Allen inserted himself into everything in our lives, I started to feel paranoid. He always seemed to know when someone had been by the house, even if they had only idled in the driveway. He'd drop subtle comments or ask seemingly harmless questions that, to anyone else, wouldn't raise suspicion. "Why is so-and-so visiting this week?" he'd ask.

To the outside world, it sounded like polite curiosity. But I knew better. This was surveillance disguised as small talk.

It also begged the question: how did he know so much? Was he spending all day driving up and down my street? Watching the house from a distance? Had he installed cameras without my knowledge?

I learned the truth later: Allen was talking to anyone who would listen—mutual friends, neighbors, even casual acquaintances—and painting himself as the victim of our failed marriage. According to him, my dad's death made me "go crazy." That narrative was getting old—but he was still clinging to it like a shield.

It hurt to realize that people I once trusted were so quick to believe him—and so quick to judge me. At first, I told myself that if someone wasn't willing to ask for my side of the story, they probably weren't someone I needed in my life anyway. Over time, I've come to accept something even harder: when people choose to stay neutral or maintain friendships with both parties, they are—whether they realize it or not—condoning the abuse. Silence and neutrality don't protect the victim. They protect the abuser.

Even after the divorce papers were signed, Allen made it his mission to monitor my every move. He'd drive up and down my road, searching for anything he could twist into a complaint. Somehow, he always knew too much—where I was, who I was with, even when I started dating again.

I still don't know exactly how he got his information, but I do know he recruited Joe as an unknowing informant. Everything I did was scrutinized, weaponized, and tied to my worth as a mother—a title Allen used not with respect, but as a tool of control and judgment.

Allen even tried to control my exercise routine. He told me that my running every morning was a problem because it took me away from the house while the boys were getting ready for school. The message was clear: running makes you a bad mom. He knew exactly where to aim to cut to my core.

But the irony wasn't lost on me. I ran early—before Allen was even awake. Even on the days the boys were with him, he was never up at that hour. But his concern was never about parenting. Beyond that—no one was going to tell me what to do with my body. Running made me stronger—physically, emotionally, and mentally. I would not stop.

As I began setting—and holding—firmer boundaries with Allen, his attempts to disparage me escalated. I started receiving messages from extended family with screenshots of bizarre Facebook posts about me. I had already blocked Allen from my accounts, and I'm not the type to ask others to manage their social media for my sake. But this time, he went too far. I asked my family to unfriend him due to the ongoing negativity. Most of them did so immediately. I believe the few who didn't simply didn't know how.

What I didn't know then is that cutting off a narcissist—emotionally, financially, or otherwise—almost always triggers backlash. For someone like Allen, being shut out isn't just rejection; it's humiliation. And narcissists don't handle humiliation quietly. The loss of control shatters their carefully constructed ego, and they often lash out to restore their dominance. What feels like self-protection to you—setting boundaries, choosing distance, or reclaiming autonomy—feels like a full-blown assault to them.

Psychologists refer to this as the collapse of the "narcissistic supply"—the emotional lifeline narcissists rely on to uphold their fragile sense of self. That supply doesn't have to come in the form of praise or admiration (though they certainly prefer it that way). It can also be fear, anger, confusion, or even pain—any intense emotional reaction that reaffirms their ability to affect you. In a twisted way, it proves their significance. Your distress becomes their validation.

During our marriage, I was Allen's primary supply. So were the boys. So was the woman he briefly worked for—the boss he would drop everything for, even long after his employment ended. It wasn't about loyalty. It was about maintaining access.

Allen needs someone—anyone—to orbit him, to reflect his importance, to absorb his moods and mirror back the version of himself he wanted to see.

And when the supply begins to run dry—when people stop reacting, stop feeding the dynamic, and stop playing the role they've been assigned—the narcissist panics. They spiral. They retaliate. Sometimes it's subtle: guilt trips, smear campaigns, or passive-aggressive jabs masked as concern. Other times, it's explosive: threats, manipulation, legal interference, or financial sabotage.

What I didn't fully understand then, but know all too well now, is that narcissistic abuse doesn't end when the relationship does. In many cases, it intensifies—a dynamic known as post-separation abuse.

When a narcissist loses control, they don't seek closure. They seek revenge. They find new ways to insert themselves, to reestablish dominance, to punish you for daring to walk away. And they almost always find a new source of supply to prop up their image while they tear yours down.

At the time, I wasn't thinking about any of that. I just didn't want Allen to have access to me or my family. He was trying to groom them, spinning stories that I'd gone "crazy" after my dad died. According to him, my grief had made me irrational—and my asking for a divorce was Exhibit A.

But he underestimated my family. We're close, and they didn't buy what he was selling.

We're also polite, which meant no one said anything to him directly—especially not in the comments section of a Facebook tirade. The idea that he could turn them against me was almost laughable. Even though as a child I had often felt like the odd one out, they didn't see me that way. They showed up. They had my back.

Blocking Allen—and encouraging my family to do the same—deeply impacted him. Months later, he was still complaining about it and blaming me. "Seventy-eight people unfriended me in one week," he whined. "You did this!"

While I'm not sure who those seventy-eight people were (my family isn't that big), what became clear is this: for narcissists, social media isn't just connection—it's fuel. They thrive on the attention, the followers, and the likes. Losing that feels like losing control.

Although they were certainly weary, Nicholas and Christopher continued to try to nurture a relationship with Allen post-divorce. I'm confident it was for my sake more than their own. They'd stay at his house and go on outings with him and Joe. They were doing their best.

The second anniversary of my father's death was a particularly weird time for them.

I planned a small gathering to honor the occasion, just as I had the year before. It was nothing terribly elaborate: just a few people, a quiet space, and the intention to remember. Allen and I were long divorced by then, so I didn't invite him.

When he found out, he was furious. He pulled out every tool in his well-worn toolbox—guilt, shame, emotional manipulation—all aimed at making me feel selfish for excluding him. He reminded me of how close he'd been with my father, how much he'd lost, how cruel I was for keeping him out.

When that didn't work—when I didn't cave—he shifted gears.

The night before the gathering, Allen picked up the boys for his scheduled visitation. As soon as they got into the car, he took the older boys' phones and disabled location sharing. "You will have no contact with your mother," he told them. "Not during my time."

Then he drove them to the cemetery.

Since, as he told them, "your mother won't let me attend tomorrow's gathering," he created his own. He brought pizza and root beer—my dad's favorites—and had the boys toast the gravestone in a makeshift ceremony.

From a distance, the scene might have looked sweet. A stepfather paying tribute with his stepsons. But up close, it wasn't that at all.

The boys had visited the cemetery before—many times. They had their own connection to their grandfather and their own ways of remembering him. This was weird. It felt orchestrated.

Later, Nicholas and Christopher came to me confused, asking why they had to give up their phones and promise not to contact me. They couldn't put the experience into words, but they could feel it. The root beer, the pizza—it wasn't a gesture of remembrance. It was a performance.

They were handed props and told to play their parts in Allen's story—a story not about grief, but about control.

Because it was forced. This wasn't about honoring their grandfather. It was theater. Allen's desperate attempt to reassert power after being told "no."

As much as the older boys tried, their relationship with Allen was untenable.

One night while the boys were at his house, Allen got into an argument with Nicholas. Details of arguments with Allen don't matter. Whenever there is conflict, he shuts down, refuses to speak, and waits for the other person to come crawling with an apology.

But this time, that tactic didn't work, and Nicholas refused to play along.

After the argument, Allen sent me a long email detailing what he described as Nicholas's "disrespect." Once again, the blame landed squarely on me. As Nicholas's mother, he wrote, it was my responsibility to teach him how to respect "adults." Of course, that was code for: You need to tell your son to respect me—no matter what. It wasn't about the facts, or teaching values, or setting boundaries. It was about demanding loyalty. And if Nicholas didn't fall in line, it was my failure.

Thus, began a new phase of our co-parenting relationship: long and scathing emails from Allen. Their content was never updates about Joe. These missives were an opportunity to criticize every corner of my life: my parenting, my decisions, my children, even my values. He didn't like the way I did anything, and he made sure I knew it.

My self-esteem, already fragile from the divorce, began to crumble. Every time I saw Allen's name in my inbox, my body tensed. My hands shook and I cried. His words echoed long after I read them. While tearing me down, he never missed a chance to remind me of his own greatness—as a person, as a parent, as the one who always knew better.

For a while, I tried using the "gray rock" technique—keeping my responses short, factual, and emotionally flat. I replied only when it involved Joe, and even then, I offered no commentary and no openings for debate. Just the basics: pickup times, doctor appointments, etc.

But even silence wasn't safe.

Allen needed a reaction—any reaction—to feel in control. When I didn't take the bait, he started taunting me for not responding to parts of his messages. "I see you chose to ignore the section about David," he'd write, dripping with false concern. "Interesting that you didn't deny what I said."

It took time for me to recognize what was happening. But eventually, I saw Allen's emails for what they were: line after line of projection, control, guilt-tripping, and blatant disrespect. He was trying to bait me and drag me into arguments so I would be forced to defend myself. And then he'd twist my words into evidence of wrongdoing. His goal wasn't communication. It was control.

And when he couldn't get that control from me directly, he turned his attention to Joe.

At first, it was subtle—almost unnoticeable. His phone calls with Joe started getting longer. At first an hour, then two. Then they began interrupting family dinners, bedtime routines, and small moments of connection that had once felt sacred. On the surface, the calls seemed innocent: football stats, draft picks, quarterback rankings. Just a dad bonding with his son.

But beneath that casual chatter, Allen was doing what he did best: planting seeds of doubt, feeding division, and slowly, methodically, driving a wedge between us. His tactics were classic parental alienation.

Allen positioned himself as the "fun" parent, the one who really "got" Joe—while painting me as uptight, unreasonable, and emotionally unstable. "I get it," he'd say. "Your mom doesn't see how hard you have it." He framed my attempts at structure and safety as cruelty, and Joe, still just a kid, couldn't see the manipulation.

He validated every complaint Joe had about our home and inflated minor conflicts into grand injustices. And any time I set a boundary or enforced a consequence, Allen reframed it as cruelty.

He made sure Joe saw him as the safe harbor, and me as the storm. Even chores like unloading the dishwasher—something completely normal—became evidence that Joe was being "treated unfairly." Allen would say things like, "You know your brothers don't have to do that stuff, right?" or "It's not like that at my house."

Joe was fed a steady stream of distorted narratives about all of us. According to his father, Nicholas and Christopher had no rules and lived free of all consequences. I wasn't a parent guiding Joe—I was a relentless taskmaster who made his life miserable. My hardworking boyfriend who owned a profitable business was labeled a failed musician and a raging alcoholic and drug addict who would never provide anything of value and didn't deserve Joe's respect, let alone a place in his life.

It was relentless, calculated character assassination—designed not just to undermine us, but to isolate Joe and make Allen his only reliable narrator. None of it was true, but truth doesn't matter when the goal is power. Over time, it worked.

Joe was groomed to see me not as his protector, but as the problem. And the more Allen reinforced that story, the more Joe pulled away. As time went on, our relationship, once rooted in deep closeness, began to fray. Joe grew colder, quicker to anger, less trusting. I could feel him slipping, and there was nothing I could do to stop it.

That's what parental alienation does—it steals your child from the inside out. And by the time you realize it's happening, you're already being cast as the villain in a story someone else is writing.

Joe wasn't old enough to see the difference between love and leverage. But Allen was. And when I tried to raise concerns about the inappropriate nature of their conversations, Allen snapped: "You are not going to stop me from talking to my child."

It was a trap. If I pushed back, I looked like I was trying to control the relationship. If I stayed quiet, the damage continued. Either way, Allen got what he wanted: power and control.

Of course, I was just trying to protect our son. When a child is with one parent, the other should still have reasonable time to connect. But Allen saw "reasonable" as hours-long calls on my time while cutting off all communication when Joe was with him. And when I raised it as an issue, I was dismissed entirely. Allen claimed Joe didn't want to talk to me because I was a bad mother—and said he'd never force him to.

The more I reclaimed my power, the more Allen fought to control the narrative. In his eyes—and soon in Joe's—any challenge, mistake, or misstep was always someone else's fault. If Joe failed a test, the teacher was stupid. If he missed a pass during the football game, the quarterback was to blame. Accountability was never part of the equation.

Since Allen was no longer welcome in my home, he weaponized Joe instead—fueling him with fire and sending him back into my space as a proxy for chaos, criticism, and pain. It may sound dramatic, but that's exactly how it played out. Joe became Allen's mouthpiece.

After visits with his dad, Joe would come home buzzing with tension. His words were sharp and rehearsed, echoing Allen's tone more than his own. "Your husband is a rager," he'd say. "Look at your track record—you won't be married long." These weren't the words of a child. They were lines fed to him, delivered with precision. He had been coached.

I'm sure it felt powerful to Joe—to be in "the know," to hold secrets, and to carry information meant to destabilize me. But kids aren't built for that kind of power. Joe didn't yet know what it meant.

That's the insidious nature of narcissistic grooming: it doesn't just tell you what to feel—it tells you who to feel it for.

One of the most damaging tactics for some narcissists is isolation, and a tactic I've come to know as "erase and replace." It's a methodical process that narcissists use to strip away your relationships and refill your world with people of their choosing. Allen did exactly that. One by one, he erased the people Joe loved most—me, his stepfather, his brothers, and our extended family—and replaced them with a revolving cast of family and friends I'd never met.

Once, Allen pulled him out of school to attend a funeral in North Carolina—for the brother of his stepfather, whom Joe had never met. But by the time they returned, there were stories, feelings, and even grief. It wasn't Joe's loss, but he carried it like it was—and to a casual observer, it might've looked sincere. But to me, it felt familiar. And fabricated.

Allen didn't just erase the people in Joe's life. He replaced them with emotional scripts—versions of loyalty, grief, and identity that served him. And Joe, still young and longing for connection, absorbed them. Not knowing yet that he was being used.

What I Know Now

Abuse doesn't always end when the relationship does. With narcissistic individuals, it often escalates—especially once you set boundaries or begin to heal. That's what post-separation abuse is: the ongoing pattern of intimidation, control, and harassment after the relationship is "over." It can show up as legal abuse, financial abuse, constant criticism, or weaponizing children and social narratives to maintain power.

For me, the most excruciating form of this abuse has been the weaponizing of my children. Parental alienation is a deliberate and systematic campaign to turn a child against a parent. It rarely looks obvious from the outside. It happens through subtle digs, carefully crafted "concerns," exaggerations, omissions, and emotional manipulation that slowly reshape how a child sees the targeted parent. Over time, the child begins to internalize the script: who is safe, who is right, and who is to blame.

What I didn't realize at first—but understand all too well now—is just how textbook my experience was. Allen followed the pattern almost perfectly. He positioned himself as the fun and understanding parent, while portraying me as rigid, unfair, or unstable. He erased and replaced—gradually stripping Joe of his connection to me, his brothers, and our extended family, while inserting new people and emotional scripts that served his narrative.

He tried similar tactics with all three boys, but Nicholas and Christopher were older and not biologically his. They saw through his attempts more easily. Joe, though, was younger and deeply vulnerable to the daily, deliberate conditioning. Allen didn't just rewrite history; he has tried to rewrite Joe's understanding of who I am.

Today, I know this: post-separation abuse and parental alienation are not "messy divorce dynamics." They are forms of violence. They target a parent's deepest attachments and a child's developing sense of self. And they leave scars that can last long after the legal documents are signed.

My Healing

The stress of my marriage didn't end when the divorce papers were signed. Freedom required far more than physical distance—it required learning to see Allen clearly, to name what was happening without softening it, and to refuse the scripts he kept handing me.

My healing began the moment I understood that I wasn't "overreacting" or "too sensitive." I was unsafe. My nervous system knew it long before my mind could articulate it. The shaking hands, the tears after every email, the dread that washed over me when his name appeared in my inbox—none of those were signs of weakness. They were signals of harm.

Healing has meant recognizing that what he calls "communication" is often nothing more than control dressed up in words. It has meant opening a long, manipulative email and choosing not to respond, no matter how many lies or provocations are embedded inside. It has meant reclaiming my mornings, my running routine, my home, and my right to live without constant surveillance. Each of those moments was a step back toward myself.

It has also meant trusting my instincts as a mother, even when one of my children has been turned against me. That has been some of the most painful work—holding onto my truth while my relationship with Joe strained under the weight of someone else's narrative.

I've had to learn how to stay steady in the storm: to hold firm boundaries even when they trigger backlash, to resist the urge to defend myself to someone committed to misunderstanding me, and to stay grounded so that if and when Joe needs me, I am still a soft, safe place to land. Healing has meant letting go of the need to correct every lie and instead living in alignment with my values, my integrity, and my truth.

I used to believe healing meant everything would return to "normal." Now I know it means building a life that is rooted in reality, in self-trust, and in peace—even when some of the people I love most are still caught inside someone else's story.

14

The Fairytale Amidst the Abuse

There is one part of my life that has unfolded like a fairytale: my reconnection with David, my first love. The mullet is long gone, but the gentle puppy-dog eyes are still there. And today, he is my husband. He meets me with tenderness, patience, and an unwavering belief in who I am and who I'm still becoming. He is both my fiercest champion and my safest place to land.

When David and I got back together, nearly twenty-five years had passed. On our first date, he gave me a quick, polite peck when he dropped me off. The real kiss came on our second date—and when it did, something electric shot through me. A surge moved from my shoulders down my spine, through my chest, arms, hips, and legs. It wasn't just a kiss; it was an awakening.

By this time, I was long divorced from Allen and our conversations should have been limited to the necessary logistics of co-parenting Joe. And yet, the moment Allen found out I was dating David, he had a new target. Allen picked him apart, blamed him for everything, and treated his mere presence in my life as a personal betrayal.

To his credit, David tried. After we started dating and before he even met Joe, he reached out to Allen to meet up and talk. His intention was simple: to establish respectful boundaries and to make clear that he had no interest in interfering with Allen's relationship with the boys. That meeting later became known—somewhat infamously in our household—as "The Lunch."

To hear David describe it, he was served a complete appetizer platter of narcissism: deflection, projection, and a desperate attempt to control the narrative. Allen spent the entire meal flipping the script, warning David about how "difficult" I was, crying poverty, and painting himself as the victim of a divorce that he claimed had taken "everything" from him. Nothing about the interaction changed David's mind about me, but he recognized that as Allen's intent.

As the months wore on, things continued to escalate. Allen's parenting—or lack thereof—involved Joe in every decision. He treated Joe like a peer his own age, which emboldened Joe to believe that he was on equal footing with the adults in his life.

One day, after a weekend with Allen, Joe came home and started taunting David—saying he "knew something" about him. David played along, assuming it was something harmless. But then Joe shared what he knew: Allen had told him that when David and I were teenagers, we had become pregnant—and had an abortion.

We were stunned. This was a deeply personal piece of our past, something I had confided in Allen during our marriage. And now, he had taken that vulnerability and weaponized it—using our child to deliver the blow.

It was sick. It was frightening. And it was not the only time. Allen justified every betrayal by saying Joe had a "right to know." He accused me of treating Joe like a baby. But Joe was a child—not an adult. He wasn't ready to know every detail of my personal life.

Allen coached Joe to believe that he was the smartest, strongest, most important person in any room. And Joe brought that energy home. He would return from Allen's house convinced that he didn't have to follow any rules in mine.

The phone calls continued too. Joe and Allen talked for hours and hours during my custodial time. Joe was barely present for the rest of us. He'd always keep his distance until it was time for an explosion. And then when the inevitable blow-up occurred, Allen would swoop in to "rescue" him.

Eventually our interactions with Allen had become so absurd that I set a new boundary: our custody exchanges would happen off-site in a public, neutral place. Allen didn't take that change well.

In retrospect, he had no problem threatening to call the police on clients at our therapy practice when they pushed back on a billing charge—people who were expressing very normal, human emotions, just a little too loudly for his comfort. So, I don't know why it surprised me when he began calling the cops on me—for doing nothing more than trying to co-parent with him.

The calls were frequent and wild. One time, the police came because Allen didn't want David to travel in the car with Joe. Another time, he claimed that David and I were abusing Joe for making him do his chores. Yet another time, he said Nicholas was the one abusing Joe. In that instance, Allen went so far as to take Joe to the police station and help him file a complaint against his brother.

Every time the police were called, so was Children & Youth, because the complaints involved a minor. Allen knew what he was doing. He was fully aware that these constant reports could jeopardize my license as a therapist.

"I am just trying to protect my son," he'd say. That was always his line. Since I clearly wasn't doing a good enough job to protect him myself, he said, he had no choice but to involve law enforcement. This wasn't concern—it was control. A deliberate, weaponized form of sabotage wrapped in the language of fatherhood.

And of course, it was nerve-wracking every time the police showed up at my door. Allen knew that, too. He knew how deeply these visits triggered my worst fears and anxieties. He loved it.

To no one's surprise, every investigation was deemed unfounded. But the emotional toll still wore us down. It eroded my relationship with Joe, and it strained my relationship with David. The constant stress, the feeling of being under surveillance, the fear that something could be twisted or taken out of context—it seeped into every corner of our lives.

It was also predictable. Each time I set or held a boundary, Allen called the police. The calls became so frequent that eventually the officers would simply show up and stay for a while, then leave. They had to follow up on every report, but it was clear, even to them, that Allen was using law enforcement as a tool to punish me for asserting boundaries.

Eventually, the officers told me they were adding Allen's name to a roll call list, alerting the station to his bogus complaints. He would now be on their radar. It brought a small sense of relief—but only that. We knew that without any real consequences, Allen would just find another way to reach us.

These interactions ended up causing the end of Christopher's relationship with Allen.

After the first time Allen called the police and Children & Youth, Christopher was concerned. He wanted to understand for himself what was going on and asked Allen for a conversation. Allen tried to justify his actions by repeating the same tired narrative—that I had "gone crazy" and that he was the only one acting rationally. But Christopher wasn't buying it. He left Allen's house that day—and never returned.

Allen, in typical fashion, responded with another onslaught of emails. He called me every derogative name he could think of and said I was "turning the boys against him."

The truth is that Christopher was almost seventeen by then. He had witnessed and endured Allen's attacks for years, and he was done. He made the decision to set a boundary—and to stick to it. That choice, that strength, that clarity... it's something I admire deeply in both my older boys.

Around this time, there was one custody exchange that made me wonder if Allen was preparing to cut Joe off.

Within thirty minutes of the start of their visit, Joe didn't comply with something Allen asked of him. Nothing major—just a typical teenage moment of resistance. But instead of requesting a custody swap or talking it through, Allen simply dropped Joe back at my house—no discussion.

"We'll talk again when he apologizes," he said flatly. It was the same script he had used with Nicholas.

The timing couldn't have been worse. That same weekend, David and I—along with Nicholas and his girlfriend—had plans to visit Christopher in Maryland for his birthday, a trip we'd coordinated well in advance. But Allen didn't care. When I reminded him, hoping he might at least consider the disruption it caused, his response was icy: "That's your problem, not mine."

We quickly scrambled to re-organize our plans so that Joe could join us. He didn't say much during the trip, but I could see the sadness in him. He was quiet, withdrawn, and a shadow of his usual self. He didn't want to be estranged from his dad. And for those few days, that's exactly what it felt like.

That's how Allen gets his way. He was trying to teach Joe the same twisted lesson he had tried to teach the older boys: that in any conflict, no matter the details, the child was always at fault. The burden of apology was always theirs. The path to reconnection is paved only by their submission.

And the punishment for noncompliance? Silence.

Narcissists use the silent treatment to gain control—it's one of their sharpest tools. It isn't just about ignoring someone; it's about withdrawing all affection and attention as a way to punish perceived transgressions. It serves multiple purposes at once: it asserts dominance, avoids accountability, provokes desperation, and gauges how deeply the trauma bond has taken root. The message is clear: You are not worthy of my time. Once you fall back in line, we can speak again.

In Allen's mind, the silence was the consequence. But the real punishment for Joe? It wasn't just the absence of his father's voice. It was having to spend more time with me and David. Joe had already been conditioned to see us not as his safe place—but as a penalty.

And it worked.

Once we returned from the trip after the weekend, an email awaited me. It was filled with accusations, claiming I had violated our custody order by taking Joe out of state.

It was both hilarious and infuriating. Allen had refused to parent and dropped Joe off without discussion or planning. But because I brought Joe with us to celebrate his brother's birthday—because I refused to leave him behind—I was the one at fault.

There was no reasoning with him and no honest dialogue. There was only Allen's version of life: how he said it was, how he believed it should be, and how everyone else was expected to fall in line.

And true to form? The next custody exchange went by as if nothing had happened. No conversation or acknowledgment whatsoever. He picked Joe up like everything was normal—simultaneously teaching our son that avoidance and emotional dismissal are acceptable ways to handle conflict.

And with that, he sucked Joe right back onto his raft. That was an analogy my therapist made, and it resonated: Allen is on a fragile raft in the middle of an ocean, and Joe clings to it—not because it is sturdy or safe, but because he believes it is his job to keep it afloat. He had been conditioned to think that if he lets go, his father might sink. He must stay close and loyal—not out of trust, but out of survival.

That's what narcissists do when they feel their control slipping—they don't let go; they pull harder. Eventually, they may try what's called "hoovering": like a vacuum, they suck their victim back in with just enough warmth and validation to mimic love, while quietly reinforcing dependency and fear.

Allen always knew exactly which emotional levers to pull—first with me, and then with Joe. He fostered confusion, guilt, and obligation—each one strengthening the trauma bond Joe didn't even know he had. Because like any child, Joe wanted to be needed. He wanted to be loved. He wanted to believe that his dad saw him, understood him, valued him.

But that wasn't what was happening. Joe wasn't being drawn close because Allen missed him. He was being reeled in because Allen needed control.

And as that control tightened, the trauma bond deepened. And the deeper it grew, the harder it became for Joe to question it. To doubt his father meant risking emotional exile. So instead, he turned on us.

David and I were always the villains in Allen's version of the story. And Joe's behavior continued to spiral.

What I Know Now

Narcissistic abuse doesn't always end when the relationship does. It often evolves and changes form. When a narcissistic ex can no longer control you directly, they may find ways to control you through your child. This is not co-parenting—it is a form of coercive control. It creates deep emotional confusion for the child, and destabilization for the parent being targeted.

This kind of abuse is rarely recognized by systems designed to protect families. Narcissists are often charming in public and manipulative in private. They use language that mimics concern—*"I'm just protecting my kid"*—when in reality, they are weaponizing that child against the other parent. What looks like vigilance is actually sabotage. What sounds like parenting is often just projection.

For the child caught in the middle, it's not just confusing—it's traumatic. Loyalty becomes currency, and affection is doled out as a reward system. And boundaries, when held by the healthier parent, can be misrepresented as cruelty or control.

This is why therapeutic support is so critical—for parents and children alike. If you are navigating post-separation abuse or parental alienation, you are not imagining things. You are not overreacting. You are likely being gaslit in both overt and insidious ways. What you're experiencing is real, and it requires care, validation, and a trauma-informed response.

My Healing

Joe's lashing out toward me and toward David is not really about us. I know that. He's a child responding to his own trauma and manipulation, parroting words and beliefs that he has been fed for years.

Once I could attach his behaviors to his own abuse and conditioning, it became easier to hold him with more compassion—even when his words cut deeply.

There were moments when Joe has scared me in the same way his father did. That is part of why it took so long to see what was really happening: my son is being abused, too. Once I accepted that, I began to reset boundaries with him. I also realized I had been walking on eggshells around my child just as I had around his father—constantly scanning for their reactions, constantly trying to keep the peace at my own expense.

I had to face how much I had blamed David for naming what was happening out loud. I wanted him to stay quiet, not rock the boat, and make himself small—because that was what I had been trained to do. Watching my husband refuse to contort himself in those ways showed me something vital: he wasn't "creating drama." He was refusing to surrender his sanity to someone else's chaos.

Healing meant learning to tell the difference between what had been ingrained in my head and what was actually healthy. It meant realizing that keeping the peace at all costs is not peace—it's self-erasure.

Healing has also meant grieving my relationship with my youngest child—and still holding hope that one day he will see clearly. It has meant being a safe, steady shore, even as the waves keep crashing. It has meant allowing myself to feel the heartbreak and the love at the same time.

And just as importantly, healing has meant allowing myself to feel the fairytale moments, too. The laughter. The connection. The kiss that wakes you up. The birthday party with guests who honor that I don't like big spectacles. The quiet mornings when I feel safe in my own home and loved in a way that doesn't demand my disappearance.

Those are all experiences I cherish, and ones I want for my boys, too.

15

The Currency of Control

As a therapist, I know that when children act out, it's usually because they feel out of control. But Joe wasn't "just" acting out. He grew to be cruel and defiant, and he learned how to refuse to follow any household rules. Allen continued to tell him that I was the villain, distorting reality for Joe to the point that he couldn't know what end was up.

When he was eight years old, Joe was formally diagnosed with oppositional defiance disorder (ODD), a childhood behavior disorder characterized by persistent patterns of disobedience, hostility, and defiance toward authority figures.

ODD is a condition in kids that goes far beyond the usual tantrums or talking back. It means a child regularly argues with adults, refuses to follow rules, and often acts in ways that seem purposely annoying or challenging. To be diagnosed, these behaviors have to happen often—over at least six months—and appear in more than one setting, such as home, in school, or in extracurricular activities.

Despite the fact that Joe had a formal ODD diagnosis and a 504 plan at school for accommodations, Allen had refused to acknowledge the situation when we were married. According to him, Joe's ODD was something I "made up." But the facts were obvious: Joe's struggles were showing up everywhere—at school, in activities, and in social settings.

His behavior was at its worst at home. Joe felt like a ticking time bomb, and we constantly walked on eggshells. There was always an argument—often multiple times a day—and Joe would sometimes just walk out. He'd just leave the house and call Allen to pick him up.

Meanwhile, as Allen's regular email assaults continued, I tried to take steps to protect myself. I created filters and set up systems to gate-keep Allen's messages—ensuring I wouldn't miss anything critical about Joe's well-being, while shielding myself from the constant barrage of vile, demeaning language. It worked, sort of.

Then came the COVID-19 pandemic and the world ground to a halt. For Allen, it was an opportunity.

Just before the shutdown, he took Joe to Louisiana for a funeral. I wasn't informed until they were already en route, which was a violation of our informal arrangement. But the bigger issue came when they returned. Allen refused to bring Joe back to my home, claiming that the "numbers game" made it too dangerous. According to him, our household—five people total—posed a greater risk than Joe staying solely with him.

It didn't matter that we were following every recommended protocol. Allen twisted the narrative to serve his agenda. And he wasn't alone. Across the country, courts were flooded with emergency filings as divorced or separated parents weaponized COVID to withhold children from one another. Even during a global health crisis, control remained the currency of power.

As the days and weeks unfolded, I questioned everything. Why had I ever thought we could co-parent peacefully? Why had I believed we could somehow get along after the divorce?

I tried to keep things amicable, but eventually, enough was enough. The self-filed custody arrangement was not working for me. Nothing was clearly outlined, and everything was vague by design. This ambiguity had served Allen well, but I was done living under the threat of his moods and needed something enforceable.

One thing was clear: nothing would change unless I took action. So, I began the process of formalizing our custody agreement through the courts.

Unsurprisingly, Allen pushed back at every step—even arguing with his own attorney at times. A formal agreement would mean an end to his "willy-nilly" style of parenting that allowed him to parent with no structure and no consequences.

In the end, with a custody agreement finalized and filed, we had structure—but only on paper. In reality, a formal custodial agreement changed little in our lives.

The lie that so many of us are sold is that the court system will protect children from emotional abuse. That once it's in writing, someone will actually enforce it. The truth? The courts rarely recognize parental alienation when it's happening in real time—and they almost never hold the alienating parent accountable. The system is built to manage logistics, not to safeguard emotional health.

The custody order became yet another tool Allen used to control my behavior. For him, the agreement was something for me to follow, while he reserved the right to ignore, bend, or break it whenever it suits him.

And soon after it was finalized, Allen made his position clear: he would no longer take Joe to medical appointments. He told me outright, "Because of that stunt you pulled, you can deal with the consequences."

Just to clarify, the "stunt I pulled" was when Allen took Joe to the doctor and had to pay for the visit. He was beyond pissed that he should have to use his money, which was really money he got in the divorce settlement, to pay the coinsurance on the visit he took Joe to. In his mind, he should have no financial responsibility and as a form of punishment, he refused to take Joe to even the most basic of appointments for his medical needs.

And he did exactly that. Beyond that one doctor's visit, every other medical appointment – and nearly every bill that came with them – fell to me. When I tried to recover his share, he'd fight back and use nonsensical math to explain why he didn't actually need to pay.

At the same time, he's convinced Joe that he had the right to make his own medical decisions. It doesn't matter that he's a child and that his doctors make recommendations. Because his father has told him it's okay, he has refused routine bloodwork, vaccines, flu shots— and anything else he personally doesn't feel like doing.

Allen doesn't just permit this defiance, he nurtures it. He planted a full-blown fear of doctors and needles in Joe's mind, shaping them into something sinister and threatening. Over time, Joe began spinning stories about traumatic medical events from his past that never happened. Allen has painted himself as the protector and the rest of us as the enemy.

Predictably, the COVID vaccine was another battle. Allen permitted Joe to get the first dose, but when it came time for the booster, he suddenly declared it unnecessary. "Joe doesn't need more needles," he said. "One is enough."

Eventually, Joe began insisting that his father was the only one who knew what was best, and the only one who loved him. In his mind, everyone else, including me, is stupid, wrong, or irrelevant.

That's the cost of psychological warfare. It is not just medical advice that Joe refuses—he ignores any information that didn't reinforce what he already believed. Allen has trained him to do it.

One of the most important aspects of our formal custody agreement was a court-mandated requirement: Joe was to begin counseling. I felt cautiously hopeful. He was clearly struggling—caught between two homes, two realities, and one parent who had no interest in his emotional well-being. Therapy, I thought, might offer him a path forward.

The judge didn't just require counseling—both parents were also expected to follow the therapist's recommendations. This included using a court-approved communication app designed to minimize conflict and document exchanges. I opted for the premium version, which flagged inflammatory language in real-time to help parents recognize and manage their tone. Unsurprisingly, I paid for it. Equally unsurprising: Allen didn't.

And true to form, he only followed the rules for about a year before abruptly announcing, "I'm done with apps. You need to grow up and communicate with me like an adult." Just like that, he opted out—because in Allen's world, rules are always optional. Accountability is for other people.

From day one, Joe resisted therapy. Each session felt like a punishment, not a place of healing. And Allen, of course, dismissed the entire process. In his mind, Joe didn't need help—because Joe was "perfectly behaved" whenever he was with him.

Soon, conversations about Joe living with Allen full-time became constant. Allen actively encouraged them.

At the time, Joe was still young enough that we monitored his cellphone use—and what I saw his father writing to him made my stomach turn. Allen's messages didn't just undermine me as a parent; he was also weaponizing Joe's confusion and vulnerability.

In one message, Allen wrote: "Make as much noise as possible." The implication was clear: if Joe stirred up enough conflict at home—if he yelled, refused to follow rules, or made life difficult—I'd eventually cave and send him to live with his dad.

This wasn't co-parenting. This was coercion. This was grooming a child to become the tool of his father's control.

Unfortunately, the therapist Joe was seeing at the time didn't recognize the signs of narcissist abuse or parental alienation that were unfolding. Sadly, that's not uncommon—most therapists aren't adequately trained to spot the subtle patterns of manipulation and coercive control in high-conflict custody situations.

Believing Allen, the therapist suggested that Joe and I attend sessions together. Given that I continued to think that counseling would serve us all, I agreed. I would do anything to help my son.

Unfortunately, it quickly became clear that the therapist was in over his head. As Joe and I talked with him, he just couldn't grasp the full picture, and he certainly didn't know how to address the toxicity behind it. Eventually, he recommended a higher level of care for Joe—something called "family-based therapy." This intensive therapy is done in the home and involves multiple sessions each week.

Qualifying for family-based therapy is a multistep process that required a lot of waiting and a lot of follow-up calls over many months. I knew Allen would not help, so I took it upon myself to go through the process. Eventually, Joe was approved, and we finally got the call to start.

The process began with an evaluation by a psychologist, and Allen and I were on the first Zoom call together. It was the first time I'd seen him in a long time, and the moment he appeared on screen, my entire body reacted. A wave of nausea rippled through me, almost like I no longer fit inside my own skin. My hands trembled. My heart pounded. A numbing sensation spread through my arms, face, and abdomen. I struggled just to stay present.

During the meeting, Allen lied. He minimized every issue. He insisted that the problems weren't with Joe, but with my household—David, me, Nicholas, and Christopher. He didn't say the words directly, but he made it clear he agreed to family-based therapy under the pretense that my household was the actual problem, and that he was simply being cooperative for the sake of the process.

The psychologist saw through it immediately and recommended a comprehensive plan: weekly sessions for Joe, Allen, and for David and me, plus alternating family sessions—one week with Joe and Allen, the next with Joe, David, and me.

It was a thoughtful and balanced plan. But still, it couldn't start right away. We still had to wait for a team to be assigned before anything could begin.

One of the hardest parts of that time was watching Joe begin to echo his father's language. It wasn't just what he said—it was how he said it. The tone, the timing, and the precision of his words cut into me like a knife. I knew those words didn't come from him. They came from Allen.

"You won't be with David very long—look at your track record," Joe would say, throwing my past back at me with chilling accuracy. Or, "You're a narcissist who gaslights me."

Joe was too young to know what these terms meant— but he'd absorbed them anyway. And when he repeated them, it felt like Allen was speaking through him. Like I was being haunted by a voice I'd spent years trying to escape.

It also broke my heart to see Joe's sense of self distorted by his time with Allen. Despite his small frame, Joe was convinced he'd play professional football. As a counselor, I've spent years helping kids and coaches navigate the line between ambition and reality. There's a time to fuel a child's dreams—and a time to help them make grounded, healthy choices.

Allen did the opposite. He fed Joe's false confidence under the guise of support, inflating his ego instead of helping him grow. The truth was hard to say out loud: Joe didn't have the size or skill to earn a Division I scholarship, let alone go pro. But Allen didn't care about preparation—he cared about projection.

Meanwhile, the tension at home grew worse by the day. David's patience was understandably running out. He couldn't understand Joe's behavior, and worse—he couldn't manage his own reactions to it. Joe knew exactly how to push his buttons, thanks to his father's coaching. He could poke and prod until David reacted. When he finally did, it often escalated to yelling—something Joe anticipated and, at times, orchestrated.

Joe's behavior created what's known as reactive abuse. He would provoke David to the point of an emotional outburst, then record it and use the footage to paint David as the aggressor. It was classic blame-shifting. And then Allen would seize the opportunity, twist the narrative, and cast David as dangerous and unfit to be around his son.

When Joe was home, our days were unpredictable. Some were calm, even pleasant. Others were so volatile we couldn't see straight. Over time, I started to recognize the pattern. The "good" days—when dinner was eaten at the table, when Joe was semi-polite or followed basic rules—were also the days when David and I tiptoed around him. We walked on eggshells to keep the peace. Most days, it felt like a coin toss.

The blowups, when they came, were like earthquakes. Joe would unleash a torrent of verbal abuse. He'd call David a fucking piece of shit, an asshole, a rager, an abuser, an addict. Any insult that might land, he used. Toward me, he hurled other accusations: that I was a narcissist and a terrible mother, favoring the older boys and holding Joe to impossible standards.

When he was done, and when the house felt turned upside down, Joe just went to bed. He had no problem resting, satisfied that he had inflicted damage and confident it would eventually be enough to break us. And it nearly did.

The toxicity in our home was unbearable. He had stopped following any rules in our home, and he'd come and go as he pleased. He wouldn't tell me where he was, wouldn't respond to my messages, turned off his phone locator, and stopped paying his phone bill. Allen taught him that I had no authority—that he didn't owe me anything. When Joe was home, David and I still stopped everything, as though his presence was some kind of honor. We still walked on eggshells.

It was devastating to watch. To hold both truths—that Joe was a child manipulated into weaponizing his love, and that David and I tried so hard to heal the fractures with ours.

Each Friday after a custody exchange, David and I would exhale in relief, knowing we had two days without tension—two days without conflict being manufactured. By Sunday night, the anxiety would return. We never knew what version of Joe would walk through the door: a sullen teenager or someone ready for battle. The unpredictability was exhausting. We lived in a constant state of emotional hyper-vigilance, always bracing for impact.

Of course, this environment had an impact. David and I found ourselves arguing constantly—about Joe, about Allen, and about what to do next. Though we knew we were supposed to be a team, we sometimes struggled to act like one. We were both hurting so deeply and so individually.

It would take a long time—through therapy, reflection, and shared effort—for us to heal from the trauma we both endured at the hands of Allen and, by extension, Joe. But eventually, we did. Together.

In many ways, family-based therapy failed our family—but not because the model itself was flawed. It failed because half of Joe's parents didn't support him being there. Allen undermined the process at every turn, spinning stories about my so-called inability to parent and painting David, Joe's stepfather, as unfit. He injected chaos into a space that was meant to foster healing.

I was grateful Joe learned a few skills in therapy—how to breathe through big emotions, how to name a feeling instead of lashing out—but the deeper work never took hold. He continued to move through the world with a victim mentality, believing every bad thing that happened to him was someone else's fault. His therapists tried, in gentle and careful ways, to help him see the damage he was doing—to me, to David—but those attempts were drowned out by the louder voice at the other end of the custody exchange.

After completing family-based counseling, Joe was supposed to transition to individual therapy—but he refused. So did Allen. With no one else advocating for continued care, the support ended. Joe met briefly with a psychiatrist that had been part of his team every two months, but he dismissed it as pointless, calling both the sessions and the provider "stupid." Allen had told him that in Pennsylvania, he could refuse therapy at fourteen—and he did. He stopped all forms of treatment but continued his defiance, disregard for rules, and blatant disrespect toward me, David, and nearly everyone else.

What I Know Now

When a child is caught between two parents—especially when one is manipulative, coercive, or narcissistic—their behavior becomes a battleground long before anyone realizes what's happening. Children don't simply absorb a parent's values; they also absorb their strategies for survival. What looks like defiance, cruelty, or apathy is often an adaptive response to an impossible bind.

A child who behaves one way in one home and the complete opposite in another isn't confused—they're trying to stay safe. Loyalty becomes a survival skill. Manipulation becomes protection. And love becomes a currency they're forced to negotiate rather than something they're free to receive.

The heartbreaking truth is that the systems meant to protect families—mental health providers, schools, courts—are rarely trained to identify the subtle fingerprints of coercive control or parental alienation. When therapists miss the signs, the child becomes more entrenched in the distorted narrative, and the safe parent becomes increasingly isolated and blamed.

If you're a parent being vilified, blamed, or rejected by your own child, it feels like the deepest betrayal. But so often, what you're seeing is not rejection—it's a trauma response. It's a child trying to survive a war they never chose to fight.

My Healing

Healing has meant learning to hold multiple truths at once:

That my son is hurting... and so am I.

My son is being manipulated... and he is still responsible for the choices he makes.

I want to protect him... but I cannot save him from what he cannot—or will not—see.

Healing means choosing boundaries, even when they are difficult to enforce. It means choosing my sanity over the chaos, even when it requires letting go of the fantasy that I can fix this alone. It means allowing time, distance, and natural consequences to do the work that my love—however fierce—cannot.

Healing looks like honoring both the mother and the partner within me. Both of them have been fighting so hard, for so long, to love well in a landscape shaped by someone else's sabotage. They deserve compassion, steadiness, and space to breathe.

Healing means knowing when to advocate, when to step back, when to pause, and when to walk away for my own well-being.

And above all, healing now looks like this: refusing to play the game. Refusing to be baited. Refusing to be broken. Refusing to let someone else's cruelty dictate the temperature of my home or the worthiness of my heart.

This is how I reclaim my power—by no longer participating in the cycle designed to destroy it.

16

House of Horrors

Years of emotional warfare—first with my mother and Al, then with Allen, and finally within my own home— hollowed me out. Every time I reached for help, the system handed Allen more power. Every time I tried to shield my children, I was the one punished.

I was exhausted. Depleted. And beginning to wonder how much more I could take.

And then—just when I thought I had nothing left—a battle I had been fighting silently for more than three decades didn't end with justice, or closure, or healing.

It ended with a death.

On a random Monday morning, I received news I had been waiting to hear for thirty-five years.

Tony never calls early in the morning, so when I saw his name on my phone screen, I knew something was off.

His voice was flat. "I just got a call. Al passed away over the weekend."

A cold shiver surged through me, starting at the crown of my head and cascading down my face, arms, and chest, settling like a tremor in my stomach. My entire body began to buzz.

"Okay, thank you for letting me know," I replied. The words were cool and professional, a tone more fitting for colleagues than siblings.

I hung up the phone and sat down on the floor in front of the bed. For over thirty-five years, I had been wishing and hoping for Al to die. It happened. He was finally dead.

The fucker was dead!

David found me a few minutes later. I looked up at him in disbelief and said, "Tony just called. Al is dead."

David erupted in celebration—pumping his fist, hooting with joy, radiating pure exhilaration. I sat frozen. Silent. *Was this even real?*

Al had tormented me emotionally, psychologically, and sexually. He stole my innocence, my confidence, and my ability to form healthy relationships. He didn't just take my childhood; he infiltrated every part of my upbringing, distorting my understanding of sex, relationships, men, and myself.

As a child, I had vivid fantasies about Al's death. As an adult, I would occasionally search the internet, hoping to discover that he was gone and I hadn't heard. I must have pictured that moment a thousand different ways. In my mind, his death would be a turning point—a celebration! The skies would open, the sun would shine, there would be singing and dancing, and I would finally be free from the invisible chains that bound me to him.

I spent the entire day in a daze, but not the kind that grief naturally brings—that quiet, stunned fog that follows the loss of a loved one. This was different. I felt suspended in time, unable to fully trust the news. Maybe it was some kind of cruel mistake—maybe Al wasn't actually gone. Or maybe, after all those years of imagining this moment, the reality could never match the weight I'd given it. Maybe it was just . . . anticlimactic?

I turned to the internet, typing into the search bar "What happens when your abuser dies?" Without much effort, I got my answer: my complicated reaction was perfectly normal.

Over the next few days, I searched and waited for Al's obituary to appear online. When it did, I exhaled. He was dead. Of course, the obituary itself—just like his life—was riddled with false narratives, so much buff and shine that a passerby would never see what kind of monster he was. He was described as having a heart of gold, exactly how people like him fool the world and make others believe they're good.

When my brother Tony told me he was considering attending the funeral, my jaw nearly hit the floor. There was no way in hell I was going, and I had to bite my tongue to stop myself from asking him not to go, either. It was his decision, of course—but inside, I was screaming, *Why would you go to this asshole's funeral? Do you not remember the hell he put us through?*

Tony said he'd only go to keep the peace during the sale of our mother's house—to pay his respects, not out of desire, but out of obligation. In the end, he didn't attend. Not because of anything I said, but because deep down, he didn't want to. Still, the whole conversation stirred something in me. It made me think about how we were both conditioned as kids to perform a certain way for the outside world. We were always made to be polite, agreeable, and compliant, even when it meant silencing our own truth.

Although my reaction to Al's death wasn't what I had imagined, there was an unmistakable sense of freedom that settled over me. He could no longer silence me. He could no longer stop me from telling the truth.

That same weekend, for the first time, I confided in one of my male cousins. I didn't share everything, but I told him enough for him to understand. His response was exactly what I had needed—and longed—to hear for years. He looked at me, his voice low and steady, and said, "I love you. I support you. And if I had known, I would've killed that guy."

Of course, he was just a child back then too—just as powerless as I was to stop what was happening. But that wasn't the point. His anger, his validation, and his love felt like an emotional embrace larger than anything I had ever received from my family. I felt protected. These were feelings I never had growing up, and they arrived like an unexpected gift—it felt good.

A few days after Al's death, Tony and I met in the driveway of our childhood home—our mother's last remaining asset, now ours to clean and sell.

Although she hadn't lived in the house for years—her stroke had made that impossible—Al had been occupying it and had died in the front room. As Tony and I faced the task of cleaning and selling, we knew we were about to board a roller coaster of emotions.

Tony found a front door key under a rock. As he pushed the door open, a wave of stale, smoky air hit us like a suffocating fog. Though our mother had insisted Al smoke only in the basement, he had long since ignored that rule. The stench was everywhere—clinging to every room, every object, even the walls.

Stepping into the front room meant stepping into filth. The carpet was stained, burned, and littered with ash and trash—a far cry from the spotless home our mom once kept. We were told Al died there, and one of the many stains might have been dried blood, but it was hard to tell. Blobs and burns were everywhere, including one burn that looked like an entire cigarette. The carpet looked more like it belonged in an auto shop than a living room.

Walking through the house was surreal. Some rooms felt eerily frozen in time, like perfectly preserved time capsules from when our mother still lived there. Others were chaotic and crumbling, overflowing with clutter and neglect—especially the spaces Al had occupied in the final years of his life.

The amount of stuff was overwhelming. In the bathroom closet alone, we found nearly twenty-five bottles of Tilex cleaner. In the basement bar, more than a hundred glasses sat boxed in a corner. The attic was overflowing with supplies, many neatly labeled and stored by my meticulously organized mother.

But no matter how well it had been arranged, there was just too much of everything. And the mess didn't stop at the back door—we found more junk stuffed into the sheds scattered around the one-acre property. The garage and its attic were also overflowing, mostly with outdoor Christmas decorations left over from the years in which we had to perform for the neighbors in the driveway.

As a therapist, I think about why people collect and stockpile in excess. There are numerous reasons why people behave like this. For my mom and Al, I suspect they filled holes that existed within themselves with material items.

Most of what Tony and I did that first day was simply look. And over a pizza that afternoon, we developed a plan. Everything in the house that was material (clothes, towels, sheets) reeked so badly and needed to be thrown away—minus a few items we would keep, including photos of our grandparents and small relics from our childhood.

A few days later, we returned to the house and realized we weren't the only ones with access. At least one of Al's three sons had been there and taken musical instruments and collectible items with clear monetary value that we had seen during our first visit.

Though incapacitated, our mother was still alive, and everything in the house—regardless of sentimental or financial worth—belonged to her. The contents were part of her estate and needed to be liquidated to help cover the ongoing cost of her long-term care. Finding out that valuable items had been removed without permission felt violating and deeply disrespectful—but in that house, such feelings were nothing new.

There was nothing we could do, but what frustrated me most was the entitlement. Al had lived in my mother's home rent-free for years. Even after her stroke when she moved into a facility, she still covered nearly all of his expenses from her own limited assets. And now, after his death, his children came and helped themselves to even more.

Tony constantly reminded me that these were her choices. She chose to be with Al. She chose to include him and his children in her life and her home. While it was easy to feel angry, he was right to point out that the fallout wasn't ours to carry. Our job was to clean out the house, sell it, and move forward. We'd leave behind everything else—the dysfunction, the entitlement, and the drama tied to Al and his family.

One of the hardest—and most important—rooms for me to clean out was my childhood bedroom. Unfortunately, it was clear that Al had moved himself into it. As a teenager, I chose a beautiful soft lavender paint for my walls, but they were now dull gray from years of smoke damage. The bed was covered in stains and buried beneath a pile of coats and hats. Trash was scattered everywhere—dirty tissues, empty containers, random boxes, and shoes spilling across the floor.

With trash bags and rubber gloves, I moved through my old bedroom with reckless abandon, throwing away all of Al's socks, pants, shirts, underwear, belts, and shoes. Al was notorious for wearing hats and I happily threw those away too, including a wool fedora that I used as a punching bag. It felt good to destroy his belongings, even if they were only material.

As I cleaned, I kept ricocheting between the past and the present. Memories from my childhood crashed into the reality of being back in that house, and every corner seemed to unlock something buried. At times, the weight of it all became too much—I had to step away, breathe, and re-center just to keep going.

Noticing this, my sister-in-law Amanda gently offered to take over and purge the room for me. It was a generous act of love. But I knew I had to do it myself. I needed to be the one to bag up Al's belongings and throw them in the trash. I needed that act of defiance and the closure that came with it.

What unsettled me most while cleaning out my old bedroom was finding remnants of my childhood still there, tangled up with his things. These were odds and ends I'd left behind—old stationery, worn-out makeup, half-empty perfume bottles. As I tossed them out, I couldn't shake the eerie truth: my belongings shared space with him. He had also lived there, slept there—and the thought of that overlap sent a chill through me.

I also found baby items—some still in their packaging, others used. I could only assume they were meant for Al's grandchildren, and the sight of them sent my mind spiraling with questions I didn't want to ask. Was he ever alone with his granddaughters? Did their mothers know what he was capable of? I have always wondered if there were other victims.

On another visit, we tackled the patio room—a sunny space off the back of the house with a pellet stove and a TV. Like the rest of the house, it was cluttered with overflowing ashtrays and half-empty soda cans.

The room was packed with hundreds of old VHS tapes and a player—a nod to the countless hours we'd spent as kids watching movies together. Like many families in the '80s, we'd rent from Blockbuster and dub the movies onto blank tapes, labeling each one carefully. Back then, they were our entertainment and our babysitters. Now, they were just clutter. We tossed them by the handful into the trash.

Later, Tony and I learned our spouses had uneasy feelings about that room and the tapes—but said nothing. It would take a while before the weight of what we may have thrown away truly sank in.

In the '80s, video cameras were rare and expensive—people didn't film casually. But Al did. He always had a camera with him.

Months after the house was sold, my best friend's dad found an old tape of me from sixth grade. I didn't remember making it, but I recognized my handwriting in the opening credits—including a thank-you to Al as the cameraman.

The video started innocently enough—me chatting to the camera, riding my new ATV, showing off for my friend. But then the camera pans. And there they were—flickering into view for the first time in decades: the camper and the van. The very places where the abuse had happened.

The last scene shows me dancing and lip syncing to the song "Hungry Eyes" from *Dirty Dancing*. My movements were awkward and childlike. But Al's camera work wasn't. He zoomed. He lingered. He turned something innocent into something deeply unsettling.

As I watched the video, I realized that all those tapes we'd so casually tossed didn't feel like clutter anymore. They felt like evidence—of what, exactly, we couldn't say. But the air around that particular memory grew heavier.

Another item we tossed was the bulky computer from the front room where Al had died. We didn't think much of it until a few weeks later, when one of Al's sons called Tony in a panic and demanded it back. He claimed it held passwords to Al's bank account, but his urgency felt strange—especially since a death certificate would've granted the heirs account access. Tony explained that the computer had already been taken to the dump and suggested he contact the trash company.

Afterwards, we couldn't help but wonder what he was really trying to recover. Our unsettling guess was child pornography. But like the tapes, we'll never know for sure.

By far, the most disturbing discovery in the house was over sixty days' worth of our mom's medications, still sealed.

After her stroke, our mother briefly returned home under the care of visiting aides—much to Al's resentment. He clashed with them constantly, driving most of the caregivers away until only part-time help remained. Insisting he could manage her care alone, he told the aides he was giving her the medications. None of them verified—there was no reason to doubt him.

But her pills came prepackaged, clearly labeled by day. Discovering so many untouched made it clear: Al hadn't been giving them to her. His arrogant belief that she didn't need all those medications had devastating consequences. Critical drugs like Keppra—meant to prevent seizures—were ignored. And in fact, that's what happened. One night, she fainted, seized, and was hospitalized. A series of strokes followed, ultimately leaving her fully incapacitated and confined to a care facility she will never leave.

Realizing this, we were sickened. Al's neglect and selfishness, and his need for control—these weren't just character flaws. They contributed directly to our mother's decline. He was a big part of the reason she was in her current state.

Despite all the pain woven into that house, there were pockets of light too. Fleeting moments of connection with David, Tony, and Amanda that stood out against the heavier backdrop. In our final walkthrough, we gave ourselves permission to remember them. The good moments. However small. However rare.

Although I had chosen two decades earlier to stay away, I always knew I'd eventually return for this very reason. It felt good when that house of horrors went on the market and sold without a hitch. The place where I had endured so much emotional and psychological torment was no longer mine to carry, and I'd never have to step foot in it again.

What I didn't realize at the time was that this moment would also quietly mark the beginning of something new—a shift toward healing that would become intentional and life-changing.

What I Know Now

When an abuser dies, the emotional impact is rarely simple. It's not like mourning a loved one—it's mourning a life distorted by that person's presence. You're left grieving not just what happened, but everything that could have been different.

You may expect closure and find only numbness. You may crave justice and feel cheated. Or you may feel nothing at all—and then feel guilty for that, too.

All of this is normal.

The body often reacts before the mind does. Shaking hands, nausea, buzzing skin, dissociation—these are not overreactions. This is the nervous system remembering what the brain has tried desperately to contain. When a trauma bond ends abruptly, even by death, the body processes the loss of danger before it processes the loss of the person.

And for those who were silenced, dismissed, or forced to carry the truth alone for decades, an abuser's death can bring something unexpected: permission. Permission to speak freely. Permission to stop protecting the reputation of someone who never protected you. Permission to finally tell your story without fear.

Closure does not arrive as a single moment of revelation. Sometimes it shows up as defiance—throwing away their belongings, refusing to attend their funeral, choosing not to play the dutiful daughter or the compliant victim anymore. Sometimes closure is simply the first breath you take when you realize they can no longer hurt you.

My Healing

Sorting through the rooms of my childhood home forced me to sit with memories I had long labeled as "dealt with." But trauma doesn't disappear just because we decide it should. It waits in the shadows and resurfaces when we're finally safe enough to face it.

Cleaning out my mom's home made everything real again: the neglect, the secrecy, the late-night shame fests, and the abuses. But for the first time, I wasn't alone. I wasn't a child being gaslit into silence. I was an adult woman with clarity, language, and support.

Healing has meant allowing the memories to come back in their own time—without judgment, without shame, without forcing them into neat boxes.

I've kicked myself for the decision to toss out the computer and the VHS tapes, because whatever was on them likely would even further validate my experiences. But over time, I've realized that I don't need the physical evidence to know the truth.

My body remembers. My instincts remember.

Piece by piece, memory by memory, I've learned that I can revisit what happened on my own terms—process it, integrate it, and finally set it down.

And for the first time in my life, I understand that that is enough.

17

The Trip to Trust

Although it took nearly nine months after Al's death for me to begin intentionally pursuing healing, the realization that I needed to heal started with my ever-curious mind... and a really bad mushroom trip.

That spring, my husband David had gone to a music festival and brought back mushrooms for us to try together. David had followed the Grateful Dead for years, played in bands, and lived a free-spirited, psychedelic-friendly lifestyle. He'd experimented with psilocybin from a young age, and while we'd talked about trying it together, I still had questions he couldn't fully answer. He warned me that the experience could be beautiful—or deeply challenging. I naively assumed it wouldn't be that intense. I'd done other substances before. How bad could it be?

We chose a warm, sunny Saturday. David lounged on the patio swing; I stretched out on the daybed. At first, everything felt easy and light. We ate the mushrooms and waited.

Every few minutes, David asked, "Do you feel it yet?" Each time, I said no. But with each ask he made, I felt more judged. What was I "supposed" to feel? Why wasn't I getting it "right?"

A dark suspicion crept in—was David withholding information to teach me a lesson? Was he trying to catch me off guard? Once those questions took hold in my head, paranoia took over. I became absolutely convinced that he was trying to control me.

With that, our experiences split. David wanted to listen to music and share the joy of watching trees dance and rocks swirl. I just wanted to lie quietly. The disconnect sent me spiraling. His playful prompts— "Look at the trees!"—landed in my brain as a command: "Do what I say!"

My internal monologue raged as David continued to narrate what he was seeing. I didn't say any of it out loud. But inside, I was unraveling. *You're not in charge of me. I just want to rest. Why do I have to do what you want?*

When David suggested walking barefoot in the grass, what I heard was *get off your lazy ass*. And the voice in my head screamed: *You're lazy. You're worthless. Rest is for losers.* That word—lazy—had followed me since childhood, echoing every time I tried to rest. I had been taught that rest was weakness, and weakness was shameful.

Not wanting to seem difficult, I got up, took a quick walk around the house, and came back. "I still don't feel anything," I muttered.

"You're not being open," David said gently. But I heard: *You're bad. You're a failure. You shouldn't be a counselor if you can't even do this right.*

My inner sarcastic teenager came roaring in: *Oh, David, you know everything, don't you? You're so enlightened. So cool. And I'm just your dumb wife who can't even trip on drugs properly.*

I'd always thought of myself as open-minded. But now, I was drowning in insecurity. When David offered to play an upbeat song, I heard: *You're boring. You're not enough. You'll never be enough.* Simple kindnesses felt like attacks. I couldn't hear his love—I only heard my own shame.

Eventually, we moved inside. I lay on the couch, frozen, convinced he didn't care. When he said, "You just want quiet, and I want music," I heard: *Your needs don't matter. Mine do.* I lay with my back to him, overwhelmed and angry, wanting him to read my mind, to show up, to prove I mattered.

When I told him I didn't want to move, that maybe I needed rest and quiet, rather than talking and chaos, he suggested that maybe I could go somewhere else in the house that was quiet, my brain twisted it. I heard: *You don't belong here. I don't want you here. Go away.*

It was all too much and I snapped. "FINE!" I yelled, storming upstairs to our sitting room. I curled up, sobbing, alone.

David didn't follow. That hurt the most.

All I wanted was for him to chase after me, to hold me, to fight for me. Instead, I spiraled: *He's just like every other man. He's selfish. He never really loved me. I've made a mistake. Again.* I ransacked our relationship in my mind, twisting every moment into evidence of betrayal. *He drinks too much. He lies. He's manipulative. He's all of them. Just another asshole.* I told myself I needed to armor up, get strong, prepare to leave. I cried harder than I ever had. This, I thought, must be what rock bottom feels like.

But eventually, the tears slowed. My thoughts softened. And a sliver of clarity returned. Was that real? Or was it the mushrooms?

I needed answers. So, I texted David.

Seconds later, he was at my side, arms around me as I sobbed. He didn't try to fix it. He just held me. "I love you," he whispered. "I'm not going anywhere. We'll be okay."

I wanted to believe him. But doubt lingered.

Later, he told me he had wanted to follow me upstairs but wasn't sure if it would help or hurt. He'd waited for a signal. And when my misspelled text came through, he rushed to me.

That evening, he brought me outside to sit in the fading sun. He handed me popcorn—my favorite—and gently invited conversation. I had no words left, just fragments. True to form, he asked questions, wanting to understand. But eventually, he saw I wasn't ready and let it go. Silence was enough.

The next day, I was still raw. We talked more, but I struggled to make sense of it all. What had been real? What had been projection? I wondered how things might have gone if my therapist had been there, guiding me through the chaos in my mind.

At our next session, I told her everything. And then, cautiously, I said it out loud: I think David might be a narcissist.

At the time, my understanding of narcissism was mostly academic. I knew about love bombing, gaslighting, and control. My ex-husband had love bombed me. Now, I feared it was happening again.

My therapist listened carefully, then gently pushed back. "David hasn't been love bombing you every day for four years," she said. "Loving someone consistently isn't manipulation. It's love."

I wasn't convinced. So, we unpacked it.

"He cooks me breakfast, lunch, and dinner," I said.

"How often?" she asked.

"Every day."

"Why?"

"Because he says he loves me and wants to take care of me."

"And how is that love bombing?"

"Maybe he wants me to believe I can't take care of myself."

She reflected it back. "So, by making you meals, he's manipulating you into believing you're incapable?"

"Yes," I said, but even as I spoke, I could hear the distortion.

"In love bombing," she explained, "he might cook occasionally, then hold it over your head. He wouldn't do it every day with no strings attached."

We tried another one.

"He makes the bed."

"How often?"

"Every day."

"Why?"

"Because he knows I like it made."

"And has he ever called you controlling for wanting that?"

"No."

Her face softened. "Real love shows up consistently, not conditionally."

Session by session, we picked apart the fears. Slowly, I began to understand that my brain had been trained by trauma to distrust love. I didn't know how to receive kindness without suspicion. After years of being manipulated, love itself felt unsafe.

What I eventually discovered was that my childhood—coupled with my marriage to Allen—shattered something foundational in me: my ability to trust anyone else. And as I moved through my healing, this distrust would expand. My husband, once a source of love and partnership, became someone I viewed as unsafe. I wondered how much my brother knew and didn't say. Even my best friend felt untrustworthy. The deeper I dove into my trauma, the more certain I became: no one could be trusted. No one but me.

My first experience with magic mushrooms was nothing I expected. Rather than fun or enlightening, the trip forced me to confront buried emotions, long-ignored patterns, and a warped sense of reality I hadn't fully realized I was living in. It shook me deeply, exposing the unprocessed pain and internal narratives that had quietly shaped my life.

Though terrifying and painful, the experience became a catalyst for change. It marked the beginning of a long, necessary journey—one that would require work with my therapist, my husband, and myself. In hindsight, it was exactly the push I needed.

What I Know Now

Trauma reshapes the way we interpret the world. It doesn't just live in our memories; it rewires how we hear words, how we read faces, and how we receive love. It can twist even the most tender gestures into something threatening. And then even kindness starts to feel suspicious.

I've seen this countless times in my therapy office—clients spiraling as they convince themselves that love is a trap, that emotional safety is just the calm before the storm. I would sit with them, helping them make sense of it, without fully realizing how much I was living it myself.

What happened during my mushroom trip wasn't just a "bad high." It was a collision between altered consciousness and decades of unprocessed trauma. Psilocybin can be deeply healing, but it isn't magic. It requires intention, preparation, and support. I didn't realize how much grief, fear, and pain I was still carrying. And when my defenses went down, all of it surged to the surface at once.

For survivors—especially those who've lived through emotional abuse, gaslighting, or betrayal—love doesn't always feel safe. Even when the danger has passed, the nervous system hasn't gotten the memo. So, we brace for impact. We interpret care as control. We scan for the hidden trap door.

That's not because we're broken. It's because our brains did exactly what they were wired to do: survive.

So, when psilocybin lowered my defenses and made my internal world louder, all those old violations came roaring back. My nervous system didn't see a loving husband asking if I wanted to sit outside. It saw another man issuing a command. It heard domination where he offered choice. It felt intrusion where he offered connection.

This is the legacy of stolen consent: you begin to distrust everyone—even the people who have earned your trust.

My Healing

Trauma taught me to expect betrayal, to assume that every kind gesture had a price, and that love was a setup for abandonment or control. Healing is slowly, carefully teaching my nervous system a different story: that consistency can be real, that care can be genuine, that not everyone who stays is secretly plotting their takeover.

Cognitively, I understand this. I teach it. I can explain trauma responses and attachment wounds all day long. The harder work is recognizing it in real time—catching the moment when my brain starts rewriting David into a villain or my best friend's text into an attack.

I know I will be working on this for a long time.

But every time I notice what's happening—every time I pause, breathe, and name it as trauma rather than truth—I loosen its hold.

Every time I choose curiosity over automatic defensiveness, I create a tiny bit more space for trust.

18

The Language of Trauma

Starting my healing process began with a question: How am I showing up in the world?

I thought about how I showed up with David, with my children, my family, my friends, and even my colleagues. Was I living as my true, authentic self—or as a version of myself I believed would be more accepted, more palatable, more . . . safe?

Professionally, I didn't lack confidence. In fact, I felt grounded and assured when teaching, researching, and presenting. I trusted my instincts, intellect, and experience. I knew who I was in those spaces.

But in my personal life, that clarity vanished.

Years of being silenced, dismissed, or manipulated had rewired something deep inside me. I began to question myself constantly—not because I lacked thoughts or opinions, but because I feared mine would somehow be wrong. Somewhere along the way, I had internalized a dangerous belief: agreeability equals safety.

Adopting other people's perspectives became my armor. It protected me from conflict, from judgment, from the pain of being told I was too much or not enough. My silence became a strategy. My flexibility, a form of self-erasure.

It showed up in small, everyday decisions—like when I'd question whether one of the boys was ready for a phone or a movie or a sleepover. I didn't rely on my professional expertise in child development. I turned to other moms, asking how they were handling things. I second-guessed myself constantly, even when I knew what was developmentally appropriate.

The truth was, I didn't trust myself—not as a mother, not as a partner, not as a woman.

That feeling of not being enough had threaded itself through every part of my life. The fear of being an imposter—of being "found out" as unworthy—was always lurking. And no amount of professional success had been able to root it out. This was work I would need to do over and over again for the rest of my life.

As I continued processing the mushroom trip that had unraveled me, what bothered me most was that David—my soulmate—had been the trigger.

David has always been my safety. He is the one person who sees all of me and loves me still. And yet, I was seeing him differently now.

I thought counseling might help us learn to communicate better. But if I'm being honest now, what I really wanted was for him to learn how he triggered me during the mushroom trip and never do it again.

I also believed the process could unfold without much effort on my part—as if my therapist might somehow read my mind. That was a pattern for me: I longed to be known without having to reveal myself. I craved understanding but resisted vulnerability, hoping others would just sense what I was feeling so I wouldn't have to say it out loud.

As a therapist myself, I know that mind-reading isn't part of the job. Yet my own expectation that someone else could do it only reinforced the distorted belief that others possessed skills I lacked. Rationally, I knew no one—therapist or otherwise—could read minds. But still, I held onto the hope that someone might be able to read mine.

When I first suggested couples counseling to David, he resisted—not because he was against the idea, but because, in his mind, we were already doing work in family-based therapy with Joe. I waited, and once the family work wrapped up, I brought it up again. I truly believed therapy could help us.

David was less than enthusiastic about it. Like many people, he worried that marriage counseling was only for couples on the brink of divorce. He believed we could work through anything with honesty. It didn't feel that simple from my side. I struggled to be fully honest—not because I lied, but because I held back my true thoughts out of fear. I feared he'd respond to my feelings with anger, or deny responsibility, or label the problem as mine alone.

It was a pattern I'd noticed: every time I neared the edge of vulnerability with David, I pulled back. I pushed for counseling because I wanted us to have a healthier way to communicate. As a therapist myself, I watched couples grow closer through regular sessions, and that's what I was hoping for. Eventually, he agreed, and we found a couple's therapist who specialized in trauma and family systems.

Our first few sessions involved a lot of work to uncover how each of us show up in our relationship and how we process stress, pain, anger, and sadness. We also spent a lot of time talking about Joe. When Joe had one of his blowups, David and I often had opposing views on how to respond. Instead of coming together, we clashed, and those disagreements had begun to erode our relationship.

One of the core challenges was how differently David and I communicated. He's an external processor—he needs to talk things through, circling around a topic until it feels settled. I'm the opposite. I process internally, silently working things out in my mind before I'm ready to speak. That mismatch created ongoing friction between us.

When I did speak up, I shared my thoughts and my perspective. David would respond with his own, and something about the dynamic always left me feeling smaller. His voice wasn't louder in volume, but in presence. It carried a weight, an unspoken authority, as if his point of view automatically held more ground than mine.

And then I would slowly begin to retreat—physically, emotionally, sometimes both. I'd go quiet, shrink into myself, and dissociate. I'd stop trying to be understood and instead focus on enduring the conversation, waiting for it to be over.

Even though I knew, intellectually, that David was simply processing out loud, my body didn't interpret it that way. Emotionally, it triggered something much older. His monologue began to feel like my mother's relentless badgering. In those moments, I wasn't just frustrated—I was transported. Back to childhood. Back to silence. Back to survival.

Our counselor encouraged us to become more aware of my body language during difficult conversations. For me, when I hunched over or curled into myself, it signaled that I was overwhelmed and shutting down. And if David continued to process out loud, it felt like he didn't care how I was feeling, like he just wanted to win, or to push his perspective until I gave in.

As I felt myself growing smaller and smaller, my voice would catch, and tears would come—sometimes in quiet streams, sometimes in guttural sobs. But even then, he wouldn't stop. Not because he was trying to be cruel, but because we were speaking entirely different languages. I was in my head, spiraling inward. He was on the outside, trying to make sense of things by talking them through.

The longer David spoke, the more it hurt. I wanted to push him away, to run, to disappear. It felt like he needed me to shatter so he could make his point. Rationally, I knew that wasn't true. Emotionally, it felt exactly like the torment I had endured growing up—where emotional overwhelm wasn't met with compassion, but with indifference or even escalation.

And here's the deeper truth: through the lens of healing, David sometimes becomes everyone. In those moments of conflict, it isn't just David talking. It's my mother, minimizing and dismissing. It's Allen, twisting my words and questioning my instincts. When something comes up about the kids, it can sound like an attack on my parenting—even when it's not. It hits a raw nerve and brings me right back to feeling scrutinized, judged, and small.

David's processing style—so different from mine—can feel like not being seen at all. Like being told I'm too sensitive or too emotional, when all I've ever wanted was to be understood. And the hardest part is that he doesn't mean to hurt me. We both believed our way was the "right" way and wanted the other to meet us where we were. That approach wasn't sustainable. Learning to understand ourselves—and each other—became the first step toward bridging that gap.

Over time, David encouraged us to keep going to counseling. To my surprise, he became increasingly open to exploring how his words and actions affected our relationship. He didn't just talk about change—he did the work. He showed up with more support, more self-awareness, and often more willingness to adapt than I was prepared for.

That was huge for me. For the first time, I wasn't being treated as the only problem. After years of being gaslit and blamed, it was hard to trust that someone could genuinely take accountability—without a hidden motive.

It also opened up a new floodgate. Even now, I sometimes catch myself doubting David's sincerity. I boomerang back to old patterns, wondering if his tenderness is just another performance, a manipulation I haven't figured out yet.

But the truth is, it's not performative. He's proven that, over time. Still, the residue of trauma is sticky. Even when you've scrubbed your wounds clean, the stain of what you've survived doesn't always wash off.

What I Know Now

As a therapist, I often tell clients that the body remembers what the mind tries to forget. Dissociation—whether through zoning out, freezing, or going emotionally blank—is not a flaw. It's a survival response, especially common in those who were silenced, gaslit, or punished for expressing needs.

What I understand now is that my nervous system reacts long before my rational mind can catch up. David's voice—through no fault or intention of harm—can sometimes pull me into a trauma state. That's not because he is unsafe. It's because I spent years in relationships where love and cruelty were entangled, where the people who claimed to care for me were also the ones who belittled, minimized, or controlled me.

This is the truth for many survivors: when we feel overwhelmed, our brain doesn't ask, "Is this person safe?"

It asks, "Have I felt this way before?"

And if the answer is yes—if the tone, rhythm, or intensity resembles a past wound—the body reacts instantly, often without our permission.

In those moments, David isn't just David. He becomes everyone who ever used their voice to overpower mine. He becomes my mother, demanding and dismissive. He becomes Allen, twisting my words, questioning my instincts, and making every disagreement feel like proof that I was wrong or unworthy. He becomes every person who ever taught me that shrinking was safer than speaking.

That's the tricky part of trauma: the present gets filtered through the past. And it all happens in a split second.

Healing doesn't mean never getting triggered again. Healing means recognizing the moment your trauma steps into the room—and learning how to gently guide yourself back to the present. It also means helping the safe people in your life understand your inner landscape so they can respond with compassion rather than confusion.

My Healing

For me, healing has meant learning to name what's happening in real time:

"I feel myself shutting down."

"My body is reading this as danger."

"I'm overwhelmed and starting to disappear."

These statements aren't accusations—they're bridges. But learning to say them out loud has been its own journey. After years of having my vulnerability weaponized against me—first as a child, then in my marriage to Allen—trusting someone with my internal world felt risky. I worried that if I said too much, if I exposed too much, if I let myself be too soft, it could all be used to hurt me later.

Speaking my truth in moments of overwhelm has taken practice. And courage. And a kind of self-compassion I wasn't raised to possess.

My goal isn't perfection—it's progress.

Every time I stay in the room instead of running, I am healing. Every time I choose connection over silence, I am healing. Every time I let my voice tremble but still let it speak, I am healing.

And yes, there are backslides. There are moments when I still run to another room. Or curl into myself and rock back and forth. Moments when my logical mind can't negotiate with the terrified child inside me.

All of that is normal. And recognizing it as normal is part of what heals me.

Even more, I can now see the reduction in frequency—and that tells me I am making real, measurable progress. Slowly, steadily, I am learning to trust myself. To trust the safety I've built. And to trust that the language of trauma doesn't get the final say in my marriage, my relationships, or my life.

19

A Map to the Past

After the chaos of the mushroom trip, I understood one thing clearly: I needed structure and safety if I was going to keep digging through my past. I also knew I had opened the door that I couldn't close now.

In Pennsylvania, ketamine was my only legal option for psychedelic-assisted therapy. I chose a structured at-home program that included consultations with a licensed practitioner, a medical review, and regular check-ins with a trained guide. While the process sometimes felt slow, I came to appreciate the safeguards. There are no shortcuts when it comes to responsible care.

I also built a support system. My therapist was fully on board, and more personally, David offered steady, unwavering encouragement. Logically, I knew I didn't need his permission—but emotionally, I needed someone I trusted to tell me it was okay to take up space to heal. His validation gave me the push I didn't know I still needed.

I just didn't realize how deep I would need to go. It would take time—time to understand why I felt I needed permission in the first place, and time to uncover the beliefs I had buried beneath layers of success, achievement, and professional armor.

The program included six ketamine sessions, spaced about a week apart. Each session lasted no more than forty minutes—far more manageable than the unstructured mushroom trip.

For the first session, I prepared my space to feel grounded. After check-ins from my guide and the nurse practitioner, and a final nod from David—my designated safety person—I lay back on my bed and waited.

The session was dark, both visually and emotionally. I expected movement, color, something cinematic. Instead, there were only faint streaks of purple behind my eye mask. I felt calm. Still. Almost empty. Afterwards, I journaled, uncertain whether anything meaningful had occurred. I even wondered if I hadn't received enough medicine.

Integration—the application of therapeutic insight outside the session—is where transformation truly begins. Like learning an instrument, real progress happens not during formal lessons, but in what happens between. I wasn't sure how to apply what I had seen—or hadn't seen. So, I waited. I listened.

Eventually, I interpreted the darkness as a message: I wasn't as close to healing as I'd thought. I had more to face. And I would have to face it slowly, piece by piece.

In my reflection time, I began to revisit the concept of attachment—specifically, my own. Years earlier, during therapy with Joe, David and I had taken an attachment style assessment. We'd skimmed the results and moved on. Now I felt a pull to revisit them with new eyes.

My attachment style is dismissive-avoidant. On the surface, it looks like strength, independence, and self-sufficiency. Beneath it, there's fear—of closeness, of disappointment, of not being safe. Knowing this helped me better understand my patterns in love and in conflict—especially with David.

I also started thinking more deeply about my early childhood. Though I had never called Al my stepfather, his presence shaped me.

So did my mom. So did my dad. I couldn't isolate my attachment style from them. The way they treated me taught me how to protect myself.

At my next therapy session, I brought all of this—insights from ketamine, from journaling, from reflection. It became clear that the same patterns that shaped my childhood were still alive in my relationships with Allen, David, even Joe.

The second ketamine session brought a shift. Still dark, but layered now. I heard water. Flowing. And then: memories.

I was nine. At the window. Our above-ground pool had been vandalized and drained.

Then another memory: a dockyard in New Jersey. Tony yelling as boys knocked my glasses off.

These weren't repressed memories—just old ones rising to the surface without clear reason or explanation. I wanted to figure out why.

As I journaled that day, I remembered something else from the boatyard. I recalled my mother telling us that Al's boat had been set on fire and sunk. It was arson, they said, and the person responsible was Al's ex-wife.

I realized the story I'd been told made no sense. How did this happen when she lived in Pennsylvania, and the boat was docked in New Jersey?

I started questioning the stories I'd been told. And then I started building. The pool vandalism and boat arson were both blamed on Al's ex-wife. Maybe she did react out of anger over the affair. But did she really travel hours across state lines just to burn a piece of his property?

I also knew Al, and his relationship with the truth was shaky at best. Pinpointing the year that he and his wife divorced felt like it could help me better understand the sequence of events in my own life. It was at least a place to start.

I am a linear, analytic thinker, and lists and timelines speak to the way I understand the world. So, I began constructing a personal timeline—part memory, part research.

And what I discovered horrified me.

There were so few concrete dates I actually knew. There were certain memories I never forgot, like the dates of my parents' divorce or my abortion. But most memories were far fuzzier.

Now, I would dismantle it. Piece by piece. And begin again.

Each new find—and each confirmed date—helped orient me. And each unknown raised even new questions. In the end, what shocked me most wasn't just the gaps, but how young I had been when so much of it started.

Therapy became a place for new discoveries, and also for grief. Each week, I brought new information to process, which came with its own challenges. I questioned what I remembered. I questioned whether my mom, my dad, and Al could have really harmed me in the ways I now suspected. I questioned everything. And yet the timeline grew.

The next three ketamine sessions were less dramatic—but still useful. I continued integrating. Journaling. Talking with David. Bringing findings to therapy.

Eventually, I pinpointed the year the sexual abuse started: I was ten. And then I searched for visual proof—and found the photo.

In it, I look joyful and am holding a fish and wearing a blue-and-white short set, with the straps pulled down to make a tube top. The sign around my neck read: "and 8 more," an homage to the nine fish we'd caught that day. The photo was taken in our backyard after a short trip with Tony, my mom, and Al. Al's camper is in the background.

I soon found another photo—same outfit, but a year earlier. This time, I looked tired. Straps in place. The contrast was startling. And that's when it hit me.

It almost seemed like the photos were out of order. Why would I look happier after everything had started?

What struck me most was that both pictures captured a little girl. In both photos, I look so small. I am a child. While that may sound silly to say, for so long, I had pictured my ten-year-old self as looking more like the adult me. Because so much of my past remained unresolved, I had trouble separating the two.

Thanks to searchable databases, I quickly found more dates for my timeline, like bankruptcy, tax, and divorce filings. The dates helped establish a clearer picture of both what I already knew and what I was just uncovering. It also helped me clarify where gaps in my memory still occurred.

There was quite a bit of documentation that I had carried with me through cross-country moves, marriages, children, and divorces. It was remarkable: there were newspaper clippings, my childhood journal, and other writings I had done for school.

One night, I pulled out my files so David and I could go through them together. I also snapped photos and texted them to my best friend. "You're a great historian," she remarked. The three of us were stunned by how many details I had documented as a child and young adult. I had already recorded so much of the history I'd been searching for—I just hadn't thought to look.

My childhood journal was especially helpful. I had started keeping it when my best friend's family moved away. I was lonely and found comfort in writing down my thoughts. I picked it up at a farmer's market—it was covered in red cloth and decorated with teddy bears wearing blue shirts and tiny blue hats. On its side was a little gold lock and a set of keys. I was drawn to the idea of having a space where I could say what I needed to say and keep it just for myself. At that point, I didn't feel like I could trust anyone with my thoughts. So, I trusted the journal.

I didn't write every day, but a habit formed early, and over the years I filled the pages with my thoughts and feelings.

As I read through my childhood journal, I wasn't prepared for how loud the patterns would be.

Over and over again, one name appeared—Al. His presence haunted nearly every page, a shadow cast over my adolescence. What struck me most wasn't just the frequency with which I wrote about him, but the intensity. My younger self, still trying to make sense of a world she had no control over, had poured her rage onto the page with heartbreaking clarity.

As I read through my entries, I was struck by how frequently I repeated the same themes—especially the stress I felt around Al. It was woven into so many of my entries, revealing more than I realized at the time.

"Al is still acting up. I hate going to church with him. People think he's my father. I hate that . . . He's not my father and never will be my dad, daddy, or father."

"Al is such a baby. God, I hate that man more than anyone on this earth! He's such a fucking baby. I wish he would go away or go kill himself"

"Al is a jerk, where does he get off saying I should get rid of my girlfriends and find a boy to go out with all the time?"

I was an angry child. Angry that a man like Al could behave the way he did and still demand my respect. At the time, I didn't yet understand the impact his presence was having on me. I didn't have the language for trauma. I didn't know why he needed so much attention, or why his outbursts came so suddenly, or why he always made everything about himself. I just knew that I hated him.

By the time my final ketamine session occurred, I was ready to move on from psychedelic treatments and to continue my healing journey in other ways.

During my final session, I saw a vision of myself standing at the summit of a mountain, its slopes lush with green grass and tall, whispering trees. I stood there—head lifted, shoulders open—face tilted toward the sun, eyes closed, as golden warmth spilled across my skin. I wore a tank top and jeans, hands tucked gently into my front pockets, grounded in stillness. In that moment, I felt it: the climb ahead would be steep, demanding, and long—but at the top, there would be light.

What I Know Now

Psychedelic-assisted therapy, when practiced responsibly, can open doors to deep healing. But those doors lead somewhere—and it's not always where you expect. Memories rise. Grief comes. And the past can feel startlingly close.

For survivors of trauma, even accurate memories can feel unreliable. Why? Because trauma fractures time. It doesn't store neatly in the brain. Instead, it gets lodged in the body, resurfacing in pieces—flashes, sensations, emotions without context.

That's why creating a timeline became such a powerful tool for me. It wasn't about proving my pain to anyone else. It was about reclaiming my story on my own terms. Laying out dates, documents, photos, and memories in a linear way helped me see patterns I'd always felt but could never fully name. It helped me recognize how young I really was when so much of it started—and how long I'd been carrying it alone.

Psychedelics did not hand me a perfectly organized narrative. They cracked open the door. Ketamine sessions brought flashes of memory and emotion; integration—therapy, journaling, reflection, building my timeline—turned those flashes into something I could actually work with.

That is the heart of it: the medicine isn't the transformation. What you do with what it shows you—that's where the healing lives.

My Healing

As a deeply linear, analytic thinker, my timeline wasn't just metaphorical—it was literal and on paper. That structure helped me create internal structure. Seeing my history laid out in front of me allowed my nervous system to begin believing what my body had always known.

Healing has also looked like patience. I did not remember everything at once. I had to accept that I might never know every fact, every date, and every detail. But I can know my truth.

I can hold space for my younger self with tenderness and say: "I believe you. I'm listening. I won't abandon you." And I can reassure her: "I've got it now. I'll take care of this. You don't have to worry anymore."

Through this work, I realized that my inner child believed she was responsible for keeping my adult self safe. That's why, when I'm triggered by David's words or by conflict, I sometimes find myself curling into a ball like a small girl. That posture isn't about my adult self at all—it's about how my younger self survived.

Releasing her from the job of protecting me—and consciously taking on that role as an adult—has been one of the most freeing shifts in my healing. It doesn't mean I'm never triggered. It means that when I am, I can recognize who is reacting, and I can gently step in.

20

The Paper Trail

I have always loved puzzles and am drawn to the challenge of fitting each piece into its place, helping little fragments come together to form a complete picture. My grandfather had hundreds of jigsaw puzzles and his love for the art helped me appreciate that they aren't just found in cardboard boxes—they exist in life, too.

As I continued to build my timeline, I recognized that information was missing in the online court records, and I couldn't find anything about Al's arrest or court appearance. My case took place long before computers were a thing, so maybe there were paper files?

Shortly after I wrapped up my ketamine sessions, I visited the police station that handled Al's arrest. It wasn't far from my home, but getting there meant silencing waves of anxiety—and quieting the echo of my mother's voice in my head, telling me to hush up and forget it ever happened. "Do not bother people," she'd say. "They have problems and don't want to hear about you."

A very young officer behind a plexiglass wall reviewed my records request and explained that, because the case was so old, someone else would need to check the archives and follow up. About a week later, a kind, though not especially helpful, patrol lieutenant called and explained that police reports couldn't be released without a court order. Still, he said the sensitive nature of the case had prompted him to call instead of sending a form letter, and he offered to answer any questions.

I asked the one thing I truly wanted to know—something I knew wouldn't be in any newspaper: had any other victims come forward? His answer was clear and immediate—no.

While I was disappointed that I couldn't obtain a copy of the report, the fact that it existed provided some sense of peace. It was further validation that it happened.

My next stop was the county courthouse, about a thirty-minute drive from my home. This was another trip that required me to dig deep and psych myself up. The first woman who greeted me tried to help, and when I asked for court records from Al's appearance, she scrambled to find someone who could assist.

Eventually, her boss—a rude, condescending woman—came to the desk and curtly informed me that I was in the wrong place. That was a trigger for me. It wasn't what she said, it was how she said it. Her tone was dismissive and made me feel powerless and small. Negative thoughts flooded in: this isn't important; you're wasting their time, Tina. Just let it go. I questioned whether I even belonged there. It was all I could do just to hold back my tears.

Determined to find answers, I visited multiple offices that day—speaking with staff, making calls, and passing through courthouse security lines many times—only to learn that the court records I needed had been destroyed. Crushed, I was told my last hope might be the jail's records.

As I walked back to my car, I recognized that I was dissociating. I felt hollow and numb. I called to update David, and then my brother, who responded that he wasn't surprised the records were gone. When I hung up, I was frustrated—with him . . . and with everyone and everything. Once again, I felt let down by the very system I turned to for answers.

When I returned home, I called the jail and asked who posted Al's bail. The woman who answered said the files were destroyed ten years after his arrest.

Finally, I understood that I would never get a copy of the record of Al's hearing. Or really, anything more than what I had kept myself for all those years.

I was so focused on surviving that I never realized there was a clock ticking down on my ability to uncover the truth. Learning that so many of the records were destroyed in such a short period of time was astounding. Most of the records were destroyed before I was even twenty-one years old.

In Pennsylvania, the statute of limitations for rape is twelve years after the crime occurs. Since I was ten years old when the abuse began, all records should have remained until I was at least twenty-two. What a failure.

A few weeks later, a staff member in the district attorney's office called and gave me the contact information for a supervisor at the county office responsible for investigating child abuse. I didn't expect much; like everything else, my county case files were long gone.

To my surprise, I was able to speak with someone who helped me piece a few more details together. She explained how the agency had functioned in the 1980s.

Eventually, I pieced together the likely chain of events in my situation.

When abuse was reported, cases are classified as either unfounded, founded, or indicated. Based on what I shared, mine would have been considered indicated, which means it was passed on to law enforcement. Whether or not the case was prosecuted didn't change its status with the agency.

The woman confirmed the name of my case manager in 1989—perhaps a small detail, but an important one for me as someone who often questions my own memory. I had his name and number in my childhood journal, and it was validating to learn he was real. He had indeed worked as an intake investigator, she said.

After the hearing, Al had been ordered to leave the home for a year and attend counseling. I learned that this aligned with their protocol—the county would not have closed a case without a safety plan in place for the child. In my case, that likely meant a conversation with my mother to confirm I was safe.

What no one understood was just how unsafe I was with my own mother. Her priority was not my wellbeing—it was maintaining her lifestyle, which included Al. Lying to authorities was easy for her. She and Al probably showed them a signed apartment lease, which was good enough.

The county trusted a mother to protect her own child, so much so that they skipped their final visit to my home. If they'd come—or asked me—I would've told them the truth: Al was back in our home within weeks of the court hearing.

As disturbing as this new information was, I appreciated this woman helping me understand what had happened. She explained that if anyone had reported Al's return, the case would have been reopened. Of course, as a child without any knowledge of how things worked, I didn't know I could report it.

I also asked her why I couldn't find any record of Al—nothing in a registry, and nothing linked to a court case. She explained that records are eventually expunged if there are no further reports. If Al had applied for a job requiring a background check or volunteered somewhere, it might've shown up. But since he worked for my mother, that never happened.

With no additional reports, his record disappeared. He got away with it.

Worse? My mom had orchestrated the entire thing. And that's when I realized—I wasn't even surprised. This was who she had always been. My mother didn't just lie to the authorities in this case—she lied to everyone.

What I Know Now

Trauma recovery often involves a search—not just for healing, but for validation. Many survivors crave some form of "proof": a document, a record, a witness. Something that confirms what the body has always known.

But systems aren't built for trauma timelines. Statutes expire. Files get purged. Paper trails disappear before survivors even find their voices. That's not an accident—it's a structural failure.

When I went searching for the paper trail of my abuse—hoping for clarity, context, or even just confirmation of what I remembered—I found instead the same thing so many survivors eventually encounter: silence, erasure, and indifference masquerading as procedure.

And still, I kept going. Not because I doubted myself—those days were behind me.

I searched because I wanted to honor the younger version of myself who still longed to be believed. I searched because every survivor deserves answers, even if those answers arrive in pieces.

In the end, here's what I know: the absence of a record does not mean the absence of a truth. Sometimes the system fails, not the survivor.

My Healing

Most days now, something new emerges—a memory, a connection, a realization about how the past shows up in my present, whether in motherhood, my marriage, or my own inner world. At first, these moments were slow and sporadic. Now they come regularly, sometimes multiple times a day. And with each piece, a bit more healing settles into place.

It is horrifying at times. It is also powerful.

Each new piece of the puzzle brings a shift inside me—a moment of alignment where something that was once tangled suddenly makes sense. It connects my past to my present and opens a clearer path toward my future.

Healing also means redefining what "evidence" is. I've learned that the most powerful validation I carry isn't a court file. It's my childhood journal. It's a photograph that suddenly clicks into place. It's a body memory rising with startling clarity.

These things—small, human, unarchived—hold more honesty than any destroyed police report ever could.

Something else has surprised me: a significant part of my healing has been happening for decades without me realizing it.

Long before I formally began my personal healing journey, I was already doing the work. My entire professional life—advocacy, counseling, teaching, researching, writing—has been shaped by a desire I didn't yet have the language to name: the desire to protect others from facing what I faced alone.

My career was a calling born from survival. I became a therapist because I wanted children to be believed. I became an educator to help future counselors recognize the patterns no one recognized in me. I advocated for families because I understood, in my bones, what happens when systems fail.

Part of me has been healing all along—quietly, steadily, through every person I've supported, every system I've challenged, every truth I've spoken on behalf of someone who wasn't ready to speak yet.

Now, the work I do is not just for others—it is finally for me, too.

21

The Ass-Backward Truth

My given name at birth was Tina Rosetta Paone. My mother said she chose it because I looked like a tiny rose.

She also told me my name was going to be Lisa, but she changed her mind because Al named his daughter—who had special needs—that name.

Not that she used my actual name all that much. I was more often called "Missy Pissy," or, on a good day, subjected to her running joke: "I should've named you Grace—maybe then you wouldn't be so clumsy!"

Other times, she skipped the nicknames and went straight for adjectives: I was labeled dramatic, a slut, and a whore. Later, when she wanted to keep me silent, she accused me of reporting my abuse as a way to break apart our family. In those situations, I had no name, I was just "an evil little girl."

So yes, I was named after a rose. And clearly, I was treated like one.

My mother often reminded me—and anyone else who would listen—that she endured seventeen hours of labor to bring me into the world. It became one of the first stories I ever heard about myself, and she played it on repeat. I was breach, but rather than use that word, she'd tell people I came into the world "ass backwards." I had caused her immense amounts of pain.

By the time I was born, my parents and Al were already familiar, friendly neighbors. After getting married, my parents had purchased the home and five acres of land. Al and his wife at the time—along with their four children—lived across the street.

One of my mom's favorite stories was from when I was a toddler, before my brother Tony was born. She'd tell it like it was just a funny, quirky moment. But looking back, I see it differently—an early sign of neglect, disguised as a charming anecdote.

The story went like this: She was shopping with me at the local mall when she suddenly and urgently needed to use the restroom. The bathroom was up a level, and rather than take me with her, she sat me on a square wooden bench and surrounded me with shopping bags.

She would tell people she was scared the entire time she was gone, worried something might happen. But still—she left me. Alone. As a baby on a mall bench.

As a mother of three, of course I understand the urgency of needing a bathroom. But no matter how desperate I got, I would never leave my baby unattended. If I had to abandon shopping bags, so be it: my child would be my only concern.

My mom saw it differently: in her eyes, the best way to ensure her packages wouldn't be stolen was to leave her young daughter to guard them. Her comfort and convenience overrode my safety.

I'd like to believe that if my dad had known more, he would have protected me, so I'd also like to think my mom was too embarrassed to tell my father this story at the time. I hope it would have been a red flag. But the truth is that I don't know what she shared with him because she had no qualms about telling it to strangers years later. But I also know that like many men in the 1970s, he took a hands-off approach to parenting, assuming my mother would handle it all, just as his mother had done.

As I grew older, I came to understand that my mother was a deeply untruthful person. It was sometimes hard to decipher the lies: they were so carefully crafted that I was constantly second-guessing myself. "I know the truth . . . I think . . . but maybe I don't."

What struck me most was the contrast between the mother the world saw and the one I knew. Outwardly, she appeared to be a good mom—providing food, shelter, and structure. But that's not what makes a mother. What was missing was the very thing children need most: safety. Emotional, physical, and spiritual safety. It simply didn't exist in our home.

Tony and I were raised Catholic—baptized, schooled, and steeped in the rituals and rules of the Church. We were taught about God and Jesus, kindness and love, and obedience and sin. The Ten Commandments were drilled into us—not just as guidance, but as sacred, non-negotiable law.

And yet, it was hard not to notice how often our mother broke nearly every one of them. She lied. She gossiped. She manipulated. She coveted—not just metaphorically—our neighbor's husband. Over time, it became clear that in our home, faith was flexible. Rules bent to her benefit. "Do as I say" was gospel, and beneath it sat an unspoken eleventh commandment: Don't question, don't challenge, don't push back.

While most commandments were treated as optional, she clung to one with unwavering conviction when it came to Tony and me: Honor your mother and father. In her hands, religion wasn't a source of comfort or morality—it was a weapon. A tool to maintain control.

Even God, as we understood him, was never safe. The God who lived in our house was moody and vengeful. If someone bumped an elbow or stubbed a toe, my mother would smirk and say it was God punishing them. If she was gossiping and something went wrong, that was divine retribution too. God didn't offer love—he handed down sentences and was a celestial enforcer, and he was always on her side.

Nowhere was her hypocrisy—or the Church's—more glaring than when I got pregnant at sixteen. Abortion was considered a mortal sin, the kind that could send you straight to hell. But there was never a discussion about keeping the baby. The decision was made swiftly and without question. Not because of faith—but because of shame. Because what mattered most wasn't doctrine—it was appearance.

The Church preached morality, but in our house, survival meant secrecy. And the greatest sin wasn't disobedience. It was making my mother look bad.

Our mother expected Tony and I to lie, too—especially to our Granny, our mom's mother. "Don't tell Granny this" or "Make sure you don't mention that" became regular instructions. Some lies seemed small, others more significant.

As we grew older, we stopped playing along. If Granny asked us something, we told the truth. After years of secrecy, we saw no point in continuing the charade—even if that's what we'd been taught to do.

Of course, a major source of secrets involved keeping things from my dad. My brother and I were often used as cover for our mother's affair with Al. Many nights after dinner, she'd tell him she needed to go back to the bindery to catch up on work, and she'd bring us along so my dad wouldn't suspect anything. While we did go to her workplace, we never just went there—we always ended up with Al.

My dad believed she worked long hours, and she did. But her evening trips to the shop, dragging us along, became a daily cover. If we asked to stay home or questioned if we were going to see Al, she'd snap "Be quiet" or "Shut up." We had no choice. From a young age, we were forced to play along with her narrative. If we didn't fall in line, there were consequences.

Once—and only once—I got the courage to speak up. When she declared we were leaving, I asked loudly, "Where are we going?" so my dad could hear. She replied, "To the shop." I pushed again: "But where are we going *after* the shop?" I made sure the word "after" hung heavy in the air.

My mother's response was instant and terrifying—she yanked my arm and hissed, "Don't you dare, Tina, knock it off."

In that moment, I realized I wasn't protecting my dad—I was betraying her. And I never tried to expose her again.

The lies only deepened once Al started living in the trailer on our property. How my parents—especially my father—tolerated my mother's boyfriend living in our backyard is something I will never understand.

Looking back, it wasn't just the deception that shaped me. It was the way love and care were treated as privileges, not rights, in our home. My mother met the bare minimum requirements of parenthood—on paper. But the deeper, emotional needs of childhood? Those clearly went unmet.

Maslow's Hierarchy of Needs defines the five levels of human needs, beginning with the most fundamental: food, water, shelter. Technically, my mother provided those. But anything beyond that—safety, love, belonging, esteem, the space to become myself—didn't exist.

Even the basics came without tenderness. Yes, there was food, but it was delivered with threats. "Eat that or I'll shove it up the other end," my mother would snap. We weren't taught how to eat—we were taught not to inconvenience her for needing anything at all.

She never modeled a healthy relationship with food. Most days, she barely ate. Breakfast might be leftover brownies or a sliver of cake, and she'd nurse the same can of soda from morning to night—not out of enjoyment, but because she didn't want to stop to pee. Even her thirst was managed for efficiency, as if her basic needs were an annoyance.

Dinner was worse because Al was there. Tony and I learned to eat in under five minutes flat—shoveling food into our mouths so we could escape the table. We didn't taste it. We didn't talk. We just got through it. That's all dinner was: another thing to survive.

Later in life, I saw the same dysfunction from the opposite angle. Allen didn't restrict food—he devoured it. He ate like he hadn't evolved to sit at a table with other human beings: fist clenched around a fork like a club, shoveling food in with no pause. There was no grace. Just consumption.

The message was the same, just delivered differently: your body, your hunger, your needs—none of it really mattered.

Even the essentials often felt conditional, like they had to be earned. Expressing a need was seen as selfish. Asking for care was met with silence, irritation, or ridicule. In her world, my well-being wasn't a right. It was a burden.

A great example? My mother never took us to a pediatrician. We didn't have a doctor. As an adult, I didn't know if that was normal for the time, so I asked around—cousins on both sides, friends, peers. Everyone else had pediatricians, regular checkups, and care when they were sick. My mother saw no need. In her world, even basic health care was optional—something she decided we did or didn't deserve.

Ironically, after her stroke, I have accompanied my mother to nearly all of her doctor's appointments. Sometimes when I pick her up she recognizes me, and sometimes she doesn't. I've held her hand as she's gotten procedures done. I've helped her steady herself and put her clothes back on after an exam. I've worked with the nurses to adjust her diaper.

I show up with tenderness, with patience, with care—and without resentment or cruelty. The irony is not lost on me. My mother—once the adult who withheld affection, protection, and emotional presence—is now incapacitated and as dependent as a child. And I, the child she failed to care for, am the one who shows up for her, over and over again.

Though I never received that from her, I give it to her. Not because she earned it. Not because I am trying to prove anything.

I'm just not like my mother. I refuse to pass on the harm. I have chosen healing over revenge.

That truth is both painful and freeing.

What I Know Now

Language becomes reality—especially in childhood. When a caregiver labels a child as "dramatic," "manipulative," or "evil," those words don't just sting—they stick. They become embedded in the child's sense of self, echoing into adulthood as self-doubt, shame, and harsh inner dialogue.

But it wasn't only the language said to me that shaped me. It was the language I was required to swallow on behalf of others.

Growing up, I carried not just my own truths but the lies of the adults around me—their contradictions, their denials, and their rewritten histories. I was taught, explicitly and implicitly, that my job was to protect their version of reality, even when it meant abandoning my own.

My mother's shame became my inheritance. She and the rigid religion she clung to taught me that being a girl was something to fear, manage, or correct. Femininity was framed as dangerous—something that could provoke sin, cause harm, or invite blame. I internalized that before I understood what any of it meant.

Weaponized religion told me that obedience was safety. My mother told me that silence was survival. Together, they trained me to distrust my body, my voice, and my instincts. They taught me that "good girls" contort themselves into whatever shape keeps the peace. And because I was a child, I believed them.

Emotional abuse doesn't always look like yelling or violence. Sometimes it looks like neglect, sarcasm, avoidance, or holy-sounding shame. Sometimes it looks like being praised for your ability to withstand pain, or being told that suffering is proof of your worth. Sometimes it looks like being handed someone else's guilt and being told it is yours to carry.

As children, we can't make our caregivers wrong—so we make *ourselves* wrong. The stories we're told—and the ones we're forbidden to tell—become the blueprint for how we move through the world. I didn't just inherit trauma; I inherited a script. It dictated how much of myself I was allowed to show, how much space I could take up, and how deeply I was permitted to believe in my own goodness.

What I know now is that healing begins with reclaiming the pen. With naming what happened, what was taught, and what was never mine to hold. With refusing to carry the lies any longer. With learning, finally, that the truth doesn't destroy—it frees.

My Healing

Healing began when I could finally say words I was never allowed to believe: I was never evil. And I was never too much.

I was a child trying to survive.

Healing has meant acknowledging the role my mother played—not to excuse it, but to understand it. Her behavior was rooted in her own wounds, limitations, and distortions—context that doesn't make the harm smaller, but helps me stop carrying responsibility for choices that were never mine.

Healing has also meant understanding that I wasn't just robbed of childhood safety; I was conscripted into maintaining the illusion of a functional home. Parentification meant constantly monitoring my mother's emotional temperature to avoid a blowup. It meant caring for my younger brother when no one else did. And it meant carrying the weight of adult secrets—my mother's affair and her lies—while pretending everything was normal and protecting her version of reality.

The emotional labor I took on didn't protect me. It only taught me to abandon myself.

The transformative part of healing came when I allowed myself to receive the care I never got. When I learned to speak to myself with tenderness and give my younger self the love, protection, and belief she deserved.

Healing also means refusing to carry that distortion forward. It means showing up for my mother now in her incapacitated state not because she earned it, but because I deserve to live without bitterness poisoning my future.

There is power in caring for the person who once harmed you without becoming like them. There is power in saying: "The harm stops with me." There is true power in choosing healing over revenge.

22

The Inheritance of Silence

As a researcher, I've long understood the concept of generational trauma. I've studied it in communities marked by profound historical tragedies: descendants of enslaved people, Holocaust survivors, those impacted by war or systemic oppression.

But I only knew about generational trauma in the context of collective suffering. It never occurred to me that generational trauma could show up in families like mine.

When I first allowed myself to consider that the abuse and neglect I endured might have roots that stretched further back—into my parents' childhoods, into the stories no one talked about—I felt conflicted. I was already sad, hurt, and angry. To then learn that the people who harmed me might also have been suffering didn't bring me peace. I didn't want excuses; I wanted accountability.

What I've come to understand is that trauma never just disappears—it moves through the generations, quietly shaping behaviors and beliefs in a family until someone is brave enough to interrupt the pattern. In many families, the "curse" is avoidance. Pain is buried and hard things are left unspoken. Generations learn to parent without ever examining the damage that shaped them.

So, I began to ask: What unspoken grief shaped my mother? What pain did my grandparents carry? What kind of emotional abandonment was passed down, quietly but relentlessly, until it reached me?

That's when I started to see everything differently.

My mother was born in a quiet mining town tucked into Pennsylvania's Pocono Mountains. Granny and PopPop—what Tony and I called our maternal grandparents—raised three daughters and a son there.

And before any of them, there was Loretta, a daughter my grandparents lost when she was just thirteen months old.

Loretta's death fractured Granny. Though she went on to have four more children, she never recovered. She became withdrawn, cold, and harsh. Their home, as it was described to me, was heavy with unspoken grief. Loretta's death wasn't just a tragic loss; it was a form of perceived abandonment that fundamentally reshaped my grandmother.

Granny never hugged us. In fact, she often seemed irritated by the very idea that we were around. Now I understand that emotional distance didn't begin with my mother—it was modeled for her, then passed on.

To add coal to the fire, PopPop worked as a long-haul trucker. As my mom and her siblings grew up, he was gone most of the week, earning his paycheck. When he came home, he brought lightness and joy—but then he left again, taking the warmth with him. Love came and went with my grandfather's comings and goings. In time, I came to see that my grandmother wasn't the only one who experienced this cyclical sense of abandonment. My mother did too.

And when I look another generation back, the roots of abandonment grow even deeper. My great-grandmother came to the United States at just sixteen, brought over by her father—who then promptly returned to Europe, leaving her alone in a country she barely knew. Within a year, she was married, pregnant, and gave birth to her first child—a baby who died within minutes. Soon after, she became pregnant again and gave birth to a little girl.

This all happened at the height of the Spanish flu pandemic, and just three weeks later, her husband succumbed to the virus. (Ironically, that baby girl—my Granny—would pass away over a century later during the COVID-19 pandemic.)

In the span of a few months, and all before she was even eighteen years old, my great-grandmother had been abandoned by her father, lost her firstborn, and became a widowed teenage mother. Though death isn't abandonment in the traditional sense, its emotional impact can feel indistinguishable. Alone in a country that never truly felt like home, she was left to raise a child while carrying unimaginable grief.

Things only got harder. After her husband's death, she moved in with his parents—alcoholics who adored the baby but despised her. The house was filled with yelling and chaos. They treated her with open contempt. When they died, they left the house to my Granny—skipping her mother entirely.

Granny often said she didn't drink because of the trauma she witnessed in that house. The screaming, the cruelty, and the instability must have been catastrophic. And she raised my mother in the long shadow of that same pain. And I have to believe it was her stories, passed down like warnings, that shaped my own view of alcohol. To me, it wasn't just a drink—it was a threat. Even one or two made me uneasy, because I had learned to equate alcohol with chaos.

Understanding all of this helped me see my mother differently. Her coldness, her emotional withdrawal, her refusal to connect—they didn't emerge from nowhere. They were responses passed down, like a family heirloom no one wanted but everyone carried. In her family, the unspoken rule was simple: don't talk about pain, don't feel it, just endure. Emotional distance wasn't cruelty. It was survival.

As a result, my mother was emotionally immature and unavailable. Her decisions prioritized her own fear of abandonment over the well-being of her children—over me. That fear ran so deep, she allowed Al to stay in our lives, even as her own daughter endured his emotional and sexual abuse. She chose to preserve her relationship with him, no matter the cost.

None of this excuses how my mother treated me. It only explains it. Despite her education and outward appearance of competence, she never developed the emotional skills to parent in a nurturing way. She simply didn't know how. No one had ever shown her. Just as she never showed me things like how to brush my hair or what to do after I got my period.

In stark contrast to Granny, my father's mother radiated love and warmth. In Italian families, grandmothers are often called Nonna, but years before I was born, one of my older cousins—still a toddler—mispronounced it as "Na-na." The name stuck.

Nana told me she loved me every chance she got. She called me "Tina, bella Tina"—Beautiful Tina. That was my name in her eyes, and she never wavered from it. Her hugs wrapped me in safety. In her arms, I felt loved, seen, and cherished.

But a barrier stood between us—one my mother had constructed. Long before we were born, she had decided that only English would be spoken in our home. Despite the fact that my father had immigrated from Italy and his entire family spoke Italian, Tony and I were kept from the language that could have connected us to our roots. We weren't allowed to learn it. We picked up words and phrases now and then, but nothing truly meaningful.

As a result, we struggled to communicate with our grandparents. While my cousins slipped effortlessly between languages, my brother and I were left behind, always needing a translation, always one step removed. And yet, Nana never stopped trying to reach us. Even without a shared language, I understood her love—through her touch, her voice, her presence.

My aunts—my father's sisters and sisters-in-law—carried that same tenderness. They enveloped us in hugs, offering affection that felt safe, unconditional, and kind. That softness, that sense of connection, is what I've tried to carry forward into my own parenting. It was the kind of love that felt like home, even when we didn't have the words.

My mother, of course, saw things differently. She referred to Nana as "a hysterical Italian woman," someone who couldn't control herself when upset. She had a label for everyone on my father's side. My Aunt Mary was "crazy," and her close, affectionate relationship with her daughter Marie was "improper."

I remember quietly admiring the bond between Aunt Mary and Marie, secretly wondering what it would feel like to have that kind of connection with my own mother. But I was taught to see their closeness as unhealthy, to believe that my mother—composed, detached, emotionally restrained—was the better model. I was warned never to turn to Aunt Mary for comfort or support.

Nana may have struggled with anxiety, but she wasn't hysterical. Nor was my Aunt Connie, who was labeled the same way after showing her emotions after my grandfather died. She wept publicly, which my mother used as further evidence of her instability.

Once again, the lesson was reinforced: to show emotion is to reveal weakness. And weakness is dangerous.

And the judgment didn't stop with family—it extended into every area of my life. Teachers, friends' parents, mentors—anyone I admired was eventually picked apart and deemed unworthy. Even the characters in the show *Cagney & Lacey*—strong women I wanted to be like—were deemed too flawed for redemption.

Now, I see it for what it was: control through isolation. If I couldn't trust anyone else, I had no choice but to rely on her. That was the goal all along.

Nana's parenting left a lasting imprint on my dad. His own childhood was far from easy—when he was just ten, his father left their home in Italy to forge a better life in America. Though the family was eventually reunited, those formative years without a father likely left a quiet ache that never quite healed. And even once they were together again, my dad faced a school system unprepared—and unwilling—to support a child who didn't speak English. By ninth grade, he had dropped out.

My dad was incredibly close to his father, and I was just a kindergartener the year he died. Looking back, I imagine that loss hit him as hard as his death would one day hit me—an earthquake that reshaped everything.

And now I wonder: while my dad was processing his grief, did my mother see an opening? Was she so starved for attention that she ran into the arms of Al, her more emotionally available business partner? Of course, if that is the case, she didn't just leave the marriage like most people would have; she allowed Al to live on our property and carried on the affair right under my dad's nose.

My father's life was shaped by a series of abandonments, and I believe those wounds influenced how he showed up for me. Early on, he wasn't there when I needed him most. But over time, he came back. He stayed. And he spent the rest of his life trying to be present and to build an exceptional relationship with his grandsons. For that, I'm deeply grateful.

Looking at the full picture—across generations, through the lens of trauma—it's clear that abandonment echoes through every branch of my family tree. It shows up in death, in survival-driven separation, in emotional withdrawal, and in the failure to protect. It's no wonder that abandonment is my greatest fear. It lives in me because it has lived in all of them.

The most frustrating thing for me is the silence. No one in my family ever talked about any of this. Generations of pain, loss, and trauma were tucked away in corners no one dared to look into. I didn't even know my great-grandmother had lost a child until I stumbled upon the death certificate while mapping out our history. That kind of silence poisons a family. It creates confusion and shame that spreads from one generation to the next. The inability—or refusal—to talk about abuse and grief doesn't make it disappear. It just makes it harder for the next person to make sense of the mess.

And yes, at times, I'm pissed. So many people in my family endured real pain and trauma, yet none of them took the time or had the tools to heal. That work fell to me. I have to be the one to say that my mother should be held accountable, but "there's context . . ."

Until me, no one chose to break the pattern. They ignored their wounds, buried their pain, and passed the weight down. It feels unfair that I had to survive this life only to realize I am also carrying damage from lives that came long before mine.

But I know I'm not alone in this. So many survivors are left holding not just their own pain, but the pain that was never acknowledged by the generations before them. And perhaps the cruelest part is this: even as we do the hard work of healing, the people around us may never offer the recognition we long for. The validation. The apology. The simple act of saying, "I believe you."

I already know what's coming. When this book is published, I can predict the reactions before a single page is turned.

From my extended family, there will be polite, perhaps even heartfelt, congratulations. They'll celebrate the accomplishment—and sidestep the content. There will be no mention of the abuse. No acknowledgment of the truth that shaped every chapter.

Or worse: I'll get subtle scolding. "You shouldn't talk about your mother that way." Or "Have a little respect for your father."

And if Al's family finds out? I don't have to wonder. These are the same people who wrote in his obituary that he had a "heart of gold." Of course, they'll deny it. Maybe they never knew the truth. Maybe they never wanted to. Either way, they'll dismiss it outright.

I know Allen will rage. He's spent years crafting his own version of reality in which he is charming and charismatic. This book threatens that. He will hate it, not just because of what I reveal, but because I had the audacity to reveal it. Because I refused to stay quiet.

And then there's Joe. He'll run to Allen's defense. I can already hear his voice, full of certainty, reciting the narratives he's been taught to believe. He still can't see what's happening—still thinks love looks like control and protection sounds like secrecy. It's painful to watch, and even more painful to anticipate, but I've come to accept that he may not be ready to hear the truth. Not yet.

Part of my healing is accepting that silence, denial, and outrage are predictable responses when you dare to tell the truth. I'm no longer waiting for anyone to validate my experience. I'm done tiptoeing around other people's comfort to protect the very systems that harmed me.

This is my story. I lived it. I survived it. And I will not be silent about it.

Another part of my healing has been recognizing that Allen's cruelty didn't appear out of thin air. Narcissism isn't something people are born with. It's a defense mechanism, a way of surviving emotional injury and abandonment by building a false self that feels powerful and untouchable. It's a carefully constructed armor—one that protects the person inside from feeling the things they were never allowed to feel, including vulnerability and grief.

Allen's history is riddled with abandonment. His mother left him as a young child. Later, when she reentered his life, she moved him across the country and told him his father was dead. That wasn't true—but Allen didn't learn the truth until adulthood.

The pain of those betrayals warped him, and he learned to use the threat of abandonment as a weapon. When things don't go Allen's way, he withdraws and punishes with silence. He demands apologies for perceived slights and makes the other person earn back his love, just as he had once been made to do.

I remember Allen telling me that when his father learned about me, he called me a "gold digger." I don't even know if that's true, or Allen just said it to sow division between me and his dad. But that comment, while dripping with misogyny and projection, might seem minor—it reveals a lot. The judgment, the emotional stinginess, and the need to cut others down before they can hurt you.

That is generational trauma, alive and well.

Al, too, was part of this pattern. From what I know about his childhood, the abuse was physical and psychological. He learned to dominate instead of feel, and to control instead of connect.

And there was another side of him, too—what some might call "loving," though it never felt safe. His affection was excessive and suffocating. Like someone hugging an animal too tightly, insisting it is out of love even as the creature gasps for air. His touch overwhelmed, and his emotions spilled out in ways that felt intrusive, confusing, and scary.

And that's also what made Allen feel so familiar. The love bombing. The intensity. The oversized gestures meant to prove devotion. By the time I was with Allen, the over-the-top emotions didn't register as a red flag—because it mirrored what I had known.

And so, the pain was passed forward—into me.

None of this excuses what any of them did—my mother, Al, or Allen. It only explains it.

And it's why I'm so afraid of what's happening to Joe.

I see the signs. The way Allen withholds affection as punishment. The way Joe has been conditioned to see my love as manipulation and Allen's manipulation as love.

Narcissistic abuse is forged from unprocessed pain—pain that's never named, never healed, and never allowed to rest. Because it doesn't leave bruises, it goes unseen. It moves silently, in the shadows. And for children, especially, it's insidious—because they haven't yet learned that love shouldn't feel like walking on eggshells.

I'm terrified Joe has inherited his father's wounds—shaped not by DNA, but by environment. And I don't know how to stop it.

Allen doesn't just seek control—he manufactures reality to maintain it.

Looking back, I'm stunned by how easily he lied. Not just about the big things—money, the boys, the divorce—but about everything. Even what he'd just had for lunch. He lied reflexively, constantly, and often for no reason at all. But the worst part wasn't the lies themselves. It was the ease with which he told them. His words had confidence and conviction. As if I were the one misremembering, the one losing my grip.

As Allen rewrote history, there was one consistency. He was always cast as the victim, the hero, and the devoted parent. And me? I was the villain. The unstable one. The threat.

When a narcissist learns to exploit the sacred bond between a parent and child, the damage cuts in all directions. The longer Joe remains in that reality, the harder it becomes to reach him—not physically, but emotionally. I want so desperately for him to see the truth, but he has been groomed to mistrust me. The more I try to help, the more he pulls away—because Allen has taught him that my love is dangerous.

And now Joe lies like Allen does.

Sometimes, it's absurd. Like when he told me Allen couldn't use money apps—although he obviously pays bills and buys things online. Other times, it's stranger. Like when Joe told me recently that some rangers had chased him out of a local park. The details of his story didn't add up, and there was no reason at all for him to tell an elaborate lie.

Like any child shaped by their environment, Joe learned it from Allen: lies aren't just used to conceal—they're used to confuse, to provoke, or to assert dominance without raising a voice.

I fight every day not to collapse under the weight of helplessness. Especially because Joe now lives full time with his father and I worry—deeply—about how that environment is affecting him.

Generational trauma isn't just something you read about in textbooks or trace back to global tragedies. It lives in families like mine. It lives in silence. In denial. In inherited coping mechanisms and unspoken grief.

I am the interruption. I am the one who chooses to name the pain, to unearth the buried stories, and to break the pattern—even as it tried to break me.

Today, as I watch similar trauma threaten to pass into my own son, I understand more clearly than ever: healing isn't just something I owe myself. It's the only way forward for all of us: me, David, Nicholas, Christopher, and Joe.

What I Know Now

Generational trauma often goes unrecognized because it hides behind normalcy. Sometimes, it's chronic emotional distance—a brother who disappears from the family in adulthood. Sometimes it's the unsaid: family conversations that suddenly fall into silence because someone got too close to the truth, and it got uncomfortable. Sometimes it's the way affection is withheld, or the way a parent shrinks from touch. Sometimes it's a look of disappointment a child doesn't yet understand—but will carry anyway.

In many families, the trauma isn't just what happened. It's what was never talked about. The silence becomes its own form of abuse.

Survivors of this kind of trauma often grow up questioning their emotions, their needs, their memories. They internalize shame that doesn't belong to them. They become caretakers of unprocessed grief that never got named—grief that wasn't even theirs to carry.

As a therapist, I see this pattern over and over. Adults blaming themselves for dynamics they didn't create. Or feeling broken because no one ever taught them how to feel. Reenacting cycles that began long before they were born. When we trace it back, we often find the same themes: parents who were emotionally immature, grandparents who survived by detaching, great-grandparents who endured catastrophic loss in silence.

Being the person who breaks a generational pattern is lonely work. You may be criticized, ostracized, or gaslit. You may be called "too sensitive," "dramatic," or "disrespectful" for speaking aloud what others pretend not to see. You may even grieve people who are still alive.

And still—it's sacred work.

If you are that person, the interrupter, know this: you are not crazy. You are courageous. You are not disloyal for telling the truth. You are not cruel for refusing to stay silent. You are doing the work your ancestors could not do, and your healing is not just for you. It sends ripples through time—in both directions.

My Healing

Healing isn't linear, and it doesn't always feel triumphant. Sometimes it feels like exhaustion. Sometimes it feels like loneliness. Sometimes it feels like pressing your back against a locked door and wondering if it would be easier to stop knocking.

But I keep going. Because I know what happens if I don't.

If I heal, my children have a chance to heal. If I break the cycle, it stops with me. If I speak the truth, my sons won't inherit a legacy built on silence.

The first part of breaking that cycle began the moment I made the decision to divorce Allen. For years, I hid the truth that our marriage was broken. I hid it from friends, family, and even from myself. I was too ashamed to admit that I was facing another failed marriage.

It wasn't until I finally internalized a truth I should have been taught as a child—that leaving an abusive relationship is not shameful but an act of profound strength—that something in me shifted. I realized that staying silent wasn't protecting anyone. It was perpetuating the very harm I had sworn my children would never know.

With that, I realized what my boys were absorbing by simply watching Allen. They were growing up in a home where a man spoke to their mother with contempt, impatience, and dismissiveness—sometimes openly, sometimes in small, sharp ways that cut deeper than yelling ever could. They were learning, without anyone saying a word, that women's voices mattered less. That a woman's expertise could be mocked, her boundaries ignored, her emotions minimized. Even when Allen insisted he was progressive, even when he claimed the title of "feminist ally," his behavior at home taught them a completely different lesson.

I knew that if I stayed, they would carry those lessons with them. They would internalize the same misogyny I had spent a lifetime trying to fight. They would absorb a pattern of harm that had already lived through too many generations of my family. Leaving wasn't just about protecting myself; it was about protecting their future—who they would become, how they would treat others, and how they would learn to value the other people in their lives.

Healing has meant talking openly with my older boys about their experiences, their scars, and their memories. Part of it is acknowledging that my role as a cycle-breaker means I cannot pretend or minimize our pain. I cannot participate in the silence that harmed generations before me.

Financial abuse and generational scarcity shaped my nervous system in ways I'm still untangling. Even now, whenever a new expense arises—a bill, a repair, something for the house—my body reacts before my brain can catch up. Panic flares instantly. My first thought is always: *I have to fix this. I have to carry this. If I don't, everything will fall apart.*

David might casually mention wanting something new, and my whole system jolts into shock, as if I am suddenly responsible for preventing disaster. I assume it's mine to purchase, mine to manage, mine to absorb—because if I don't, the fallout will somehow land on me.

That belief was wired into me long before Allen, but he exploited it so relentlessly that it became instinct. Hyper-responsibility became my default setting—not because I craved control, but because I grew up believing that survival depended on absorbing the weight alone.

With time, healing has slowly begun to feel like peace.

I know I will never get the apologies I deserve. I will never receive validation from the people who harmed me. The people I most wanted to understand me never will.

But healing gives me something else: freedom from needing their permission.

I am the one who turned pain into purpose. I am the one who faced what everyone else ran from. I am the one who chose honesty over silence. I am the one who broke the pattern.

I am the legacy shift. And that is no small thing.

23

Unseen Radical Grief

We're taught that grief usually belongs to the death of a loved one—marked by funerals, sympathy cards, casseroles, and quiet nods of understanding. That kind of grief is socially acceptable, expected, and supported.

But what happens when the thing you need to grieve isn't a person, but a childhood?

What happens when the loss is safety, innocence, and basic emotional care?

That kind of grief has no rituals. No one brings a lasagna to acknowledge a mother who was physically present but emotionally absent. There is no eulogy for the childhood of the woman who performs through pain and smiles through fear.

Growing up, Tony and I didn't think much about how things were—we were just two Gen X kids doing what Gen X kids did, or so we believed. Even now, Tony will say, "That's just how it was back then." But as I've peeled back the layers, I know what we experienced wasn't just a generational quirk. It wasn't "just the '80s." It was abandonment.

By the time I was eight years old, and Tony was six, we were so-called "latchkey kids." Except we didn't have keys!

Most afternoons, we'd walk home from the school bus stop, slip in through the sliding door off the back patio, and take care of our homework and chores before watching TV or playing until our parents came home. Sometimes they were home early, other times not.

It usually worked out fine. But sometimes the sliding door was locked. And without keys, we had to get creative.

At the back of the house was a small basement window next to a metal panel with a hole that we called the "cat window." It was actually the dryer vent, but it's how our cat came and went.

When we were locked out, one of us would kick in the cat window, wiggle around the pipes, drop onto a wooden box, then crawl down and unlock the sliding door from the inside. The first time we did this, we told our mom—and got scolded for not putting the panel back. The next time, we replaced the panel and said nothing.

This didn't just happen a few times. We became experts. Even our friends remember us breaking into our house this way. We never told our mom again. It wasn't worth the yelling. We learned early that keeping the peace was often safer than telling the truth. Even at that age, we knew—don't upset her. Just survive.

Summers were even more extreme. We were home alone all day, every day, just the two of us, with no adult supervision. We made our own breakfast and lunch, watched TV, and kept ourselves entertained. We never complained. We knew the rules. If things weren't just right, our mother's anger would ignite—so we did whatever it took to keep her calm.

Yes, she made sure there was food in the fridge, and that we had a roof over our heads. But the day-to-day emotional labor of existing? That was ours to manage. Our mother was always somewhere else—physically present at times, but even then, emotionally vacant. We learned more about how the world worked from the television than we ever did from her. That wasn't always a good thing. Hollywood is not real life, and being raised by it meant I was exposed to adult themes and situations long before most parents would have considered it appropriate.

I also understand something now that I didn't back then: I didn't look like I needed help. I looked like the daughter my mother wanted the world to see—put together, high-achieving, and fine. I didn't look broken, so no one stepped in.

Growing up, hygiene only seemed to matter before church. In the parking lot before mass, our mom would inspect our faces and, if needed, lick her thumb and scrub us clean. I hated everything about it—her breath, the wet thumb, and the roughness of it all.

The rest of the time, Tony and I rarely bathed. It never seemed odd—our dad washed at the kitchen sink, and we often counted a dip in the backyard pool as good enough. When puberty hit and we became more aware of body odor, Tony started showering and I started using perfume.

No one ever pulled me aside to say otherwise, so I didn't change—not until college, when my boyfriend showered every day and I decided to try it. It stuck. I felt better, cleaner, more confident—less like I had to hide.

In grade school, I didn't wipe after using the bathroom. No one ever taught me. I just pulled up my underwear and went back to class. I remember lying to a doctor once during a school physical, saying there hadn't been any toilet paper in the bathroom earlier that day. There was—I just didn't use it. I don't know why. Maybe it was faster. But deep down, I also may have believed if my body smelled, Al would stay away.

As an adult, that realization wrecked me. I sobbed for that little girl. I wanted to scoop her up and reassure her that she was never the problem. That she was always worthy of love. I just didn't know how to love her yet.

As children, we instinctively know how to respond to physical pain. We cry out, clutch our bloody knee or elbow, and—if we're lucky—someone rushes in with a bandage, a kiss, and a soothing word.

But when the pain is invisible? When it stems not from a fall or a bump, but from the slow, steady erosion of our sense of self at the hands of someone who claims to love us?

Children aren't built to understand emotional manipulation. Truthfully, most adults aren't either. The damage is quieter, more insidious—and infinitely harder to name.

Narcissistic harm is stealthy. It seeps in over time—through gaslighting disguised as guidance, control masked as care, and a constant reshaping of reality to serve someone else's needs. You start to wonder if you're the problem. You learn to hide your pain, not because you're brave, but because no one seems to see it anyway.

And sometimes, what looks like success is just another response to trauma.

In my case, I became an overachiever. A perfectionist. I was (and still am) organized, efficient, and relentlessly high-performing. That's the cruel irony of narcissistic abuse—it can make you exceptional, but only because you were taught that your worth depended on it. And the world? It rewards us for it. It cheers us on without ever asking what it cost to become this capable.

For most of my life, I apologized for everything—my needs, my feelings, and my presence. I said "sorry" for taking up space, for speaking too loudly, for asking questions, for crying, and even for things that had nothing to do with me. It wasn't about guilt. It was about safety. When you grow up walking on eggshells, you learn quickly that assuming blame is often easier than risking someone else's anger. Apologizing became a reflex. A way to shrink myself into something softer, smaller, more tolerable.

Even now, I catch myself apologizing for things that don't require it—as if existing still requires permission.

Healing, for me, began with grieving my childhood. Not just what was taken, but what never existed in the first place.

I had to grieve the love I never received from my mother. The secure attachments I never knew. The safety I never felt. The hugs that were never safe.

I had to grieve the loss of my Italian family and my heritage—cut off from connection at a time I could have really used it.

I had to grieve my innocence that was stolen by a child molester. The normal teenage milestones I missed because I was too busy running. The early confidence that was crushed before it could grow.

Learning to love my little girl self has been one of the most transformative parts of loving my adult self. The more I reflect on what she endured—the violence, the abandonment, the silence—the more awe I feel for her bravery. She survived what so many couldn't. She held on long enough for me to grow up and come back for her. And now, she's safe inside of me. She is me.

And that grief didn't end in childhood. I also had to grieve parts of my adulthood—especially the years lost while I was married to Allen.

What makes this grief particularly sharp is knowing that I didn't just lose more pieces of myself in that relationship—I missed some of the most important moments in my sons' lives. And I didn't even see it clearly until much later.

I grieve the years I spent disconnected, trying to manage Allen's moods instead of delighting in the chaos and joy of motherhood. I grieve the silence I kept, the moments I couldn't protect them from, and the times I wasn't fully present—not because I didn't love them, but because I was trying to survive a storm I didn't yet have the words to name.

This kind of grief is messy. It comes layered with guilt, with shame, with a thousand internal questions like, why didn't I leave sooner? Why couldn't I see it?

But I know now: when you live under the influence of a narcissist, time distorts. Reality bends. You learn to question your instincts until you no longer recognize the sound of your own truth.

Understanding narcissism changed everything. Once I learned to name what I had lived through—emotional abuse, gaslighting, parental alienation—it allowed me to hold compassion for the woman I was back then. The woman who was doing the best she could with the tools she had.

Grief has come in waves: sadness, rage, regret, disbelief. It has required me to sit with uncomfortable truths, to let them rise up and move through me without numbing or dismissing them. As I worked on this book, my depression kept me from having the energy to complete my morning run.

Eventually, all of this processing of my grief led me to something else: acceptance.

Not the passive kind. Not resignation. But true, radical acceptance—of what was, of what never will be, and of who I am now because of it.

I know the grief process worked because I can talk about my past without editing out the details that make others uncomfortable. I can name the harm without softening it.

I can care for my mother now, in her fragile and incapacitated state—not because she deserves it, but because I've made peace with who she is. I refuse to become her. I will be the mother she never was.

I know the grief process has worked because my body feels different. I no longer brace at every raised voice or slam of a door. I can sit beside my children and be fully present—not dissociating and disappearing because of some echo of the past.

My healing also shows up in funny ways. On hard days, my dad used to show up with a pizza in hand—always with light sauce and pepperoni—as if it could fix anything. He showed up with pizzas on good days too. For my dad, pizza was the perfect choice for every mood and every occasion.

To this day, I cherish pizza. It's less about the meal and more about the ritual and the memory of feeling cared for. I love getting pizza to soothe me after a hard day. Sometimes David will pick one up to surprise me because he knows it makes me smile. I even default to the pizza emoji when I'm texting friends. It's my way of saying, "Have a slice and take it easy."

I know I'm healing because I no longer chase love. I don't shape-shift to be accepted by others. Although it's still a work in progress, I am learning to show up for others as me—fully, authentically, and without apology.

What I Know Now

Radical acceptance is the moment you stop arguing with reality and allow yourself to say, without pause: Yes, this happened. To me. In my childhood. In my marriage. To my children.

For a long time, I believed grief only applied to death—the loss of a person or a relationship. Now I understand grief also applies to the death of dreams, innocence, safety, and versions of ourselves that never had the chance to grow.

What I learned to mourn was the absence of what every child deserves: consistent care, emotional safety, comfort, and love. I grieved a mother who was physically present but emotionally unreachable. I grieved never being taught how to care for my body, how to feel safe in it, or how to trust others with it. I grieved the small but sacred rituals of childhood—bedtime stories, someone brushing my hair and tucking me into bed, a gentle voice saying, "You're okay. I've got you."

This kind of grief is radical because it dares to acknowledge what was never offered. It asks us to mourn the intangible: the accomplishment that wasn't celebrated, the hug that never came, the comfort that was always just out of reach. For survivors of childhood trauma, grief is often about the internal parts of ourselves we were forced to abandon in order to survive.

Grief like this is messy, nonlinear, and often tangled with guilt and shame. We question whether we're "allowed" to grieve what we never had. We compare our suffering to others. We minimize our pain because there was a roof over our heads and food in the fridge.

But the grief of being unseen, unheard, or unloved is real. And it deserves recognition.

My Healing

As first, I had to acknowledge that I had something to grieve. I began with my childhood and grieved the love, care, and kindness I didn't receive. I grieved not feeling safe. I grieved not getting to be a carefree child.

I grieved the ordinary teenage experiences I missed—late nights out, parties at the lake, silly moments in the woods with friends. In early adulthood, I grieved the freedom to explore, to be carefree, and to make mistakes without them being weaponized against me.

In my marriage, I grieved the partner I thought I had but never did. I grieved the idea of a "true" partnership that never actually existed. I grieved the realization that what I thought was love was a lie—that what I thought was family was, in fact, a web of manipulation, gaslighting, and parasitic behavior. I had to mourn the fact that there are people who don't love, but control. Who don't connect, but consume.

I also had to face the most devastating grief of all: my children did not have the best version of me. I grieved the ways I wasn't fully present. The times I was managing Allen's moods instead of savoring their childhood. I could not protect them, and have had to sit with the reality that each of them experienced their own form of abuse—and that I was in the house where it happened. That truth doesn't mean I didn't love them. It means I was surviving something I didn't yet have language for.

Over time, grief—held with compassion—has become one of my greatest tools for healing. I now see my grief not as weakness or indulgence, but as evidence of my strength. I'm no longer hiding the truth of what I lived through. I'm no longer apologizing for what it cost me to survive.

Healing isn't about erasing the grief. It's about allowing it to exist without shame, without editing, and without apology. It's giving yourself permission to say: I missed something essential, and I get to mourn that.

Grief has given me access to a deeper kind of love—for my boys, for David, and for myself. It has allowed me to sit with my sons and talk openly about their experiences with Allen, modeling that it's okay to name what happened and to feel however they feel about it.

The little girl inside me—the one who didn't bathe, who thought smelling bad might keep her safer, who broke into her own house because no one gave her a key—finally knows she was never the problem. She was always worthy. And now, she is safe.

Radical grief is not clean. It's messy and nonlinear. But when held with tenderness, it becomes a doorway. A way to move from survival into something fuller, softer, and more free.

24

The Anatomy of Abandonment

People use a lot of words to describe narcissistic abuse—toxic, manipulative, controlling, crazy-making. But those words barely scratch the surface. If you've lived it, you know: narcissistic abuse isn't just "difficult." It's a full-body, soul-level erosion. It erodes your trust and your identity and quite literally rewires the brain. You stop knowing what's real. You stop knowing yourself.

For years, I had mostly associated narcissism with the grandiose kind—the loud, boastful, entitled types who dominate every room they enter. Those adjectives never quite fit my experience.

It wasn't until I learned about quieter, more covert forms of narcissism that my past finally began to come into focus. Suddenly, memories that had always felt foggy and confusing snapped into place with unsettling clarity. The subtle digs, the manipulations disguised as concern, the way I had been made to feel too emotional, too demanding, too much—these weren't just isolated moments. They were patterns. And they had shaped me.

For me, understanding the vocabulary and the patterns helped me name what I had spent years trying to survive without understanding. Because when you're in it—when you're living through it—it's easy to excuse the occasional cruelty, the inconsistent affection, and the mind games. You tell yourself it was a bad day. A moment of stress.

But narcissistic abuse doesn't show up once and leave. It becomes the air you breathe, so constant that you stop noticing the way it's poisoning you.

I had the language and understanding of narcissism to recognize Allen as a narcissist. But what I hadn't realized—what truly floored me—was just how many narcissists had been woven into my life. I simply didn't know.

Looking back, I realized that my mother, Al, and Allen all followed the same patterns. They had no real empathy. Everything had to be about them. They needed constant praise, yet couldn't tolerate even gentle feedback. They demanded control, twisted facts, crossed boundaries, and punished me for having needs. They blamed me for their anger, for their lies, and for their failures. They couldn't stand being questioned.

At the time, I didn't know any of that. I just knew I always felt off around them—confused, anxious, ashamed, and somehow always to blame. I thought I was the problem. That's the most dangerous part of narcissistic abuse: it convinces you that you're broken, and they're just "misunderstood."

And so, whether or not the people in my life ever receive a formal diagnosis stopped mattering to me. In every relationship that revolved around a narcissist, the rules were the same: they got to shine, and I existed only to reflect their light. If I stopped reflecting—if I asserted myself, set a boundary, or asked for what I needed—I was punished. Sometimes with silence. Sometimes with shame. Sometimes with rage.

Learning the language of trauma gave me something I'd never had: clarity. Narcissistic abuse doesn't exist in isolation—it thrives in systems, especially families, where one person dominates and everyone else adapts to survive. In those systems, we take on roles. The narcissist demands the spotlight, and others—enabler, scapegoat, golden child, lost child, truth-teller, caretaker, mascot—play their parts to keep it there. Even the flying monkeys have a role, doing the narcissist's bidding, knowingly or not.

In small families, roles can overlap or shift depending on the narcissist's needs.

In my childhood, both my mother and Al displayed narcissistic traits. But it was my mother's refusal to protect me that made me the scapegoat—I carried the blame, shame, and tension. In my marriage to Allen, the roles shifted: I became the enabler. Joe was the golden child. My older boys, the scapegoats.

And today, Joe is the flying monkey, bringing back to Allen whatever small details he can use to distort reality and further try to shame me.

None of this was conscious, of course. It just . . . happens. That's how these systems work. You learn to read the room, anticipate the narcissist's needs, and fill the void left to try to manage the emotions.

This isn't love. It's a trauma bond.

And I can tell you from experience—trauma bonds are brutal. They convince you that if you could just be better—quieter, prettier, more patient, more grateful—the pain might stop. But it never does.

Because when the narcissist harms you, they don't apologize. They do everything they can to pull you back in with false promises, selective kindness, or guilt-laced affection. The trauma bond rewires your reality until you believe you're the problem.

But the truth is: the abuse is not about you. It never was. And healing from this kind of harm requires a radical, unwavering acceptance of three things:

This was real.

This was wrong.

And this was not your fault.

It means reclaiming your voice after years of being silenced. Setting boundaries after a lifetime of being told you don't deserve any. It means rebuilding your sense of self from the rubble they left behind.

Let me be clear: narcissistic abuse is abuse. When it happens in childhood, it's emotional and psychological child abuse. In adult relationships, it is domestic violence.

My mother trained me to ignore my instincts and to stay quiet at all costs as she presented our family to the world as flawless. No one saw the fear, the silence, the emotional terror behind closed doors—because my mother would never allow that. Image was everything. She wore that mask so well that even one of my older cousins, when I started researching this book, said, "I remember your mom being a really good mom."

That's how convincing the illusion was.

The smear campaigns were also there, long before I had the words to name them.

I remembered how Al and my mother vilified Al's ex-wife, painting her as greedy and unstable. I believed them, even though a lot of the stories didn't make sense. I was a child and these were adults. That early training—learning to internalize distorted narratives—set the stage for how easily I would believe Allen's lies, too.

Smear campaigns were one of my mother's favorite tactics to try to control me, too. When I was in my twenties, I finally told Tony everything that had happened to me as a child. I hoped—desperately—that disclosure would ensure he took steps to protect his children from being alone with Al. To their credit, he and his wife Amanda immediately set that boundary.

Predictably, all hell broke loose. As soon as our mother learned about this new rule, she lashed out. She harassed me, belittled me, and accused me of stirring up drama. I was the villain, the troublemaker, and the one ruining everything.

Later, Amanda told me my mother had turned her rage on them too—insisting that I was a liar, a whore, and a manipulative force trying to divide the family.

By that time, I'd come to accept the full-scale character assassinations. For my entire life, she did everything she could to make it seem like I was the problem.

When I used to think of abandonment, I pictured a stray animal left on the side of the road, or a newborn dropped off at a fire station by a desperate young mother. I never thought to use that word to describe myself.

Now I see it. As a child, I was abandoned. My mother leaving me alone to watch her shopping bags as a toddler was just the beginning. Every time I thought there might be someone to turn to, someone who could help, I was reminded: "No one is coming to save you, Tina."

I felt let down by everyone—my parents, the school, the judge, the lawyers, the child welfare system. No one acknowledged the psychological torment I was enduring. They all left me in an abusive home with no protection.

One of the hardest parts of my past to unravel was why my father did nothing to help after I finally found the courage to tell him what happened. He said he'd take care of me. Then after his conversation with my mother and Al, he told me to let it go.

What had happened in that house to change his mind?

For years, I believed my father had chosen to protect himself over protecting me. I came up with countless theories to explain his silence. Maybe he still loved my mother and would do anything she asked. Maybe he was involved in something shady—some lingering, mafioso-type entanglement—and she had threatened to go to the police. I spun elaborate stories to make sense of the absence. But underneath all of them lived the same painful truth: I felt abandoned.

I asked my dad for clarity on his actions—or rather, his inaction—more times than I can count. He never gave me an answer, at least not one that made sense.

This only made things more confusing. I got to know my father as one of the most loving and empathetic people in the world. He didn't exhibit any of the traits I had come to recognize in narcissistic personalities. I would ask him, again and again, why he didn't protect me. He never gave me an answer. That silence was its own kind of abandonment.

Then, after he died, I found a book tucked away in his house—one of those keepsake journals meant to be filled out by a parent and child. I had given it to him years earlier, and had already filled out with my responses, hoping he might add his own over time.

He never did. My dad was never much of a writer, so I hadn't expected much. And sure enough, most of the pages were blank—empty spaces that mirrored so many of the unanswered questions I had carried with me since childhood.

But one response stood out. It was the page where I asked him why he didn't help me when I was a kid. His answer was short. Simple. "Your mother," he wrote.

It was a stunning admission, and one I desperately wished I could ask him about. He had never blamed my mother before—not out loud, not to me. What had shifted in him? What had caused him to write her name now, in this one quiet corner of a mostly blank book?

And then, all at once, something inside me cracked open.

What if my father's marriage to my mother was filled with the same kind of gaslighting and manipulation that had defined my marriage to Allen? What if he, too, had been worn down by confusion and quiet control? What if he had been slowly hollowed out, losing pieces of himself one small compromise at a time?

I had never considered that possibility before. Now, I feel it with conviction.

My mother's ability to manipulate people knew no bounds, clearly. For years, I believed my aunts and uncles knew what was happening and chose to side with my mom and Al. My mother told me they didn't want to get involved. She told me they wanted me to forgive and forget, just like she did. She also insisted that if my grandparents ever found out, they would die from the stress.

I still struggle to comprehend how much hate it must have taken for her not only to abandon me herself, but to convince me that everyone else had too. It hurts. Why would a mother do this to a child? What was going on for her that she wanted me to feel pain? Why didn't she want to protect me?

Only recently did I learn the truth: no one in my family knew. When my aunts finally heard my story, they were stunned. They hadn't ignored me; they had simply never been told. And yet, even then, they didn't quite know how to respond. A silence about the truth settled between us, and it stayed.

Throughout my teen years, I wrestled with the weight of abandonment—sometimes rooted in real events, other times the result of the logic of a child. The courts failed me. The institutions failed me. The people who should have stepped in didn't. Children & Youth abandoned me when they failed to check in. I had also felt abandoned by David when he didn't agree to run away with me after I told him I was pregnant.

The message was clear: I was on my own. The only person I could count on was me.

My mother isolated me and taught me to be silent, and Al used that silence to teach me that my body wasn't mine. By the time Allen showed up, all the pieces were in place.

What I Know Now

For most of my life, I didn't believe I had been abandoned. That word felt too dramatic, too extreme—reserved for children left on doorsteps or characters in tragic movies. I didn't see myself that way. I told myself, *"I wasn't abandoned. I had parents. I had a home."*

Now I know better.

Abandonment isn't always physical. Sometimes, it looks like being left alone in a locked house as a child. Sometimes, it's not being believed when you tell the truth. Sometimes, it's being surrounded by adults who should have protected you—but didn't.

Sometimes, abandonment is silence.

Even as a therapist, it took me decades to apply the words I used for clients to my own life. I could define narcissistic abuse, domestic violence, trauma bonds, gaslighting, and parental alienation with clinical precision. But naming it in my own story? That was different.

When it's your mother, her boyfriend, and your husband—the lines blur. The harm becomes normalized. You stop seeing violations as violations. You stop valuing your instincts. You stop noticing that what you're calling "love" is actually control.

When I finally began to put the pieces together—through my body sensations, through my reactions in my marriage, and through the stories I had been conditioned to tell about myself—everything shifted.

I finally realized that the deep shame I carried didn't originate with me. It was planted and cultivated. And that shame had one goal: to keep me quiet.

Because that's the thing about narcissistic systems—whether in families or relationships—they're built on silence. On distortion. On making sure the person being harmed doesn't trust their own perception.

When I finally had the language to name what I had endured—narcissistic abuse—it felt like stepping into the light after years underground. Suddenly, so much made sense. The confusion, the guilt, the constant second-guessing. None of it was mine to carry.

I was never too emotional. I was never too sensitive.

I was never the problem.

The truth is, I was raised in a system where people demanded control and called it love. Where affection was withheld to punish. Where reality was rewritten to maintain someone else's power. I was trained to abandon myself long before I ever learned to speak up for myself.

And when I finally did try to speak up? I was erased again. Labeled dramatic and unstable. A whore. A liar. An evil little girl. The smear campaigns were designed to make sure I never found my footing.

Now I know what's true:

Narcissistic abuse is abuse.

Emotional neglect is abandonment.

Parental alienation is child abuse.

Sexual coercion—even in marriage—is rape.

Naming these truths isn't disrespect. It isn't betrayal. It isn't revenge. It is breaking the chain.

My Healing

Healing from narcissistic abuse and lifelong abandonment has been painstaking. It has required me to see clearly for the first time. To sit with truths that once would have shattered me. It has involved grieving the family I needed but never had, the safety I deserved but never received, and the versions of myself I had to silence in order to survive.

Healing has meant stepping out of roles I never chose but was forced into—scapegoat, enabler, truth-teller, emotional caretaker. It has meant holding my ground even when others called me difficult or dramatic simply for refusing to carry their shame any longer.

But most of all, healing has meant choosing myself. Over and over again.

I used to wonder whether I'd ever stop feeling like that little girl—left behind, left out, left to figure out the world on her own. Now I know that the antidote to abandonment isn't reunion or justice. It's reclamation.

I have reclaimed my story. My voice. My boundaries. My right to be believed. My sense of safety, love, and belonging.

Healing isn't about pretending it didn't happen. Healing is about finally telling the truth.

25

Triggers, Tremors, and Truth

I had run from the chaos of my childhood straight into an early marriage—and then straight into the arms of a monster.

Allen saw everything: my self-doubt, my shame, my longing to be loved. He didn't have to break me. I was already fractured. All he had to do was offer the illusion of safety and then weaponize my hunger for it.

What I now understand is that Allen didn't stumble into control—he studied me. He mapped the cracks in my life and inserted himself with precision. He knew about the college fling my first husband had early in our relationship—it was something we kept in the open to make sure it never happened again. He also knew how alone I felt during my husband's military deployments.

So, when Allen became the one to "break the news" of another supposed affair—timed perfectly while my husband was deployed—he cast himself as the rescuer. The trustworthy one. The man who would never abandon me. But Allen's version of love was never about partnership.

There's a word I've since learned that perfectly describes the kind of narcissist Allen is: parasitic.

Parasites don't just coexist—they feed. On your time, your energy, your reputation, your labor, your money. And by the time you realize what's happening, the damage is done. You're depleted. Disoriented. Wondering if you were ever whole to begin with.

That's what Allen did to me. He latched onto my vision, my work, and my credibility. He embedded himself so deeply into the world I built that he made himself seem indispensable. But it was all extraction. I was the one paying the bills, buying the groceries, and covering the cost of family outings. Every meal, every gift, every act of generosity—it came from me. And yet, Allen managed to make it all look like it came from him.

That was Al, too. On paper, it looked like he was in a relationship with my mother. But in reality, he was a shadow—attached, dependent, and demanding. He lived in my mother's house, rent-free, and worked at the shop only in the narrow ways he wanted to, always positioning himself as irreplaceable, while creating chaos behind the scenes.

He also spent recklessly, regardless of whether there was money. My mother kept the business afloat; Al rode its wave. And in the end, when she was incapacitated, he took it. He believed it was his all along—just like Allen believed my business was his, taking it all in our divorce and then unceremoniously shuttering it without a care for the employees and clients left behind.

This is the parasitic pattern of narcissists. They attach themselves to strong, competent, compassionate people—not to build something together, but to feed off them. And when they've taken all they can, they move on. Often without consequence.

Allen's financial abuse began long before I named it. I never got paid back for the engagement ring, of course. I funded the trip to Disney, our weddings, and the cross-country move. The groceries were paid for from my account, as were 100 percent of the household expenses. And as I took on more and more jobs to make ends meet, Allen barely even looked for employment.

He knew I would keep things afloat—because I always had. Long before we met, I had already mastered the art of surviving financial instability. As a teenager with little support from either parent, I worked constantly. It wasn't just a way out of the house—it was survival. I worked to cover the gaps in my tuition, to keep gas in my tank, to afford lunch, and car insurance. I even paid my own way into school band and other extracurriculars—not because I had the time, but because they gave me a fleeting sense of normalcy.

While other kids were just being kids, I was budgeting, hustling, and making sure the pieces held together.

My therapist at the time provided her observation that I did "far more than any eighteen-year-old should have to do." She was right. I was exhausted. I had support from a few trusted adults—my boyfriend's family, a school counselor, my friends at work—but none of them could replace the unconditional love and safety I needed from my own parents.

So, by the time I married Allen, I was already used to carrying the load. Working hard. Figuring things out. Making ends meet. I didn't immediately see that he was manipulating me into yet another version of the same dynamic—one where I gave everything, and he provided nothing in return.

There was something else too. It took me years to understand that what happened in my marriage wasn't "marital obligation" or "keeping the peace." It was sexual abuse—so normalized in my mind that I didn't name it until recently.

Here's how it played out: in our marriage, I repeatedly told Allen over and over again that I didn't want to be touched, didn't want to have sex, and didn't feel safe in my body. But it didn't matter. He manipulated, pressured, and punished until I gave in. If I didn't comply, he became irritable, hostile, or withdrawn. When I finally gave in, I left my body entirely—dissociating, bracing, going still—because it was the only way to endure something I never consented to.

He often threatened to cheat on me if I didn't "meet his needs," as if infidelity were a reasonable consequence for my boundaries. He kept a running tally of the days, weeks, or months since we'd last had sex, reciting the numbers with growing intensity, as if my body were a bill he was owed. In the house, my body was treated like open territory: constant pinching, grabbing, poking, and groping—always justified by the same line: "You're my wife. I should be able to touch you whenever I want."

It didn't register as abuse at the time because it mirrored what I had already survived. Al had done the same things when I was a child—taking what he wanted, insisting my body existed for his use, convincing me that compliance kept everyone safe. That conditioning ran so deep that Allen's behavior felt familiar. Expected. A terrible kind of "normal." I internalized the belief that if I wanted harmony, if I wanted to prevent anger or avoid punishment, then this was simply part of my duties.

It took even longer to admit the deeper truth: Allen was never a parent. He never had the capacity. He lacked emotional intelligence, parenting skills, and empathy. He had no insight, no depth. And many of the stories he told me about his childhood—the pain, the abandonment, the trauma—were told to me in elaborate, exaggerated ways meant to gain my sympathy and lower my defenses.

He was the fraud. Not me.

My older boys—Nicholas and Christopher—suffered under his control in ways that still leave me sick with grief. They were ignored, demeaned, and emotionally manipulated—all while I believed I was protecting them. I wasn't. I was surviving. And in that survival, I missed so much.

Of course, I blamed myself. I told myself over and over that I hadn't been the mother they deserved. Healing has meant looking that shame directly in the face—and talking with my boys, honestly and openly, about what happened. I've taken responsibility for what is mine. I've asked hard questions. I've listened. And in doing so, we've built a bond stronger than it's ever been.

Even their father—my first husband—saw it. He had once considered Allen a friend, and watching him harm our boys left him devastated. He, too, carried regret for not seeing it sooner.

Unfortunately, that same opportunity for healing hasn't been possible with Joe. His situation is more fragile. He is Allen's biological son—and their connection is deeply enmeshed. The manipulation runs deep, and the damage is still unfolding.

For years, I fought Allen at every turn. I documented every custody violation and lie. I kept meticulous records, believing that someday—when it got bad enough—I'd take it all back to court. I truly believed that with enough evidence, justice would catch up to him. That someone would see what was happening and intervene.

Healing changed that.

I've come to understand that our legal system is just another broken institution. It's no different from all the other systems that fail survivors. Family court isn't built to hold narcissistic abusers accountable—not in any real or consistent way. Not when the abuse is emotional, psychological, and invisible to everyone but the victim.

I know this because I lived through it. If I am an adult still struggling to recognize the kind of abuse I endured, how does a child going through it ever stand a chance?

And with Joe, it's so subtle and insidious that I know—deep in my bones—that no courtroom is going to fix it. There will be no intervention and no dramatic unveiling of truth. I had to stop exhausting myself trying to prove what Allen had done. Instead, I've chosen to pour my energy where it matters most: into my relationship with Joe.

I worry deeply about Joe's future. The space between us has grown so wide that sometimes we barely speak. I drive him places. I wait in the car. I help him out when needed. But the silence is suffocating. The distance is deliberate.

Allen used every weapon in his arsenal to sever the bond between me and my son. And the heartbreaking truth? It's working. He's reshaped Joe into an extension of himself.

This is textbook parental alienation: little by little, Allen undermined my role as a parent and cast himself as the fun one. The "understanding" one. And eventually, Joe started repeating his lines.

I see it all the time now—in the words he uses, the way he reacts, and the stories he tells. The evidence is everywhere, disguised as normal teenage behavior, but laced with a script I know too well.

How I know this is happening comes in the form of daily reminders.

Take the time Joe was in a car accident while traveling for a sports tournament. No one called me. I only found out because I reached out, panicked, like any mother would. I wasn't even listed as an emergency contact. And when I tried to advocate for him—tried to be his mother—he texted me, accusing me of "making a scene" and "threatening" the league director. He told me to stay out of his business.

That's what Allen has taught him: my care is a threat, my presence a disruption.

Here's another example. A few months after Joe began living with Allen full time, I invited him to Christopher's college graduation party. He responded that he'd "need to check his calendar." When someone gently suggested that his brother's graduation might be something to prioritize, Joe's rage exploded. It was instant and intense— frightening in just the same ways that Allen's rage appeared the day I left him.

Joe screamed at David, calling him a "piece of shit" over and over. Then he turned on both of us, hurling accusations with venom that felt too rehearsed to be his own: we were liars, thieves, and horrible people.

It was like watching a familiar storm roll in—one I had spent years trying to survive.

Joe tore everything off the walls of his room, flung his clothes and belongings from the closet onto the bed, packed a single box, and stormed out. The chaos of that day felt almost cinematic: a scene pulled straight from Allen's playbook. And I stood there, heart pounding, watching a child I loved more than life itself become a mirror of the man I had spent so long protecting him from.

Then came the triangulation.

Joe reached out to Nicholas, pulling his older brother into the drama. Suddenly, I was getting texts—"What's going on, Mama?"—as if Joe were the victim and David the aggressor. It was the same tactic Allen always used: twist the story, recruit allies, manufacture chaos.

Joe didn't return until after Christmas, while David and I were out of town. He let himself into the house, went straight to the tree, and opened every single gift—alone. Then he sent me a photo: wrapping paper strewn across the floor, a smug look on his face. When I asked him why he did it, there was no apology. Just a flat response: "You weren't there."

Joe is beginning to love the way Allen does—with detachment, conditions, and control. He's learned that love is earned through loyalty. That silence is power. That anyone outside the borders of Allen's carefully curated world is a threat—even his own mother.

Some days, I let myself hope. Maybe when Joe goes off to college, he'll meet people who challenge the narrative. Maybe he'll begin to question the foundation he's been handed. See the contradictions. Feel the manipulation. Remember who David and I are—and how fiercely, unconditionally, we have always loved him.

But I also carry another truth. A harder one. I fear that Allen has shaped Joe in his own image—and that my son may continue down a path of entitlement, manipulation, and emotional detachment. That the child I raised, the boy I love so completely, won't be lost to death, but to Allen's narcissism.

This is what so many people—especially the court system—fail to understand.

Parental alienation isn't a theory. It is a devastating psychological warfare tactic, often deployed by narcissistic parents to punish, control, and destroy. They use it to exert power, maintain superiority, and retaliate against their former partner—especially after a separation threatens their fragile self-image. The children become tools, and in that process, learn to distrust the parent trying to protect them.

The worst part? It works.

It teaches a child to weaponize their pain and redefine loyalty. It flips love into suspicion and turns the protective parent into the enemy. Slowly, the child is conditioned, and by the time you realize what's happening, you're already cast as the villain in a story you didn't write.

Allen didn't just alienate Joe. He taught him to hate. To reject me as his mother. And to erase our home and to believe that I was the one manipulating him all along.

It's not easy to live in a liminal space between hope and heartbreak. And it's impossible to parent a child you can no longer reach. This is what it means to mother through trauma. I don't know how this particular story ends. I don't know what lies ahead for Joe as he graduates high school and steps into the world as his own person. For now, Allen has gotten what he wanted, and Joe lives with him full time. I fear that if Joe ever decides to assert himself and question the version of the world he's been fed, it won't end well.

I do know this: I will never stop believing in the boy I raised. I will never stop loving him. I will never stop holding space for his return.

And if he does come back, I'll be here. Always. Loving him with every fiber of my being. Without conditions or expectations. Just love.

What I Know Now

For as long as I can remember, the narcissists in my life took what they wanted without asking.

Al stole my bodily autonomy before I even understood what autonomy was. My mother violated me in her own way by insisting I tolerate it—minimizing, dismissing, and outright denying the truth because my "fuss" was more inconvenient to her than acknowledging the harm being done to her daughter.

Later, in my marriage to Allen, my body was treated like community property instead of my own. I was pulled into unwanted kisses, grabbed without warning, and touched because he felt like it. My butt was pinched every time I bent over to pick something up in my own home. I was guilted into intimacy, reminded it was my "job," told how long it had been, accused of being cold or unlovable if I didn't comply.

The message, over and over, was this: Your body is not yours. Your needs are not yours. Your boundaries do not matter.

Now I'm fully learning and understanding consent, and how mine was never given in these situations.

Now the biggest challenge for me is learning how to be a mother to Joe.

For years, I believed I understood parental alienation. I could define it clinically, cite the research, and explain the mechanisms behind it. But living through it? That's different. That's the kind of knowledge that doesn't stay in the mind—it settles in the bones. It presses on your chest at night. It hums through the hollow places in your body that grief carves out. It weeps through your ribcage when no one is watching.

Losing Joe in this slow, silent, strategic way has been the most agonizing grief of my life. And obviously I've known grief intimately.

Allen didn't need to win custody through the court system; he won it through influence and manipulation. He planted doubts, twisted narratives, and positioned himself as the parent Joe needed to protect. Over time, a familiar pattern emerged—one I recognized from my own childhood. The loving parent got cast as the problem, while the parent causing the harm became the one the child defended.

This is how narcissistic abuse repeats itself across generations: it teaches children to question the parent who sets boundaries. It encourages them to see compassion as weakness. It rewards loyalty to the abuser and punishes any closeness with the healthier parent.

Even with my training and experience, I wasn't able to stop it. That's the part that's been hardest to accept. There are no emergency hearings for the day your child calls you an "ass" for the first time. Family court is not designed to recognize or intervene in the kind of psychological manipulation Allen uses. There are no legal remedies for subtle emotional erosion, and no judge can see what actually happens behind closed doors.

I can't control Allen, the courts, or even Joe's current perceptions—but I can control my consistency. And I will be consistent in one thing above all else: Joe will never have to doubt my love for him. I drive him to where he needs to go, make sure his basic needs are met, and stay available even when he pulls away. I don't do this because he acknowledges it—I do it because I'm his mother.

My commitment to radical acceptance means that I must understand that Joe's healing won't happen on my timeline. I've had to accept that he may not fully understand what's happening until he has distance from Allen.

Recently, I've begun to see small signs that he is questioning things. That gives me hope.

My Healing

Healing has meant letting go of the idea that I can protect everyone I love from harm. I couldn't fully protect my older boys from Allen, and I can't protect Joe from him now. What I can do is protect myself, speak the truth about what happened, and refuse to let shame keep me silent.

My healing has depended on being honest with myself about the roles I played—both the ones I chose and the ones I didn't. I've had to acknowledge that my survival mode in my marriage with Allen made it hard for me to see what was happening to my children at the time. I've had to face that reality with my older boys, have difficult conversations, and do the work of repairing our relationships.

With Joe, that process isn't possible yet. His relationship with Allen is still too enmeshed, and the influence Allen has over him is too strong. I've learned that pushing won't help. This is what healing looks like for me now: staying grounded in reality, staying connected to the truth, and holding space for my son to come back when he is ready.

26

The Body Remembers

Understanding narcissism and narcissistic abuse—how it operates in both families and relationships—has been one of the most eye-opening parts of my journey. That knowledge has helped me reframe my past and reclaim my present. But knowledge alone isn't enough. Healing comes through integration—taking what I've learned and actively applying it to my life.

I've had to ask hard questions: How does this apply to me? Where does this pattern show up in my behavior? What can I do differently now that I know better? The more I integrate, the more I heal. It's not enough to know something intellectually; I have to feel it, sit with it, and use it to shift the way I show up in the world.

So much of who I've been as an adult—how I've loved, how I've reacted, how I've coped—can be traced directly back to childhood. But now, I'm learning to recognize those roots without being strangled by them. I'm learning to choose differently. And in that choosing, I am slowly but surely changing the course of my life.

I've lived most of my life in a state of constant alert. My shoulders are tight. My jaw is clenched. My breath stays shallow, ready for whatever comes next. I am always scanning, always assessing—listening for the shift in tone, the warning in a sigh, the silence before the storm. At night, the faintest sound wakes me. During the day, I flinch at every unexpected noise. It's like there's a threat I can't quite see but can always feel.

I used to think I was high-strung. Now I know the word for it: hypervigilance.

Therapists say it's a form of survival. You see it when a deer freezes in place, its ears twitching in every direction to track the danger. That's the posture I learned in childhood.

In our home, unpredictability was a constant. The rage had no schedule. I learned to read the subtle signs: a narrowing of the eyes, a shift in breathing, the pitch of a footstep in the hallway. Anticipating the explosion felt like the only way to stay safe.

Even now, I notice things most people miss. The flicker of irritation behind someone's smile. The tightening of a jaw. The way a hand moves just slightly too fast. My nervous system still reads those things like a language—an early warning system. When I sense anger or volatility, my brain lights up in sirens: Danger, Will Robinson. Danger!

For most of my life, I didn't know what to call this. I thought I was just overly sensitive, someone who couldn't take a joke or needed too much quiet. I didn't realize my body was carrying the residue of decades of betrayal and chaos. I thought I was just "on edge" or "too rigid." I didn't know I was wired for war.

What I've learned—what so many survivors learn—is that trauma doesn't end when the abuse ends. It lives on, coded into the body. The mind may rationalize, minimize, forget—but the nervous system remembers everything. The body keeps score.

As a child, I remember my knees hurt a lot. The pain was sharp and unrelenting. "Hush up. It's just growing pains," my mom would tell me, brushing it off as the price of getting taller. But it was more than that. I noticed it more on rainy days, as if my body could predict the weather before the skies changed.

A few weeks after I moved into my college dorm, away from the chaos, the pain vanished. My knees no longer cried out. I guess my mom was right all along, I thought.

Now I know better. The body knows. And triggers never ask permission. They show up uninvited and break down the door.

Yes, I've done the work. I've gone to therapy. I've named the abuse. I've mapped the cycles. I've reparented myself. I've broken generational patterns.

And still—when a trigger from my past surfaces—my body reacts. Suddenly I'm ten years old again. I'm frozen. My hands shake. My stomach flips. My heart races.

Sometimes it happens through sight. I'll see an old man in a plain white T-shirt, trucker cap, wire-frame bifocals, and jeans, and I don't register a stranger—I see Al. My entire body tenses before my mind even catches up. If I see someone with beady eyes, a thick beard, bushy eyebrows, and a heavy frame, I think of Allen. The resemblance doesn't need to be exact. My body doesn't need a perfect match. It reacts to suggestion, to familiarity, to threat.

It isn't always strangers either. Sometimes I look down at my own hands, and I see her. My mother. The woman who didn't protect me. The woman who, in so many ways, handed me over to harm.

The crunch of gravel in the driveway still makes me brace. As a child, that sound meant my mother was pulling into the driveway, and I had only seconds to prepare for whatever mood walked through the door.

I listen and notice everything. I hear the shift of weight on a carpeted floor. The creak of a drawer. The tension in the tone of a voicemail.

David is loud by nature. He walks hard and slams cabinet doors. I joke that he's a bull in a china shop. He laughs, because it's true—and I love him for it. But my body doesn't always get the joke. When I hear him, my body braces itself. Just for a split second. Just as quickly, I remember: It's him. It's okay. And the butterflies settle.

But not all moments resolve that easily. If I hear David's voice rising on a phone call—even if it's about something innocuous like a billing mistake—my body tenses. I know he isn't angry with me, but my body still perceives the threat: raised voices mean something bad is coming.

Even something as small as him calling my name from downstairs can flood me with fear. My first thought isn't "he needs help." It's that "I'm in trouble. I've done something wrong. I'm about to be punished." My brain doesn't wait for tone. It reacts to memory.

And then there's smells. Marlboro Reds are my undoing. That brand, specifically. Cheap coffee, too—the kind that comes in the red plastic Folgers can.

When I was pregnant with Christopher, I began to regularly smell smoke that didn't exist. No one else could smell a thing. Around the same time, I also began experiencing migraines. One of them landed me in the emergency room, and since I was pregnant, I was wheeled straight to labor and delivery to be monitored.

What started happening after that became strangely consistent: I'd smell smoke—it would come and go for days. And it always ended in a crushing headache. Over time, I began to connect the dots. The phantom smoke was my warning sign. The debilitating pain always followed.

In one scary episode when the boys were young, my migraine mimicked a stroke. I was home alone and we were moving through our usual nighttime routine when I suddenly couldn't speak. The words were there but blocked—stuck under pressure. It only lasted a minute or two, but it scared me. I called a friend who lived down the street, and within minutes she and her husband were at my door. She took me to the hospital while he stayed with the kids.

Once my speech returned, it was replaced by a blinding headache. In the emergency room, after a battery of tests, including a spinal tap, the diagnosis was simple: migraine.

I managed the pain as best I could while still in Reno. When I moved back to Pennsylvania, I found a neurologist who worked with me for months as I documented my symptoms. Eventually she gave a name to what I was experiencing: olfactory aura. In short: under stress, my nervous system makes me smell things that aren't there.

The migraines were impossible to prevent, even with medication, but at least I knew what it was. The pattern was clear: a smoke smell would linger for days or a week, and once the migraine hit, it disappeared.

Over time, and as I learned more about narcissistic abuse, a possibility began to emerge, one I hadn't considered before: maybe my body wasn't just reacting to physical strain and stress. Maybe it was remembering.

Almost every waking moment, Al had a cigarette in one hand and a cup of coffee in the other. It was his default posture—like a signature. Sometimes he let the cigarette dangle from the corner of his mouth, the ash growing long as he ignored it, never once lifting a hand to tap it. Other times, he smoked with slow, deliberate intention—inhale, exhale, pause. And then there were the times he puffed so fast and hard you could almost see the cigarette disappear.

He smoked constantly—at least a pack a day, sometimes two. Ashtrays were everywhere: on every table, at work, in the trailer, and at every house he stayed in—including ours. It didn't matter where we were, the air around Al was always thick with smoke.

He smoked in the car like it was required for the engine to run. In the winter, the windows barely cracked open, smoke curling into the air and drifting straight into the backseat where my brother and I sat, trapped in the haze. Every time we got in the car, the cigarette was already lit.

Restaurants were no different. When the host asked "Smoking or nonsmoking?" there was never a choice. I remember wishing I could sit in the clean air of the other section—the side where the light felt brighter, the air felt lighter.

After every meal, we waited. We waited while he lit another cigarette. We waited while he drank another cup of coffee. We waited because that's what you did with Al. To suggest otherwise—to hint that we could just leave—would be seen as rude or disrespectful. Everything stopped for his cigarette and his coffee.

By the time Al died, I knew without a doubt that stepping into the smoke-filled house would trigger a migraine. There was no avoiding it. And I was right.

I mentioned all of this to my neurologist, explaining my belief that the migraine auras—particularly the smoke smell—were tied to my childhood trauma. I could tell she wasn't fully convinced. But that was fine: I didn't need her validation. I knew what I was experiencing. I could feel the connection and see the patterns.

Most telling of all—after we sold the house, the smoke smell started showing up far less often. And strangely, it returned while I was writing this book, arriving and lasting up to a week during the hard chapters that forced me to sit with old memories and unspoken truths. It also shows up when David and Joe have an intense argument.

I don't think anyone would question my ongoing discomfort around touch. Al's violation of my body wasn't limited to his sexual abuse. Later, after he was caught, his full-body bear hugs became a steady part of my life. Even as adults and close friends, my brother and I only hug on holidays like Christmas. For us as children, the language of touch was never safe or simple.

Allen made my aversion to touch even worse. He had a habit of sneaking up behind me and tickling me without warning, or poking me when I bent over to pick up something off the floor. He always thought it was funny. I found it alarming, intrusive, and violating. And I told him I hated it—more than once—but that only seemed to encourage him. He turned it into a game. He'd jump out from around corners just to startle me, laugh when I screamed, and egg the boys on to join in. What felt like "fun" to him was a complete invasion of my nervous system.

Eventually, I stopped feeling safe in my own home. I couldn't walk from one room to another without bracing for impact—waiting for the jolt, the "tickle," the moment of being caught off guard. I began squatting down to retrieve things off the floor, rather than bending over in a way that left my backside exposed.

This all might sound small, maybe even silly, to someone else. But living like that—constantly on edge, never knowing when your body would become a joke or a target—is a terrible way to exist.

And there was something deeper, darker, more insidious in how Allen treated my body. Sex happened on his terms. Always. He draped his entitlement in performative affection—saying the kinds of words that might sound loving to someone on the outside, but to me felt manipulative and hollow. I wasn't a partner; I was a possession. If I said no, I was met with resistance. "You're my wife," he'd say. "I should be able to touch you whenever I want." And if I pushed back further, he'd remind me, "I'm not Al." As if that alone was enough to grant him access. As if his version of coercion didn't count.

And sometimes, if he was really frustrated, he'd not-so-subtly hint that he had other options (subtext: other women) if I didn't please him.

Trauma isn't always loud or obvious. Sometimes, the most powerful triggers are quiet—hidden in the subtle ways my body still braces for control. It's not always about touch or sensation. Sometimes, it's about power. About feeling like I don't have a choice.

Alcohol is one of those triggers. Not because of a single traumatic event, but because of what drinking represents: risk, unpredictability, and vulnerability.

For someone shaped by trauma, vulnerability has never felt safe, and for years, I didn't drink at all. In college, I was always the designated driver, a role that gave me purpose and control. Eventually, I turned alcohol into a litmus test—people who drank were irresponsible and reckless.

That's what trauma can do—it pushes you to extremes. In my nervous system, a beer didn't mean "relaxation" or "social connection." It meant danger. Unpredictability. Just like a kiss could feel like a prelude to sex, a drink could feel like a prelude to disaster. There was no middle ground.

When David and I got back together, I had to work hard to rewire my thinking. His world was steeped in music and spontaneity—a life shaped by nights at concerts, cross-country road trips, and friendships forged over shared drinks and lyrics shouted into the night.

At the time, even just him mentioning it—"I think I want a beer"—was enough to make my stomach drop. My body braced for whatever awful thing was about to happen.

But love is patient. And so was David. So was I.

It took both of us, working actively and intentionally, to chart a new path. Through therapy and honest conversation, David learned he didn't need to drink to excess to enjoy himself or feel free. He showed me—over time, with gentleness—that I was safe with him.

Through this process, I learned something, too: that I could sit next to someone I loved, with a glass of wine in my hand, and not fall apart. I even discovered that I liked it. That a drink could be warm, shared, even joyful.

Now, one of our favorite weekend rituals is going wine tasting. It's not about the alcohol—it's about connection, trust, and the quiet, daily ways we've rewritten what safety looks and feels like.

Alcohol wasn't the only trigger. Car rides became another battleground.

David inherited his driving style from his dad—tailgating, weaving between lanes, and sudden braking. He gets easily frustrated by other drivers, which makes me feel even more unsafe. But the difference is: David sees me.

When I flinch or grip the seat, he reaches over and gently squeezes my leg. It's his way of saying, I've got you. You're okay.

With Allen, it was so much worse. If I reacted in the car—flinched, gasped, expressed concern—he'd throw his hands in the air and snap, "Fine, you drive then!" And so, I did. Every time we got into the car, it was my role to chauffeur.

With Allen, it was never about sharing responsibility. It was punishment. A way to paint me as controlling while excusing himself from any effort or accountability.

Learning how to cry again has been one of the most profound parts of my healing journey. It's taken years to stop thinking of tears as weakness—or worse, manipulation. Reclaiming my right to cry has been one of the quietest, most powerful acts of defiance I've ever made.

As a child, any time I cried—often for good reason—my mother would accuse me of being dramatic. "You're always performing," she'd sneer. "Stop trying to be an actress." My pain wasn't just dismissed; it was ridiculed. I began to question my own emotions. Was I actually hurting? Or just being too much?

Eventually, I stopped crying—not because the pain ended, but because I learned that showing it would be used against me. That lesson was seared into my skin during the nightly tirades in my bedroom as a teenager. Any tears I shed became ammunition. "You're too emotional," she'd say. "You can't handle anything."

My childhood journals document my struggle between speaking the truth and controlling my emotions while doing so. At the front of one notebook, I wrote what I must have intended as a mantra, equal parts plea and armor: "You may think you hate someone, but if you don't speak out, no one will ever know why. Have faith in yourself, never give up, and most of all—never, never, never let them see you cry. It's a sign that you're weakening and you're ready to give up. Trust me. I know what I'm talking about. Fight for your rights!"

I tried. Over and over. But no matter how hard I fought, my mother broke me down. Al broke me down. Over time, I internalized the message: crying wasn't just unsafe—it was failure. And weakness was never allowed.

Allen only made that confusion worse. His relationship with emotion was the opposite of mine—loud, theatrical, often disconnected from reality. Not long after we moved back to Pennsylvania, his pet prairie dogs died. I'll never forget the scene: Allen sitting cross-legged on the patio, cradling their limp bodies and sobbing so loudly that his grief echoed down the street. Neighbors heard it. He made sure of that.

He mourned celebrity deaths with the same intensity. (The passing of Paul Walker from *Fast & Furious* was one particular household tragedy.) The depth of Allen's emotion never matched the distance of the relationship. Grief was a performance. A show of feeling that didn't require vulnerability—just volume.

Witnessing all of this only reinforced what I'd already learned from my mother: there was no safe way to cry. Public grief was manipulation, and private grief was weakness. Either way, I continued to keep my emotions locked up inside, believing they had no rightful place in the world.

I used to think healing meant scrubbing away this whole ugly past and starting clean.

But now I know: real healing means remembering it all and choosing differently anyway.

It means understanding why my body still reacts, why my breath catches, why my fists still clench at the sound of raised voices or the sight of a white T-shirt.

It means noticing the trigger, feeling the wave, and reminding myself: I'm not there anymore.

It means allowing myself to cry—not the choked-back tears of survival, but the deep, guttural kind that wash something loose.

Yes, my story is still being written. But this time, I hold the pen.

What I Know Now

When I first became a therapist, I was trained to listen for the words—what people say, how they say it, and what goes unsaid between the lines. But over time, I learned to listen to something else, too: the body.

The shallow breath.

The clenched jaw.

The way a client shifts in their seat when a memory begins to stir.

The flinch that comes before the conscious awareness of fear.

I learned, as so many trauma clinicians do, that the body holds the truth long before the mind is ready to name it.

What I didn't expect—what still humbles me to this day—is how deeply my own body remembered. Long after I had named the abuse, mapped the patterns, and even forgiven myself, my nervous system still sounded alarms in the presence of familiar shadows. Not because I was weak, but because I had survived.

Survival leaves marks. It rewires the brain. It lives in the muscles, the breath, the pulse. For many of us—especially those who experienced abuse in childhood—the nervous system becomes our first therapist, our earliest protector. It learns to scan, to brace, to freeze. And it keeps doing so, long after the danger is gone.

This is the paradox of healing: we can be safe now, and still not feel safe.

We can be free, and still flinch.

We can be loved, and still brace for punishment.

That doesn't mean we're broken. It means our body did its job.

My Healing

When clients come into my office and say, "I don't know why I'm reacting this way," I smile gently and say, "But your body does." That knowing, that deep cellular recognition of threat, doesn't ask for permission. It doesn't need language. It simply is.

I've felt it in myself—in the migraines, the phantom smells, the sudden tears, the silent flinches, the body aches, the nausea, the panicky wake-ups at 3:00 a.m., the anxiety, the depression. I've smelled smoke when there was none. I've clenched at cabinet doors closing too loudly. I've felt my stomach drop at the sound of my own name.

None of these are signs of failure. They are echoes. Tremors from an old earthquake.

And what I know now is this: we don't heal by ignoring our reactions. We heal by listening to them.

The work of somatic healing isn't about erasing the past. It's about teaching the nervous system what the mind already knows: you're not there anymore. It's about practicing presence. Grounding. Creating new pathways in the brain and body that say, this is now. This is safe.

And yes—this work takes time. It takes support. Sometimes it takes somatic release, or trauma-informed yoga, or simply a hand on your heart and a deep breath in the mirror.

Sometimes it takes sitting with a friend, naming the pattern, and choosing not to run.

Sometimes, healing sounds like crying again after years of silence.

Sometimes it looks like joy—a glass of wine with someone you trust, a car ride where your breath stays steady, a moment of laughter without looking over your shoulder.

Most of the time, it takes all of these things. All of these small moments . . . but each one is not a small thing. These are victories. Proof that healing doesn't just live in insight—it lives in the body, too.

And with tenderness, patience, and support—you can also relearn. The body that once protected you can become the body that lets you rest.

27

The House with the Broken Alarm

As an educator, I regularly attend conferences—sometimes as a presenter, other times as a participant. A few years ago, I sat in on a session about complex post-traumatic stress disorder (C-PTSD), and it felt like my mind exploded. This! I thought. This is what I've been living. This is me!

C-PTSD doesn't come from a single traumatic event—it comes from enduring trauma over time, often at the hands of people who were supposed to protect you. It doesn't just make you afraid; it reshapes your entire nervous system. It builds slowly and silently, layering over itself until your body starts speaking a language you never consciously learned: hypervigilance and dissociation. It changes how you see yourself, manage emotions, and connect with others.

It doesn't just affect how you respond to danger—it changes how you live.

Imagine your body is a house with an alarm system. With C-PTSD, the alarm doesn't just sound when there's a real threat—it blares every time the wind blows, or a leaf brushes the window, or someone knocks softly. You live constantly on edge, scanning for threats that aren't there. Your body braces. Your breath shortens. Your system doesn't know how to stand down, even when you're finally safe.

One of the most powerful things I've discovered is the concept of radical acceptance—the willingness to stop minimizing, stop explaining things away, and simply name what happened. For years, I denied and downplayed what I had endured. I told myself it wasn't that bad. That others had it worse. That maybe I was too sensitive, too reactive, too emotional.

It took me a long time to even use the word "trauma" to describe my experiences. My mother's voice was ever-present, echoing in my mind, downplaying everything: *It's no big deal.* I internalized that message so deeply that I thought trauma was a word reserved for people only who had been through something truly devastating. I didn't think my experience qualified.

Radical acceptance showed me the truth: what I survived was devastating. And it was time to shine a bright light on it.

My mother's obsession with appearances—the desperate need to control how we were seen—was passed down to me like a birthright. It's why, for years, no one knew the truth about my marriage to Allen. And no one knew what my older sons had endured—or what my youngest continues to face—because I kept it hidden. Just like my mother had. I wore the mask. I smiled in public. I protected the image, even when it was killing me inside.

Even after I left Allen, I stayed quiet. He had already twisted the narrative and painted me as unstable, selfish, and unfit. After a lifetime of being gaslit, I feared that telling the truth would only prove him right in the eyes of others. Speaking out felt too dangerous.

The truth is, our world is built to protect abusers—not survivors, and certainly not children. This brutal reality still fuels my work in social justice. Time and again, I've watched the so-called justice system fail the very people it claims to protect. Survivors are silenced. Children are disbelieved. And the ones who cause the harm? They walk away untouched.

It's no wonder so many victims stay quiet. When you're trapped in abuse, the world teaches you that speaking up will cost you more than staying silent. That no one will believe you. That you will be blamed. And then shamed.

Healing has broken me of that belief. I know the truth. I know what happened to me. I am not willing to stay silent anymore.

Although my early experiences weren't great, I've been involved with therapy in one way or another since I was thirteen years old.

My first therapist hardly spoke to me directly. I remember her more as someone who would chat casually with my mother as we walked out of the building than someone who helped me navigate what I was going through. After about six months, the sessions ended—abruptly.

In high school, I found refuge in the counseling office. I visited my school counselors often—though I was terrified my mother would find out and punish me for it. But those counselors never broke my confidence, and they gave me a place to land when everything else felt like freefall. I didn't share everything—I was still guarded—but I shared enough. Enough to survive.

That experience deeply influenced my early career choice to become a school counselor. I wanted to be that safe space for other kids—the one I'd needed so badly. I wanted to create the kind of sanctuary that had once held me together in high school. Working in schools allowed me to give back, to show up for children in ways I had only dreamed of being supported myself.

As an adult, my relationship with therapy evolved. I've worked with a number of counselors—not because any of them failed me, but because I've learned to recognize when I feel stagnant and need a new voice to push me. As a therapist myself, I know that some people thrive with long-term therapeutic relationships, finding deep comfort and security in working with the same person for years. But for me, healing requires movement. I seek out new perspectives, new techniques, and new ways of understanding myself.

Each shift, each new counselor, has brought me closer to myself. Therapy has never been a linear path, but it has always been a sacred one. And I've learned to honor when it's time to begin again.

One of the most transformative experiences I've had was during an intensive somatic release and breathwork retreat. It pushed me far beyond my comfort zone, and it shifted something profound within me.

I arrived with an open mind and a hopeful heart, but also a lot of anxiety—especially walking into a space with three hundred other people. Vulnerability in a room that large is no small ask.

The facilitators offered some helpful education before we began, explaining what to expect and encouraging us to simply feel what we feel. They reminded us that no two experiences would look or sound the same—and that was okay.

I set up my space with my blue yoga mat and wrapped myself in my Mama Bear blanket that Nicholas had given me, pulled up my hood, and slipped on an eye mask. I had no idea what I was about to encounter within myself, but I hoped it would be powerful.

As the breathwork began, rhythmic breathing merged with music that vibrated through the room. At first, I felt a pulsing energy in my hands, like I was holding a large, invisible sphere. And then, without warning, the tears started. Something about that moment—the music, the breath, the energy—I could feel it unlocking something buried.

As the session deepened, memories surfaced. I found myself returning to childhood. I saw myself on the witness stand, not testifying, staying silent. What I hadn't realized until that moment was how much anger and disappointment I had been carrying toward that little girl. I had been asking her, why couldn't you have been stronger? But in that moment, I finally saw her strength. I finally understood that she was surviving the only way she knew how. She didn't need shame—she needed acknowledgment, protection, and love. And she needed me, the adult version of her, to see it.

The tears turned into sobs. Deep, guttural, body-shaking sobs. I could feel the trauma leaving my body with each exhale. The guided process helped me access memories and energy I didn't even realize I was still holding onto.

And then, very unexpectedly—I found my voice. At first, I was terrified to use it. But then I did. I screamed. I yelled. I released what had been festering inside for decades. I expelled the toxins.

I'm deeply grateful to myself for having the courage to walk into that room and trust what would unfold. That retreat didn't fix everything, but got me serious about starting a meditation practice. I started small: just ten minutes a day. At first, I relied on guided meditations, but over time, I found my rhythm in the sound of ocean waves. Now, nearly every morning, I carve out that quiet space for myself. Meditation has become a steady anchor in my life.

This practice hasn't just helped me reconnect with my body—it's strengthened my connection to my mind. It's taught me that I have the ability to regulate my nervous system when I'm triggered. That I have the right to slow down, to rest, to take time for myself without needing to earn it. That I can use the skills I've cultivated—mindfulness, breath, presence—in everyday life, not just when I'm meditating.

One of the most consistent and powerful tools for me in this process has been writing. Not just this book, but also in my journal. One especially helpful technique I used often was what I called Socratic writing, where my therapist brain can meet my wounded self on the pages of my journal. These written dialogues helped me uncover the roots of distorted beliefs and reclaim the truths that trauma had buried.

A significant part of my healing has been connecting the dots—tracing how my early childhood experiences, especially my malformed attachment style, shaped the way I navigated the world both as a child and as an adult. Those formative years were critical, not just because of what happened, but because of what didn't happen.

I have heard the term "inner child" so many times in my life, but I never truly paused to consider its weight. The inner child is not an abstract concept. She is me. She holds my earliest memories, the pain and joy of my first attachments, the ways I learned to survive. She also carries the scars: deep feelings of shame and guilt, chronic overworking, a constant need to achieve.

In the beginning, I struggled to see myself as a child. My adult mind kept projecting grown-up expectations onto my younger self. Of course, it did—I had been over-parentified from a young age, always feeling older than I was. So, the work began with recognition. I had to truly see the little girl inside me. To understand her. To give her safety. To forgive her. To love her.

I began reconnecting with things I once loved as a child. I started coloring again and discovered how soothing it felt. I did arts and crafts for no reason other than joy. I painted rocks. I hot-glued things together. I allowed myself to play without purpose. It awakened a part of me that had been asleep for far too long.

And there's the reconnection with my loved ones, too. That requires radical honesty.

In my twenties, during a visit back home, I had found the courage to talk to Tony about what happened to me. I wanted him to protect his own children from Al, but I was also terrified, convinced he would reject me or deny everything.

But when I told him what had happened, he was devastated. He cried—something I'd never seen him do—and he hugged me tightly.

"I'm sorry I didn't protect you," he said. I'd approached that conversation hoping to protect his child from the horrors I had endured. But I came away with so much more: I got my brother back. I felt heard. I felt loved.

This honesty extends to how I explain my reactions to David, too. I would never ask him to change who he is for me, but sharing how certain things trigger my body allows us both to navigate those moments with more awareness and care. That mutual understanding has brought us closer—and that kind of acknowledgment has been essential to my healing.

So now, when he is speaking and I feel myself drifting away, I say "I'm full," and he knows I need to pause and regroup. So he stops and just sits with me.

Most people see being late or forgetting something as a small mistake. For me, it can feel like a betrayal. If David says he'll be home at six and walks in at six-thirty, I don't just feel disappointed. I feel forgotten. I feel unsafe. That's the language of my nervous system.

Time means trust. I'm hypersensitive to "future faking," a favorite tactic of Allen's. When someone says they'll do something and doesn't, it feels like the beginning of abandonment.

David gets that now. If he forgets to take out the trash, he doesn't deflect. He doesn't excuse. He says, "I'm sorry, baby. That was my job." And that small act—accountability—softens everything. What hurt the most in my past wasn't just broken promises. It was the denial of harm and the refusal to see me.

What I Know Now

In trauma therapy, we often say the body tells the truth—even when the mind can't. I've seen this play out over and over, both in my clients and in myself.

Complex PTSD (C-PTSD) isn't simply a diagnosis. It's not even formally recognized in the DSM-5 (Diagnostic and Statistical Manual of Mental Disorders). It's a lived experience. It develops when a nervous system grows up in chronic unpredictability—not from one catastrophic event, but from the slow erosion of safety over time, especially inside relationships that were supposed to offer protection, care, and attunement.

When your body learns that safety is conditional—or nonexistent—it adapts. And those adaptations are permanent unless consciously healed.

The metaphor I come back to again and again is the house with the broken alarm. It doesn't matter if the storm is over or if the structure is finally safe. The alarm still screams. It still jolts you awake in the middle of the night. It still insists something is wrong—even when nothing is. That isn't a malfunction. That's survival.

So many survivors carry this silent, relentless alarm inside them. They call it anxiety, panic, irritability, reactivity. But underneath those labels are very real physiological responses—learned, protective patterns that once kept them alive.

Hypervigilance isn't an overreaction. It's a nervous system doing its best to protect you, especially when no one else did.

Clinically, C-PTSD includes symptoms like emotional dysregulation, dissociation, shame, relationship difficulties, and distorted self-perception. But in the therapy room, it often shows up more subtly:

The client who flinches when the phone rings.

The mother who believes she's failing because her child cries.

The professional who excels at work but feels hollow at home.

The partner who panics when someone is ten minutes late—not because of the clock, but because of the history.

Beneath all of it lies the same quiet truth: I was never safe when I should have been.

For many survivors, healing begins not with worksheets or exposure exercises, but with something quieter and far more radical: permission. Permission to tell the truth. To stop minimizing. To grieve what was lost—and what was never given.

Permission to finally say, "This happened. It mattered. And I am still here."

My Healing

So much of my own trauma recovery has been a return to reality—*my* reality. Not the version handed to me by abusers. Not the sanitized story shaped for public consumption. But the raw truth that lived inside my bones long before I could speak it.

Still, radical honesty wasn't enough. I had to relearn safety.

That's where somatic work became essential for me. C-PTSD lives in the nervous system; it isn't something we can think our way out of. My body needed to be invited back into presence—slowly, gently, with care.

For me, that looked like grounding techniques—breathwork, sensory orientation, self-holding. It looked like mindfulness and meditation. Like creative expression through writing, art, and music. Like trauma-informed movement: yoga, dance, walking, running. Like learning how my nervous system operates and why it responds the way it does. And most importantly, it looked like building relationships rooted in safety, consent, and reciprocity.

What I know now is this: healing doesn't require burning down the entire house just because the alarm is broken.

I learned to reset it. I rewired the system. I painted the walls, opened the windows, and slowly made that house—my body—a home again.

Not perfect. Not silent. But *safe*.

And when I reclaimed my voice, my body, my time, my joy—it felt nothing short of revolutionary. I didn't just heal in private. I healed by reentering the world on my own terms.

28

Taking Back What Was Mine

My entire career is rooted in one unshakable belief: when we see injustice, we must name it—and then we must fight like hell to dismantle it. Through healing, I've applied that same philosophy to me.

There's no doubt that my professional journey was heavily shaped by my past. Through my university work, I fight for others because I know what it's like to be unheard, dismissed, erased. Through my counseling practice, I support people just like me who are on paths towards understanding and healing.

Today, I speak truth—loudly, clearly, and without apology.

After nearly five years of relentless legal battles, my brother and I finally regained guardianship of our mother. We had documented everything—every dollar gone, every misstep ignored, every abuse of power—and used it to build a case that couldn't be denied. For this work, I was invited to Washington, DC, and testified before the United States Senate Special Committee on Aging.

I shared my mother's story, but I spoke for so many more—for the millions of families failed by the very systems that are supposed to protect them. And the irony wasn't lost on me: I've become more of a mother to my own mother than she ever was to me.

Even with the healing I've done, it remains easier for me to fight for others than it is to fight for myself. I'm working on that.

That's the other side of healing—the quiet, internal revolution. While I've stood on national stages to confront injustice, the most transformative work has happened in the most private corners of my life.

Reclaiming my spirit has meant reclaiming my "no." It's meant drawing lines not just in the courtroom or on behalf of others, but within my own relationships, my body, and my time. Naming abuse publicly is powerful—but so is quietly refusing to let it back into your inbox. The boundaries I once set to survive have become the boundaries that now allow me to thrive.

When I found the words that got Al to stop touching me—if only for brief periods—that was a boundary I had set. When I told my mother that he would never be allowed around my children, that was another. Years later, after my divorce from Allen, when I said he was no longer welcome in my house . . . then in my driveway . . . then in my inbox—those were boundaries, too. Each one was hard-won. Each one chipped away at the years I'd spent believing I wasn't allowed to protect myself.

Perhaps those early lessons were essential—because the only reason I've been able to navigate co-parenting with Allen is because of the boundaries I've learned to set. But with Allen, for reasons I couldn't understand at the time, it was so much harder. Not just to set the boundaries—but to even realize I had the right to set them in the first place.

In many ways, I had internalized Allen the same way I had internalized my mother: as the authority, the one who was always right. And if he was right, then I must be wrong. If he was reasonable, then my discomfort was overreaction. If he was calm and I was upset, then I was the problem. That's how the gaslighting worked. That's how I became conditioned to believe that setting boundaries was selfish or irrational or cruel.

So, for a long time, I didn't.

But healing changed that. Slowly, I reclaimed the right to my own space, my own peace, my own truth. And with that reclamation came boundaries—not out of spite or pettiness, but out of necessity.

I will not speak with Allen on the phone; his calls are never about Joe's needs. They are traps, laced with blame, manipulation, or attempts to provoke me. I've eliminated texting altogether, reserving it only for true emergencies. All other communication happens via email—and even then, I respond only to what is absolutely necessary and only if it directly involves Joe's care.

These are the gates I keep. And I get to decide who walks through them, and under what terms.

Boundaries are the language of healing. They're how I remind myself that I'm allowed to feel safe. That I don't owe anyone access to my time, my energy, or my peace. Especially not someone who has repeatedly shown me they will use it to cause harm.

When even that was too much at times, I recruited a gatekeeper to read through the emails and only deliver information related to the actual custodial issues.

All of this worked. It stopped the tirades. Eventually, Allen stopped communicating with me entirely—even about Joe.

Every time I set and held a boundary, I felt a little more grounded in myself. I was no longer willing to hand over my safety, peace, or autonomy just to avoid conflict. I had finally learned: I didn't have to play the game just because someone else insisted on keeping score.

Professional boundaries have been important to set too. I love my work—it's meaningful, impactful, and uniquely suited to my passions. And early in my academic career, I said yes to everything—because I had to. It was how you got tenure, how you proved your worth. But nearly twenty years later, as a full professor, I have learned to say no. No to the extra committees, no to the side projects, no to the asks that only came to me because others assume I'd say yes. Colleagues have told me they admire this shift—they also want to learn to say no without guilt.

For all the ways I've learned to say no to others, learning to say yes to myself—to rest, to pause, to soften—has been the hardest. Setting boundaries with abusers was necessary for survival. But setting boundaries with the relentless expectations inside my own mind? That's the work of healing.

Even now, I sometimes wait for someone to grant me permission to rest when I'm sick. When David gently suggests I stay home, or colleagues assure me they've got things covered, I feel relief—but also guilt. I still hear my mother's voice: You're not sick. You're well enough to push through.

She never stopped moving. Multitasking wasn't optional—it was proof you weren't lazy. She skipped water to avoid bathroom breaks, scolded employees who stepped away, and taught us that comfort was selfish. By first grade, Tony and I were working in her smoke-filled bindery, surrounded by dangerous machines. At home, our after-school time was spent completing her work tasks—and if we took breaks, we were lazy.

That mindset followed me into adulthood. From the outside, it looks like discipline. Inside, I'm exhausted, stretched thin, and struggling to allow even the smallest pause. When my husband takes time off, I feel a flash of anger—but it's not really anger. It's envy. I was never taught to rest. I was taught that lazy people are bad people. And I don't want to be bad—so I don't stop.

But I'm learning. My lifelong inability to relax—to feel good without guilt—is a sign of my trauma. I understand now that those beliefs were never mine. They were planted in me by people who didn't know how to love themselves, let alone love me. And now, I know better.

Rest isn't weakness. It's not selfish. It's allowed. And it's essential.

One of the most personal acts of reclamation has been taking back certain words and pieces of language that had been stolen from me.

"Princess" is such a simple, lovely word. David has always called me his princess; it's one of the ways he loves me. But the first time he said it, I felt sick. A memory I buried came rushing back: Al used to call me his princess too. He used it in those moments of fake tenderness after an explosion. I was his "princess" when I stayed quiet, didn't resist, and let him touch me without protest. It was a word of manipulation, not affection.

So, when David used it, I froze. When I explained why, he immediately asked if I wanted him to stop. I said no. Al didn't get to keep that word. I wanted it back. David understood and followed my lead. For the first time in a very long time, I felt heard.

David still calls me his princess, and I love that part of our relationship. It carries no darkness—only light. It's a word that belongs to us now, and to me.

When we got married, David wrote me a song called "Yes, My Princess." Before the wedding, I pulled my brother aside to explain—just in case the word triggered anything for him too. He said it didn't. But that's what trauma does: it makes us brace, over-explain things, and try to protect others from the echoes of our own pain.

The second reclamation was the Italian language.

Although my father's family spoke it fluently, my mother forbade my brother and me from learning it. With that decision, she cut us off from our culture, our grandparents, and a deep sense of belonging. I've carried that disconnection all my life—always feeling not Italian enough, not connected enough.

Over the years, I made small attempts—like enrolling in an Italian class in college—but life kept getting in the way. Then one day, Christopher showed me a language app he'd been using. It was simple and accessible. I gave it a try.

Now, every day, I complete at least one lesson. Word by word, I'm restoring a connection that was broken before I was even born. I may never speak fluently—but that's not the point. This is about reaching back through generations to honor my grandparents, my father, my culture—and the parts of me that were once erased.

Reclaiming language is not just healing. It's a declaration: I get to decide what belongs to me.

Another reclamation was water.

As a child, I was thrown into the pool to learn how to swim. That moment—meant to teach—instilled fear instead. I became terrified of water. Then later, when Al assaulted me in the pool and tore off my bathing suit, I stopped trusting anyone near me in the water.

In college, I signed up for a scuba class, determined to face the fear. I passed, eventually, thanks to a gentle, patient instructor—and earned my scuba certification. Still, the fear lingered.

Fed up with living like this, I decided as an adult to teach myself how to swim—really swim—not just survive in water, but move through it with purpose and grace. Every Friday morning, I showed up at the pool. Slowly, patiently, I practiced. And eventually, I did it. I taught myself how to swim—and then I started competing in triathlons.

Reclaiming the water wasn't just about athletics. It was about showing myself that I could return to what once scared me and create something empowering in its place.

One of the casualties of prolonged abuse is often the quiet, joyful pieces of who we are—the passions that once gave us life. For me, that was music. Not just listening, but making it. Playing instruments, singing, dancing—expressing myself without fear or apology.

As a child, music was everything. I played flute, clarinet, trumpet, saxophone, and piano. I sang in choirs, performed in musicals, joined every ensemble I could. In college, I minored in voice performance and thrived on stage. Performing wasn't scary—it was grounding. It was who I was.

When we moved to Reno, my dad bought me a grand piano. Even with young kids and a full schedule, I played. When we moved again, I shipped it across the country. But life got harder—and Allen convinced me to sell it. He framed it as my decision, a sacrifice to help with bills. I told myself it was true. But now I see it for what it was: one more piece of myself given up to make his life easier.

I used to love dancing. But somewhere along the way, I became the woman who stayed seated at weddings and family functions. I couldn't feel the music anymore. I second-guessed every move.

And now, looking back, I can pinpoint the exact moment I began to doubt my musical ability: it was the day I married Allen. Allen had mocked me so cruelly at our wedding ceremony that I felt shamed. And shame silenced something deep in me.

Years later, when I reconnected with David—a professional musician—I found myself especially intimidated. He's an extraordinary pianist and producer. When I sang around him, I braced for the same criticism I used to hear from Allen. But it never came.

As part of my healing, I purchased a guitar and started lessons. My progress is slow, but meaningful. I've even begun singing again while I play. My confidence is still fragile, especially around rhythm and performance—but I can feel her returning: the musical me.

Even now, when David offers suggestions, I sometimes shut down. I feel overwhelmed, insecure, defensive—like I'm hearing my mother's voice or Allen's critiques. That's what trauma does. It can make love feel threatening. It can make support feel like control.

But I keep playing. I keep singing. And little by little, I'm reclaiming the music that always belonged to me.

Another vital part of my reclamation has been reconnecting with my physical body.

For years, I carried pain, fear, and memory in my muscles, skin, and joints—places I learned to ignore, dissociate from, or control just to survive. Some parts were easier to reclaim. Running every morning helped me feel present and strong. But other areas—more intimate ones—were far harder to navigate.

As a survivor of sexual abuse, I didn't believe sexual healing was even possible for me. I certainly never imagined it could feel safe.

Once, when I was in therapy with Allen, I made a collage to illustrate how I felt about sex. One side was filled with sharp objects, dark images, and frightening faces—that's what sex felt like to me. The other side showed hearts, softness, connection—what I longed for it to feel like. When I shared it with him, he wasn't moved. He was offended.

Eventually, I stopped trying to connect with him. I gave up on being understood and simply complied. Sex became something I endured to avoid being cheated on—because Allen would remind me what I "owed" him and hint at consequences if I withheld. I stopped listening to my body. I went numb.

David helped me change that. Through our relationship, I learned what love really feels like and what sex could be. He was attentive to everything—not just my words, but the way my body responded. If I tensed, even slightly, he stopped and asked questions. If I said no, he listened. Every time. No anger, no guilt, no manipulation. Just a quiet understanding that consent is constant.

With David, touch doesn't come with a cost. Intimacy isn't something to endure or perform—it is something shared. Over time, my body began to soften, to trust, to remember that it belonged to me. That I could say yes. That I could say no. That both would be honored.

It's still a journey. Trauma doesn't vanish; it lingers, flares, resurfaces. But now, I meet it with curiosity, not shame. And I'm no longer alone in the process.

Healing myself doesn't mean I'm "fixed." Even now, when David gives me feedback while I'm learning or exploring something new—like music—I can feel old wounds flare up. My nervous system still struggles to tell the difference between help and harm. He'll say something kindly, and I'll spiral. It's a reflex I'm still working through.

But this much I know: these steps I took allowed me to take back my power. I've reclaimed my body, my pleasure, and my right to say yes or no. I've learned what it means to be safe inside my skin. To be loved without being used.

Part of my healing has meant re-learning how to show up in all relationships—not just romantic ones, but friendships, too. It's easier to talk about healing in the context of leaving a toxic partner. That kind of betrayal is big and loud, but it took me years to understand how the narcissists in my life worked to keep me cut off from deep connection with others. Not explicitly, not in ways you can always name. It was always subtle.

For my mother, isolation came dressed as criticism—especially toward anyone I admired. She had a talent for dismantling the women who made me feel seen, strong, or safe. Mrs. Kelly, the only teacher I ever trusted enough to share my truth, was dismissed as an "old biddy." My aunts, whose warmth and emotion offered me comfort, were labeled "hysterical" for simply showing feelings.

For Allen, isolation from friends came in the form of withholding approval, like expressing concern when my best friend was in town for business and wanted to have dinner. I don't always understand the motive, but I do understand that it was sowing just enough doubt that I began to pull away from people who loved me.

For both of them, the goal wasn't just control—it was disconnection. Because people who are deeply connected are harder to manipulate. They have perspective. They have support. They have exits.

And this is important: neither my mom nor Allen ever had someone they call a lifelong best friend. They moved through relationships with ease, always trading in one model for the next, depending on their whims.

That's what scares me most when I look at Joe. I see patterns that remind me of my mother and Allen—the shifting stories, the emotional distance, the absence of meaningful friendships. Like Allen, Joe has never had a consistent friend. No anchor person. His friendships rotate constantly, orbiting around performance, convenience, or shared interest, but never really rooting in anything lasting. His friends seem to serve a function, and then disappear. I am only now seeing that this has started to change for him. He has begun to create meaningful friendships in his final years of high school.

Like everything, however, the situation with Joe continues to evolve. Since Joe started driving, I noticed him reaching out to me and Dave more—calling, texting, and showing up. I noticed him having more friends and enjoying time away from his father. I noticed that is making a difference for him and speaks volumes to me—that Joe is starting to notice that perhaps the narrative he has received from Allen all of these years isn't making sense anymore. In the past several months, Joe says he loves me—without prompting.

What I Know Now

Healing is not an event—it's a journey. And what we put into that journey is exactly what we will get out of it. I can't expect to heal by ignoring the past. I can't expect to heal by repeating the same patterns and calling them progress. I can't expect to heal without making shifts, without choosing differently, without doing the uncomfortable, necessary work.

Healing will be something I do for the rest of my life. It happens in small, everyday moments—in the pauses, the choices, the boundaries, the reflections. It's hard and messy and astonishingly beautiful. And every bit of work I've done, and every bit I will continue to do, has made and will continue to make a profound impact on the person I am becoming.

If you are considering reclaiming yourself, know this truth: it will take time. It will be hard. It will be messy. You will want to give up. But if you stay with yourself through it all, you will emerge knowing exactly who you are—and who you have always been beneath the layers of survival.

My Healing

Writing this book has forced me to confront just how deep my mistrust runs. I grew up conditioned not to trust the people closest to me, so it's no surprise that there were moments I questioned everything—even those who have only ever loved me. At one point, I even convinced myself that David and my best friend were conspiring behind my back. I can see the irrationality of it now, but at the time, it felt real. That's the legacy of psychological abuse: it rewires your sense of safety. It trains you to anticipate betrayal, even in places where love is steady and true.

For me, healing has meant learning to trust my instincts again—to differentiate between a red flag and a trauma response. To identify safe people. To take small emotional risks. To believe, slowly and cautiously, that not everyone is waiting to hurt me.

I'm learning to let people in.

Gently. Deliberately.

And for the first time in my life, entirely on my own terms.

Epilogue

Healing from narcissistic abuse is deeply personal—and profoundly complex. For me, it was never going to be just one therapist, one breakthrough, or one method.

There were times when I felt like I had tried everything: cognitive processing therapy, trauma art narrative therapy, eye movement desensitization and reprocessing (EMDR), talk therapy, parts work, energy healing, sound baths, yoga, mushrooms, somatic writing, ketamine, meditation, marijuana . . . the list goes on and on.

Every modality offered something—a new perspective, a release, a reconnection. And over time? All of it helped.

That's not to say I haven't resisted—oh, I have! I've rolled my eyes and dismissed things as "not for me." And sometimes I've been right. Not everything fits. But I've learned that the things that resonate tend to stick, and the ones that don't? I leave them behind.

Over time, I have become more open. And that openness, that willingness to try—even when I'm unsure—always brought new insight.

Living in a safe environment has made healing possible. It still wasn't easy, but it was possible. I know that my healing won't be used against me, and that getting better won't be twisted into evidence that I'm "too much" or "too broken."

I don't have all the answers. But I've learned that sharing the process can help. Maybe my mess can light the path for someone else. If even one part of my story sparks recognition, relief, or hope in another, it's worth every word.

My work BFF always reminds me to "take your fucking flowers." In other words: receive the recognition you've earned.

For too long, I couldn't. I was too busy hiding in competence and masking pain with productivity.

But the truth is: I was always strong. I was always brave. I just couldn't see it through the fog of abuse. What healing gave me wasn't those qualities—it gave me the clarity to finally see them in myself.

I've done big things—earned awards, published work, and finished triathlons. But the most radical thing I've done is learn to love myself. Not for what I achieve. Not for what I overcome. But for who I am. And for who I've always been.

Healing meant unearthing the version of myself buried under years of coping and self-protection. Writing this book became part of that process, too. I started it hoping to help others. In the end, it helped me too.

I didn't heal alone. My people—my chosen family—stood with me. My beloved David. My brother. My boys. My best friend. My family. Even my father, whose memory continues to whisper in his signature way: *Reeeeeelax. Taaaaaaake it eeeeeeasy.*

This, too, is healing: Slowing down. Remembering to breathe deeply. Letting in joy. Resting without guilt. Trusting what is good.

While my healing will continue in many ways for the rest of my life, what I've done so far has helped me finally feel whole. Not stitched together with shame or patched up with duct tape, but truly whole.

Because I now know: I am not broken. I am not an imposter.

I am a survivor. A scholar. A mother. A fighter. A healer. And yes, a badass.

The environment I have now makes it safe enough for me to continue on this path. I don't take that for granted, and I will never give it up again—I have finally learned that I can trust myself and my intuition. I can trust people who show up for me time and time again. I can trust love.

I began this journey unsure of where it would lead. I now understand: healing is not a destination. It's a lifelong path. My story is still unfolding—especially with my son, Joe. But I did what I set out to do: I found her. I found Tina.

And I'm learning, finally, to take my flowers. I fucking deserve them.

So do you.

Acknowledgments

I want to acknowledge and thank those individuals who have helped me throughout my life, through my healing journey, and through this book-writing process. I am forever grateful to have crossed paths with you. Know that I love you.

There are countless others whose names may not appear here, yet whose words, quiet encouragement, and simple acts of kindness helped me keep going. This book holds pieces of each of you. Thank you.

To my husband David—my rock—my love—my soulmate. You have been the love of my life since I was sixteen years old. When we reconnected as adults, you brought with you a steadiness, devotion, and depth of love I had never known. You celebrate every accomplishment, lift me when I falter, and hold space for every chapter of my healing—every breakthrough, every setback, every step forward, every tear. Walking this healing journey with you by my side has been one of the greatest gifts of my life. Your presence has been an anchor, your love a safe haven, and your belief in me a constant light. Thank you for loving me the way you do. *You make me feel love, baby.*

To my three boys—you are my *why*. You are the reason I needed to heal. To end the generational cycle of abuse—to show you how to heal—and to show you there is a way out of what we once assumed was normal.

Nicholas, you have been through everything with me and have taught me how to be a mother. Your charismatic smile and boundless energy are contagious, and I hope you continue to share that light everywhere you go. I am endlessly proud of the man you've become and grateful for every moment we've walked through together.

Christopher, you inspire me and teach me more than you will ever know. Watching you chase your dreams has given me the courage to chase my own. Your humor, your heart, and the way you see the world have been making me smile since the day you were born. I am so honored to be your mom.

Joe, my baby boy—my heart. Your smile can light up an entire room when you let it shine. You are so smart, so capable, and I know that one day you will stand firmly in your own truth. No matter the distance, no matter the season, I will always be here for you. Always.

To my brother, Tony—thank you for every pizza, every call, and every text as I pieced this story together. You are the only one who truly knows what it was like, because we lived it side by side. We survived it together. My hope is that this book also becomes a voice for you—a doorway to your own healing from the narcissistic environment we grew up in. I love you. And I love that you brought Amanda into our family, and how she has supported my healing, knowing that it will help you, too. I am forever grateful.

To my editor and BFF, Jennifer Gabriel—I couldn't have done this without you! Who would have guessed that two girls who met in nursery school would spend a lifetime circling back to each other, our lives unfolding in astonishing parallels and us reconnecting as if pulled together by some invisible force? Now here we are—decades later—bringing this story into the world as a light for others who are healing. Your encouragement has been constant and your support unwavering. You took my words and shaped them with clarity, strength, and power. And truly—any friend who loves me enough to build an entire church from scratch just so she could marry me to David is the kind of friend whose devotion becomes a chapter of its own. I am endlessly grateful—and forever in awe of you.

To Barbara Kelly—thank you for being my voice when I didn't have one. The impact you made on my life is deeper than you will ever fully know. As an educator myself, I understand how rare it is to see the true reach of our influence. Please know that yours was profound, and I carry it with me still.

Daddy—in life, your presence held a steadiness that reminded me to "reeeeeelaaaaaax," "take it easy," and breathe. In death, you gave me the most valuable gift I can imagine. Your passing struck like an earthquake—one that split my life open just enough for the truth to pour through, forcing me to change and to break the cycle of abuse for my family. I love and miss you every day.

To all of my cousins, my aunts, and my uncles—thank you for being an extended family that offers love in all its enduring forms.

Michele Herron, you have seen me through all of the ups and downs—finding ways to make me laugh no matter how hard the circumstances.

And to the women whose presence wrapped around me with a steady, resolute grace—Evelyn Campbell, Mary Brennan, and Lynn Romeo—your energy has shaped me more than you know.

To my mother figures who stepped in and stood steady: you have left a lasting imprint on my heart.

To my mother-in-law, Pat Hawkins - thank you for the love and acceptance in the moments when I needed it most. You are the mother I always wanted.

To Daisy Pyatt—Your practical lessons on how to move through the world have stayed with me as my own foundation. Your kindness has never wavered.

Through my professional work, I've been lucky to cross paths with extraordinary women who became far more than colleagues—they became confidants, truth-tellers, and friends.

Nicole Pulliam—thank you for always reminding me that the fucking flowers are mine to take, and for being a relentlessly positive force in my life, even on the days when I couldn't find the light myself.

Krista Malott—two decades of knowing you have made me a better writer, a sharper thinker, and a braver woman. We've written scholarly articles, yes—but we've also collected stamps in our passports, memories in our pockets, and a friendship that has traveled with me throughout the years.

Cindy O'Connell— What you taught me about running turned into a masterclass in endurance. You gave me the stamina to keep moving forward when I needed it most.

To Jeanne Wermuth, Dawn Frigerio, Teresa Tecee, Ardella Main, Renee Bell, Charlotte DiNenna, Cheri Brown, Bonnie Marino, Linda Brown, Cathy Walkowitz, and Rosann Ventura: you may never know the depth of your impact, but it was there. Your presence in my life helped me find my footing when the ground felt unsteady.

I was also fortunate to have role models who demonstrated a strong, compassionate way of being a man, treating women with dignity and care. Erich Uhlenbrock, Jack Casey, and Bob Edgington each offered steady guidance, kindness, and integrity at different points in my life, reminding me through their actions that goodness in men not only exists, but endures.

I believe counselors deserve far more recognition than we often receive, and I want to honor those who walked beside me when I needed them most. Thank you to Maureen Coffey and Mary Lou Graham, who supported me in high school; to Phyllis Shanken, who reconnected me and my dad; to Richard Perkins, who guided me in early adulthood; and to Stacee Paley, who helped me navigate the turbulent transition of my divorce and find my footing on the other side. Each of you helped lead me to the place where I was finally ready to write this book. And to Laurie Berman: you pushed me to make it finally happen—thank you!

To everyone who helped me heal, grow, and reclaim my story: I carry your love with me. Thank you for helping me come home to myself.

This work was supported, in part, by a Creativity and Research Grant from Monmouth University.

About the Author

With her unique blend of credibility, authenticity, and compassion, Dr. Tina Paone is well-positioned to speak to—and for—the millions of survivors navigating their own healing journeys. *UNBROKEN* is more than her story. It's a mirror for those still finding their voice.

Dr. Paone is a licensed professional counselor, registered play therapist-supervisor, counselor educator, and tenured professor with over 25 years of experience in the mental health field. She has spent her career training future therapists, leading social justice initiatives, and helping survivors of complex traumas reclaim their lives.

Her lived experience is as powerful as her professional expertise. She writes with clarity about surviving childhood grooming, emotional neglect, a coercive marriage, and post-separation abuse. This memoir brings both her worlds together, offering a rare and vital dual lens: the deeply personal, and the clinically informed.

Dr. Paone's current clinical work focuses on supporting survivors of narcissistic abuse and family systems seeped in trauma. She is also a sought-after speaker and workshop facilitator in anti-racism and social justice forums. Her reach continues to grow across personal, professional, and digital spaces as she advocates for a deeper understanding of narcissistic abuse and trauma recovery. Learn more at drtinapaone.com.

www.ingramcontent.com/pod-product-compliance
Lightning Source LLC
LaVergne TN
LVHW021233080526
838199LV00088B/4330